Accidental Life

purposefully stumbling into meaningful existence

Jim McCracken

Accidental Life: Purposefully Stumbling into Meaningful Existence
Copyright © 2019 Jim McCracken
All rights reserved.

Print Edition
ISBN: 978-1-7335713-0-2
Published by Jim McCracken, 2019

No parts of this publication may be reproduced, stored in a retrieval system, or transmitted in any form or by any means, electronic, mechanical, photocopying, recording, or otherwise, without the prior written permission of the copyright owner.

This book is sold subject to the condition that it shall not, by way of trade or otherwise, be lent, resold, hired out, or otherwise circulated without the publisher's prior consent in any form of binding or cover other than that in which it is published and without a similar condition including this condition being imposed on the subsequent purchaser. Under no circumstances may any part of this book be photocopied for resale.

Scripture taken from the NEW AMERICAN STANDARD BIBLE,
Copyright © 1960, 1962, 1963 1968, 1971, 1972,
1973 1975, 1977, 1995 by The Lockman Foundation
All rights reserved
Used by permission.
http://www.Lockman.org

Cover design by Amie McCracken
Interior design by Amie McCracken
Cover images by Deb McCracken and family

***To** my wife, Deb – my faithful sidekick in all adventures, organizer of chaos, mystical prompt, factual critic, shaky heroine, and iridescent–eyed beauty!*

No one has more fun than...

*ced**For** my three girls, Ellie (Belle), Sarah (Pooh) and Kate (Bop), their chosen men, and the tribe of grandchildren they've so perfectly spawned and crafted*

***In loving memory of** my dad, William E. McCracken, who should have written the stories of his vast travels, who would have been pleased (and maybe surprised) that I finished this book*

***Thanks to** my beta readers – Deb, Kate, Michael Kelly Blanchard, Len Woods, Karl Kemp, Kevin Riley...offering fair doses of encouragement and realistic expectations; a unique thanks to Amie McCracken (not related, but one more serendipitous, "accidental find"), who applied her friendly and professional expertise to typesetting, formatting, cover design, and generous advice*

chapters

A Magical Setting	**9**
What Is This Book?	**10**
Part One: The Silly Years	**13**
Inglorious Accidents	14
Romantic Hardhead	29
Street Cruisers	41
KO'd in Detroit	52
Second Fiddle's Fine	58
The College Experiment	66
A Thundering Velvet Hand	74
Part Two: More Serious Times	**89**
Hitchhiking and Hijacked	90
Presidents and Pygmies	106
Family Planning	116
Acapulco Gold	120
Home Sweet Hospital	128
Inner-city Slaughter	141
A Skeleton from the Closet of My Personal Journal	148
In Camp with the Kurds	151
A Man's Been Shot!	160
Career Development	170
Helping People Die	179
Helping People Get Hitched	195
Big Bending	205
Success in Reverse	221
Part Three: Season of Serendipity	**229**
Breaking Good	230
A Season in the NFL	239
Seconds of Turkey	257
Good Dog Bad Dog	268
Son of the Highlands	278
Exiled on Patmos	287
Poetry in Motion	**301**

a magical setting

I am writing while "exiled" on Patmos, the very same Greek island on which the Apostle John received and penned the Apocalypse. This seems fitting (not that this book is anything approaching the great Biblical book of Revelation) because Patmos is a mystical place that I could never have foreseen or planned as the setting for composing my book. An apparent "accident" of fate. But fate has nothing to do with it. This setting is not the result of some haphazard series of good and bad luck, nor some weird, pre-written divine script. I believe there *is* One in heaven overseeing all the events, places, people, and stuff of our lives. At the same time, I believe we make very real and consequential choices. How those two realities intersect, certainly God alone knows. Maybe the big difference between us mere humans is that some of us come to recognize those two intertwined roles, and some of us don't. To me, it makes all the difference.

what is this book?

My first job right out of college was selling life insurance. One of the first things I learned was that "Accidental Death" pays double the benefits of "normal death." "Normal death" doesn't. Now, nearly forty years later, I've learned that "Accidental Life" also pays *double* benefits! "Normal life" often doesn't.

Here's what I mean…

If you count on your DEATH being a routine heart attack or quietly slipping away in an old folks' home, then don't buy the accidental death insurance rider. Save your pennies, cross your fingers, and hope for a boring, normal death scenario that is safe-enough to justify "I just need to be able to bury myself."

Likewise, if you count on your LIFE just being a series of safe bets, responsible plans, careful activities, comfortable situations, balanced diet, and budgeting for the old folks' home…then don't allow for risk and serendipity. Save your money and time for a future that may or may not arrive. Plan on a normal life scenario of boring and safe-enough adventures, one that concludes "I just need to play life safely and be able to reach the retirement center with enough financial security to last until…I die." Ugh, when you put it *that* way…. Exactly my point.

I think it's often that way. Many people want to sneak through life carefully, with a goal of peacefully, safely reaching...death. Odd, if not poignantly sad.

"Jim, you seem to be able to fall in a pile of horse manure and always come out smelling like a rose."

Although certainly an exaggeration, my parents were onto something as they repeatedly told me this over the years. It was somewhat true, but not in the way I thought as a youngster. Sometimes I thought I was just lucky, a winner, one destined for something great. And although I might mess up, fail, and fall short here and there... everything would eventually end up good, if not great!

Later in life, a true and wise friend, Lorenzo, would ask me in the midst of a difficult trial and one of my attending discouraged funks, "Did you think life was going to be easy?" It didn't take me but a few seconds to honestly answer, "Yeah, I did." I had grown up in what I remember to be a *Leave It to Beaver* home in middle America with a Mom and Dad who were happy, intact, handsome, talented, successful. I had one brother and one sister - one older, one younger. The perfect sampling of siblings. I figured we kids would probably end up just as charming and charmed as my folks. I was healthy, did well in school, rode my bike freely without fear or helmet, went to the circus on my birthday, and enjoyed annual vacations in exciting places. I was convinced it was just a matter of years before I'd find myself riding a horse on a ranch out West alongside my beautiful wife and fantastic children (probably three, of course). I'd be traveling the world seeing all sorts of exotic wonders and eating interesting foods. I'd win in sports, sing in public, speak to masses, fly planes, climb mountains, survive accidents, rescue lives in great peril.... And somewhere in there, I would certainly appear on "The Tonight Show" with Johnny Carson for doing something noteworthy and entertaining. How and why that all might happen wasn't even a conscious question. It would just *happen*.

And here's the weird thing...it *has* happened...so far. All those things and more! Well, except for the Johnny Carson appearance.

Many of the rich and real experiences recounted in this book did just seem to happen. But, as I look back, there *was* a thread of purposeful continuity behind ostensibly random occurrences. There was an invisible Hand in all the workings. It manifested itself to me in a belief in serendipity. The risk of venturing into unknowns and the unguaranteed in order to just "see what happens" might not be as crazy as it appears at first blush. I had an anticipation of finding life accidentally. It *would* just happen.

Now in retrospect of sixty years, as far as what my gut instinct said, I was right. However, as far as the *way* it's worked out, there's been a lot more to experience and learn.

So…through the vehicle of personal stories, I want to commend for consideration "Accidental Life."

- It involves resisting some planning.
- It involves letting go of some attempts to control it.
- As a latter chapter reveals…it may actually involve *Breaking Good*!

This may *sound* like a call for an "ill-planned life" or "out-of-control life." On the contrary:

- "Accidental Life" is a *humanly* unplanned life…but that is *not necessarily* the same as an ill-planned life.
- "Accidental Life" is a *humanly* uncontrolled life…but that is *not necessarily* the same as an out-of-control life.

I would like to invite the reader along on a journey of life. A coming of age story…and beyond. A multi-cultural road trip, if you will. The twists, coasting, crashes, and stopovers along the route may themselves reveal a curious path to *real* life.

This is NOT a book of *teachings*…although I am a teacher and the book potentially teaches.

This IS a book of *stories*…personal, real, varied, some funny, some sobering, hopefully all entertaining, touchable, and provocative.

part one: the silly years

The day is ending, the way is long; my life already begins to stumble on its journey.
- Po Chü-i

nuclear family, front left

inglorious accidents

From the wonderful movie *The Princess Bride*:
Fezzik to Westley who's been "mostly dead all day"—
You just shook your head. That doesn't make you happy?

One theme of my growing-up years could be described as a series of inglorious accidents. I apparently wasn't satisfied with or destined for *cool* accidents....

Like my second grade friend, Dougy, who got a broken leg at recess when the teeter-totter he was on came crashing down, buckling his leg under it (not mentioning the bum who purposefully jumped off the other end and got away scot-free). I'm sure it hurt, and he did cry some, but that was all over soon. For the next several weeks, Dougy was the rock star of Mrs. French's class. Clip-clopping his cool plaster cast around the classroom, signed by everyone, gained him all kinds of heroism and sympathy.

And if that wasn't enough, Dougy was, at the mere age of 7, already one of those trend-setters that saw an opportunity. He wore shorts to school because it was easier to get over his cast. Nobody wore shorts to school. We weren't even sure it was lawful at Groveport Elementary. And Dougy wore not just any shorts. He wore khaki shorts with extra pockets and clips and zippers, just like Jungle Jim in the movies. He also had a pair of blue jean shorts that he rolled up just above the knees. *How do some guys instinctively know what's cool?* Anyway, Dougy's accident jump-started his elementary school career of fad forming. I even tried to hitch-hike off Dougy's fashion trend-setting by wearing my not-quite-as-cool khaki shorts. As soon as I hesitantly entered the classroom that day, I knew I'd made a big mistake. My skinny legs with knotty knees didn't look anything like Dougy's stocky, strong, cast-enhanced pillars. The laughs, comments, and name-calling erupted within seconds of my entering, and I couldn't wait for the school bell to end my first and last day of sporting shorts. But that's another topic. Back to my penchant for inglorious accidents.

Unlike Dougy, I, on the other hand, not only didn't have cool accidents, I had ones to be ashamed of. Unmentionable ones. Like a butt cut.

The lead-up to the butt cut incident was potentially cool. I played summer Little League baseball and had just finished a game in which I got to slide into home plate, which gets one really dirty, which is really cool. However, I didn't get hurt on the field of sport. That came in the bathtub after the game. My mom had put some Calgon bath crystals in the water (heaven knows why for a baseball player) and even warned me to be careful because the tub would be extra slippery. *Then why do such a hazardous thing for an already proven accident-prone kid?* Of course, within seconds of stepping in the tub, I slipped, felt a pain in the butt, reached back to feel a gaping wound in my left cheek, saw lots of red in the water, involuntarily screamed, then cringed as my Mom ran in on my nakedness, and then got shaky as I heard phrases from her like "Oh my!", "really big cut", "hospital", "stitches for sure." I had fallen against the porcelain soap dish mounted in the tile wall, which broke a corner off, leaving a sharp knife-edge to slice my behind deep and wide.

So how do you get a kid to the hospital with a two-inch bleeding slice that goes sideways on his butt-cheek? If I bent or sat, I opened the deep wound causing it to bleed as if bottoms had arteries. Well, what you do is lay the kid face-down in the back seat of the car all the way to the hospital. A very undignified and intensifying position. Nothing to look at to distract or lend light to the situation. Only the dark, stinky car seat to grind my face into the facts: *You've done it again. You're off to the hospital for some more pain and embarrassment. You'll have to show your bum to at least one nurse before a doctor will see it.* And I was right.

The social embarrassment factor didn't start with nurses. It started by entering an overly-populated waiting room where I had to stand for what seemed hours. Stand because I couldn't sit. That might have been tolerable except that every compassionate gentleman and gentlewoman offered this poor kid their seat, often insisting I accept their kind gesture. I was in a quandary as to how to be respectful to these thoughtful adults while not giving away my "condition." My Mom at least tried to intervene, but her dramatic, deeper meaning-filled "It's okay, he *can't* sit," to me didn't hide the fact. It seemed instead to scream out loud, "He's got a big cut on his butt!"

Not one, but a couple of nurses had to "now just let me take a look" before the doctor finally took over with the inevitable stitching utensils. Once he had closed-up my gaping cheek with synthetic stitches (which meant yet another embarrassing event of removing the stitches a week later), the doctor gave me a serious look. He said he wanted to give me some important advice. I braced. "Now, since this laceration is sideways, you need to be very sure you never go down any playground slides, because your bottom will go 'b-b-b-b-b-b-b-b-b-b-b-b-b-b'!" (which sound he made by doing the old rapid up-and-down finger on the lips raspberries). *Hilarious, Doc.*

Incident over? Oh no...more mileage! My family has to get mileage out of these kinds of things. Although it was, thankfully, before the age of computers and Facebook, it was not before the age of age-old gossip; the age of "Children are to be seen and made storylines of, not heard." Of course, family and neighbors had to know. It was an accident that required a hospital visit, after all. I get that. Maybe I'd do the same. But what I don't get is why Mom insisted on showing her close friend, Mrs. Featherstone, my "stitches" when she came over to visit. "Just let her see, Jim. Don't make such a big deal out of it." *Not that she'll see my bared bottom, of course. She'll look beyond that and only see my "stitches", right?* Mileage.

Such was one of my several childhood inglorious accidents. Not to belabor the point, but in order to make my point and validate it, let me in brief fashion relate a few other unsavory, if not humiliating, youthful accidents.

The butt cut fiasco was not my first rodeo. Previously, there was the time I learned to *not* dance on the point of a nail. (Many years later in seminary, I would hear of the quasi-theological question "How many angels can dance on the head of a pin?" That impractical platitude had about as much appeal to my adult mind as this childhood "lesson" did at the time!) Anyway, per usual, I was warned in advance. My dad was doing carpentry work in the garage, and had old two-by-fours with nails sticking out of them lying on the floor. He faithfully pointed them out to me and clearly expressed the potential threat of stepping on one. Being quite young, I don't remember how many minutes it took for me to test his hypothesis. For some inane reason known only to little boys, I put my little Keds on a nail point. Nothing. I pushed a little. Nothing. I put a little weight on it. A slight sense of indentation in the sole. I stood up on it and decided to see if I could spin! (Who knows why complex-brained, biped children do things quasi-brained arthropods wouldn't?) Next thing I knew, I was hopping around the garage on the good foot, hollering, with a board dangling from the now bad foot. Dad swooped me up, removed the offending board and nail, ran me to the kitchen sink, yanked off my Keds, and stuck my foot under cold water. This is my youngest remembrance of lots of red blood flowing from my body, mingling with water. Off to the hospital. Only a cleansing and some meds, but somewhere along the way I vaguely remember hearing what would be a running lecture over the years to come – "What were you thinking when you...?"

Then there was the hapless episode that earned me the lovely family nickname "Fang." A guest had shown up at the house and I was called upon as usual to hold the dog since her friendly nature required her to jump on everyone who visited. I bent over Candy with both sets of fingers in her collar. She lunged, I plunged...face-first with hands unavailable to catch myself. I came up from the concrete without a trace of blood this time. But also without the lower, inner triangles of my upper front teeth. Not baby teeth, but the ones you live with forever. What was left, and would define my smile for a number of years before I was big enough for porcelain caps, were two matching, pointed fangs. Thus, the nickname followed. Another accident that would not only *not* gain me heroic attention, but be a shameful source of squirrelly, closed-lipped smiles instead.

Seeing a pattern here?

you'll shoot...

Next came a real doozy! Dad's in South Africa on business (no insignificant factor to me in this particular mishap) and I'm a freshman in high school. It's evening basketball team practice and there's a ball coming off the backboard and rim. I go up to rebound the ball and coming down with it, I do what I'd been taught to do – spread elbows and knees to clear the area of defenders. Only one problem as I come down spread eagle - my buddy, Steve, goes up late with his knee.

Now, I know childbirth is the biggie that no one is supposed to question as the mother of all pains (pun intended). But there's a pain for guys that might, for a brief period of time, rival it. I rolled on the shiny maple floor for a good little while before getting up and punching Steve. Not sure he deserved it, but my pride was hurting as well, so he got punched. I retreated to the locker room to find I had a "bigger problem" (euphemism intended) than the usual knee to the groin, "just breath deep and walk it off" situation. Once home and obviously needing a doctor, the post-puberty teenager had no one to call on but Mom. Poor Mom. Poor *me*! Dad's on the other side of the world in a coal mine and I'm once again exposing my private parts to my mom.

And to the hospital. This time several nurses and doctors feel the need to weigh in. I'm equally scared and mortified as I'm repeatedly examined up close and personal. Technically, it's called testicular torsion. If the accumulated blood and water doesn't go away in the next twenty-four hours or so, the testicle might have to be removed! Now it's getting beyond just plain embarrassing for me and my mom. We go home to wait it out, and Dad needs to know. Poor Dad. An ocean away, he makes what was a meaning-filled decision to me. He cut his trip short and flew home. The one huge comfort in this mess - Dad would be here for me.

Let me leave off this humiliating story by saying just this: The obscenely large swelling did go down, I did not require surgery, and I now have three daughters. Enough said.

I wasn't finished yet, not by far. I must admit that the next major accident could be classified in the cool category, but since it ranked probably number one on the pain spectrum, it deserves an honorable mention.

In our Midwest, Erie Canal village, there was a low area in town behind Norm's Market and the shabby pink bar next door. Just the right combination of precipitation and hard freeze in the winter created a natural, rustic hockey rink. Matches involving anywhere from four to twenty players could spontaneously generate. In order to keep warm, there was always enough construction wood and trash behind the two establishments to keep a good fire going. No one worried or even thought about burn laws in those days. One other great natural feature was the presence of pond reeds and Catalpa, or Cigar Trees. During time-outs, we became proficient at picking and trimming these long bean pods into Ohio Cubans. There was nothing pleasant about smoking the homemade stogies, but that was beside the point. We were a motley group in our layers of sweatshirts and figure skates with semi-melted soles and toes from standing too close to the fire.

Hockey started young, but we continued on into high school, getting a lot more serious and sophisticated in our skills, but not in our gear. No one ever wore mouth guards, helmets or even shin pads. One particular day my sophomore year, it was just a handful of us, including my two best childhood buddies, Rick and Keith. As a set-up to my upset, Rick was a stocky guy who played linebacker in football season. I was lean. During a loose puck moment, Rick and I were on an obvious collision course en-route to the prized black disk. It was time for one of those climactic moments in hockey called "checks." Succinctly put, Rick went low, and I stayed high. Undercut, I went over his back and landed on my right shoulder. I immediately knew something was really wrong. Not only was the pain excruciating, but the strange angle of my whole arm where it attached to my body was...*wrong*!

It took a lot of help from my two friends to get me into Keith's parents' maroon station wagon and then home. There was no one home, so they got me in the house, and very slowly and carefully helped me remove my layers of gray jersey. The cringing look on their faces was not comforting. The ball of my shoulder was not where it ought to be in the socket, but was somewhere in my former armpit. My upper arm, instead of hanging straight down my side, was pointing out at about 45 degrees. And it ached liked crazy! For some reason, which I can't remember now, I wanted to wait alone for my parents to get home. Faithful pals Keith and Rick somewhat reluctantly left me propped up on the corner of the couch with my arm supported by pillows.

I had somewhere between thirty minutes and an hour to sit and ponder this new muddle...and my parents' response. I wasn't worried about some big display of anger. That wasn't their character. It was the timing. As they say about humor and many disciplines – timing is everything. My mom was picking my dad up at the airport from one of his long business trips overseas. I would be the dampener on Dad's homecoming, making his jetlag worse with an immediate U-turn to the hospital.

It was all one hairpin turn kind-of sentence. "Hey, Jim, what's up... what's wrong?"

At the hospital, they called it a "massive dislocation" of the shoulder. And then the scary news started unfolding. Since it hadn't gone back into place on it's own, they would be "popping" it back in place... with me awake. And (this was the comment that really got my heart pounding) they would do their best to *not* break my collarbone in the process. *You have got to be kidding me!* But they weren't, and they started to position assistants around me as I sat on a chair. They must have thought it would help to explain what they were doing, but inside I was moving rapidly up an ascending scale of anxiety with each revelation. A nurse was in front of me to help "hold him down." *No!* A male doctor or nurse or assistant (it didn't matter what he was) was behind me to "push on his clavicle" (I knew that was the thing they were trying to not break). *Oh no!* The main doctor (it *did* matter what he was...or I wouldn't have let them do what they were about to do) stood to my right and was going to "put one hand under your arm to leverage against, while I pull your arm up, out and down with the other hand." And then the final warning: "Now, Jim, honestly, this might hurt more than the initial accident, but we have to do it. Sorry...." *No, no, no, they can't be doing this with me awake and....*

I don't know if one would call the sound a "pop" or a "crack" or a "thunk." All I knew was that I let out an embarrassingly loud yell and got woozy and the doctor said something like, "Okay, it's all over, Jim. You're fine. Let's get him to x-ray just to check that collarbone." I had experienced pain before, but this was of a different kind. It was the unwanted gift that kept on giving with a very slowly pulsing, deep, profound ache. And the x-ray...just in case? Have you ever had someone manually break your collarbone and tell you in advance they might do it?

As I grew in age (I would love to add "and in wisdom", but can't), my accidents incorporated the newly acquired means of motor vehicles. It's not that I had a lot of traffic accidents. I only had two...technically. Other slip-sliding, near misses, and unreported bumping into this and that didn't count as official accidents. I considered those as driver's "continuing education." And since one of the two official accidents was honestly quite innocent, involved black ice at only 20 miles per hour, and had relatively unimpressive results, we can leave its details out...except for the fact that I did end up in court and the cop got chewed-out by the judge for wrongly ticketing me. That *is* pertinent information in the next story...but still doesn't warrant it's own accident report. On the other hand, wrapping the gold Impala around the old oak tree *does* have sufficient merit as a bona fide accident. So....

Why did big things always happen when my Dad was out of the country? He was selling more mining machinery, this time in Australia. I was on my way home from a date and, as usual, was pushing the envelope of curfew, meaning I was already past it. I was trying to turn the clock back by flying about 85 mph down a straight country road with virtually no traffic. Now, in my defense, when something runs into the road in front of you at night (which a cat did), you instinctively hit the brakes (which I did...hard!). It's natural. Once I missed the cat (there went the evidence) and I realized that my tires screeching on the pavement was going to draw attention in the neighborhood, I let off. But the brakes didn't - they locked. I pumped the brake pedal, only to have the car begin to drift across the lanes, up a slight grassy ramp in a yard, and launch me in my Dad's Impala off the ground and broadside into a very solid oak tree. The car wrapped around the tree, spun round it, dropped, and stopped. Somehow, I ended up totally inverted with my head on the brake pedal and my feet at the ceiling. No, I didn't have my seatbelt on. I had been warned, of course, but once again, you see the pattern.

When the police officer arrived on the scene, I was still shaking and had surprisingly escaped with only a few cuts, bruises, and a mouth full of tiny glass shards. But I was sure I would be getting a whopping ticket! After investigating the scene, the officer asked me how fast I was going. Being the honor student, church youth group leader, and former Boy Scout that I was, I answered, "About 55" (since I knew that was the speed limit). He stared me down, with anger behind his eyes, saying, "Son, I've got 175 feet of black skid marks on dry, level pavement, and you hit that tree on an impact of at least 50 miles per hour... and you're telling me you were going 55? And you know what makes me so mad? I can't do a thing about it. I can't use any of that as evidence to cite you!" As I processed my second big escape that night, the officer generously pleaded with me to learn something from this close call. He was a good cop, and I was a very fortunate and alive young man. He had a right to be angry and concerned about me. Oh, and did I mention...this cop was the same one who got chewed out by the judge just a couple months earlier?

Dad in Australia, despite hearing about his newly purchased gold Impala being totaled, was mostly relieved to hear that I was okay. A

golden crash

good man. Good parents. A good cop. A double escape. It was all coming together to bring about some genuine reflection in an otherwise carefree teen-ager. I even sat down with our pastor to get some perspective about what God might be showing me. *Accidental Good? Hmmm....*

One final accident wraps up my youth and serves as another life marker that, in time, would be used to help direct me toward a genuine path of wisdom. It was the summer before my senior year in high school and I was feeling like I had life by the horns. I had done well in school and sports, had a girlfriend, had a paying lifeguard job, and was currently on a two-week vacation with friends of the family at a beach resort on Traverse City Bay in Michigan. Life was full of fun and great expectations, one of which was the ambition of winning a medal in the pole vault event that coming senior year in the Ohio State track and field championships. That would very possibly be my route to a college scholarship.

It was a warm and slightly windy day on Lake Michigan. I was a decent water skier and was on a roll. I had pushed my limits in choppy water, but was still vertical. The beast pulling me was a new experience – a 22-foot Boston Whaler with twin outboard 80 Mercs, which left a wide, turbulent wake that crisscrossed in the middle for a frothy, bumpy ride. For you landlubbers, that's a lot of boat and motor on a big body of water.

As much as I was loving the challenge of skipping across double wakes, I realized I was getting pretty exhausted and, quite sensibly for me, hand-motioned to the driver that I would circle wide and then drop off. As I leaned right into the last turn and swung wide, I got the usual whip-effect that makes one go faster than the boat and often causes unwanted slack in the rope. That's always a momentary, anxious "pause" during skiing for me. The rope goes limp, while conversely, the nerves go tense. The skier has to work his posture and arms in such a way as to hopefully cushion the inevitable *yank* of the rope when it's once again tugged straight. As I tried to pull the slack out by raising my hands above my head, the rope went taut quicker than I expected, and jerked me forward. I fell hard, face-first into the water and felt the rope's handle grips rip from my hands with a jolt. Even though it had been a convulsing forward crash and tumble across the water, and I felt shaken up, I instinctively began to swim back to get my ski. As I stroked through the water, my left hand felt strange and cold. I looked at it, not really expecting to see anything unusual, only to discover half of my ring finger gone! The flesh was torn off about the mid knuckle, and the bone was sticking out another quarter inch and was snapped off ragged.

Shock. I stared. I turned it to look at each side. I searched around me as if I might find the rest of it floating nearby in the churning Great Lake. It began to trickle blood. More red blood mingled in water....

I started to cry, but quickly remembered and counseled myself that I was in a hundred foot deep water. I knew it as fact from the sonar we'd used fishing in that area a few days before. I almost immediately calmed. However, very disturbing and specific thoughts tore through my mind: *This can't be happening! What am I going to do? What's this going to mean? No! Can't we go back just a few seconds and do this differently? No, no! I won't be able to play guitar any more. This is grotesque! Will I be a freak? What will my girlfriend think of it? What will my parents say this time? No, no, no! Will I be able to pole vault and get a college scholarship?*

The boat with my friends approached and they asked if I was all right. For the record, I hate hysteria and sure didn't want any at that moment. So, despite being a shambles inside, I simply held up my hand and said, "I lost a finger." They thought it was sophomoric joking by holding my finger down. They laughed. As I moved closer to the boat's ladder, I turned it around palm toward them and again said, "No, I really did lose a finger." At that sight, their faces changed to sickness. They helped me onboard and raced the boat to shore, where they by-passed the docks and atypically beached it on the soft sand. I sat on a log for a good while waiting on a car for the next stage - the hospital, of course.

I remember quite distinctly my conscious frame of mind and general thoughts as we approached the shore and while sitting on the beach waiting for conveyance to the hospital. I couldn't help myself several times from unwrapping the shirt one of my friends gave me to put on it. I needed to see it. *Why isn't it bleeding more? It looks like a chicken bone. Is that tendon or ligament? What will they do with this piece of flesh hanging on that side? It seems like it should hurt more than this.*

At the hospital the attending surgeon was very encouraging, telling me I was "lucky." He told me that he'd had a woman nearly lose her arm in the same way a few weeks before. Then of a guy who was hot-dogging, had put the towrope handle between his knees, fell forward, and was emasculated! I started feeling lucky. He even told me that of all the fingers I could have lost, this was the best one, the least necessary for a right-handed guy. His talk actually worked. In short order, I was seeing just how fortunate I was...and had been many times over in my short life. Strangely, I was becoming okay with this accident, and began to look at it as a potentially good thing. It would make me stronger, a better person, maybe smarter, maybe more moral....

I was so okay with it that I asked if I could watch the surgery. The surgeon was a good man. I think he knew what I needed right then. He put a mask on me, sat me up on the side of the gurney, and explained everything he was doing. He even answered my questions. The reason it didn't bleed and hurt as much as I would have expected was due to the fact that it was pulled off, as opposed to cut off. A cut finger would sever the vessels and nerves in a way that allows the blood and pain to flow unrestricted. But the way my finger was pulled off stretched everything like rubber bands that, when finally torn, snapped back into my finger and hand, allowing everything around them to swell and squeeze, constricting blood flow and pain. That may all sound like superfluous facts to a kid looking at his dismembered hand, but it wasn't. It was helpful in the moment to focus my mind on something I *could* grapple with, and not the future I couldn't anticipate or handle.

The surgeon chipped-off and filed bone, removed some flesh, re-attached other, and finally pulled it all together by suturing it up. *How odd.* I was aware that I was accepting it. *I lost a finger.* It was a freak accident. And importantly to me, I hadn't done something really stupid this time to make it happen. It hadn't been the result of negligence. I remember thinking, *It's not like I was rushing while using a table saw in shop class.* That sort of thing would have eaten away at my thoughts. Instead...*Maybe I needed this to happen?* It was an accident, but somehow I knew it had purpose. It could somehow be something useful for "good." I didn't really know how, but I believed it. And still do.

Now, lest you the reader start having this mental picture of me as some grotesque monster full of holes, scars, missing limbs, or worse...let me presume to say that I'm not half bad to look at. I actually had a very normal childhood and youth including girlfriends, academic and sporting accomplishments (yes, I placed at State in the pole vault and eventually got a half-ride scholarship at the university), and incidentally, found I could get a laugh by asking for a ten-percent discount when buying gloves! I would re-learn to play guitar through improvising chords. My friends even thought my ripped-off finger was kind of cool. Sympathy essentially helped get me a new girlfriend. And now four decades later, I'm still in excellent shape and health.

still 10 fingers

More significant, however, than any physical consequences of these and many other bodily accidents I've experienced, is the impact they have had on my mind, my heart, my soul, my spirit. My life. Older people often offer quips like: "Trials are good for us." "It's the tough times that make us." "Crises in life are the potential for a better person." "You'll look back on this apparent set-back and be glad for it". And they're right! These are good people. They are the wise ones. They say such things because they're true.

I wouldn't want to go back through any of the physical accidents of my childhood and youth. I certainly wouldn't want to go back through a single one of the much greater accidents, fear-filled times, failures, and tragedies of adulthood. But...I wouldn't give up the fruitful benefits of having been through them either. They *do* have the potential for producing good in a life that can't be produced by easy and happy times. Back in those youthful years, I didn't really understand it like I do now. But the truth that real life, real living, can *appear* to come accidentally – that's an immense reality to me now. I'm a believer in "accidental life." What may seem negative on the surface - mishaps, upsets, misfortunes, disasters, calamities - can, in actuality, be downright glorious!

Inglorious accidents? I'm okay with some. After all, Westley had been "mostly dead all day." In answer to Fezzik's *"You just shook your head. That doesn't make you happy?"*, I could say, "Yeah, it actually does make me happy."

romantic hardhead

*Beauty is something wonderful and strange
that the artist fashions out of the chaos of the world in
the torment of his soul.*
- from *The Moon and Sixpence* by W.S. Maugham

I love beauty. And I've always had good taste concerning things of beauty. I know there are other perspectives on the subject. "Beauty is in the eye of the beholder." One of the first Technicolor-haired rockers, Todd Rundgren, made a valid proposition that "love between the ugly is the most beautiful love of all" (my guess is that he was kind of paving his own road to romance with that quip). But seriously, although there is certainly some subjectivity and preference regarding what is beautiful, I think it's a fair observation to conclude that aesthetics and beauty are more important to a certain segment of the population than to others among us. Some of us just naturally notice a prism rainbow spilling across an end table from a pair of reading glasses. Some of us simply *have to* pull the car off the road to watch a rainstorm crawl across a prairie. Some of us can listen to a piece of music without having to do something else at the same time. Some of us will risk asking a stranger in a Hallmark store what the scent of perfume is that she's wearing. Guilty...but I did explain I was asking in order to buy it for my wife. And some others just don't.

Mrs. Sims was absolutely gorgeous. There wasn't anything wrong with her. Her blond hair slightly curled at the shoulders (this was 1967), her sleek form, the long fingernails, shiny lipstick, her tanned complexion, the classy dresses and heels. Even her voice had a caressed crispness. The floral wafts when she passed your chair or leaned over your deskwork was overpowering. She was perfect. And I was among the admirers in her fifth grade class.

It wasn't a sexual thing. We were ten-year-old boys in an age of much more genuine naivety than today. Typically, a premature knowledge of such things didn't outstrip our hormonal capacities. We were admirers, and the corny expression "puppy love" might aptly apply. Proof of our immaturity and ineptness in romance was evidenced in the way we got attention. Tripping girls and insisting they had cooties was still in vogue. I even had a brief mental fling with a classmate, Candy. Twin fountain-like ponytails along with her big smile and deep dimples caught my attention for sure. But those childish features were no competition for Mrs. Sims's refined makeup and hairspray. We also managed to get the less-than-welcomed attention of our teacher through the normal shenanigans of prepubescent boys. And when those misbehaviors were flagrant enough, the punishment of that era still included swats. That's what we called them. Out in the hall, bend over and grab your ankles, look at the wall, and...*swat!* A wooden paddle compacting your corduroys and BVDs against your cheeks. Typically, one or maybe two was considered sufficient reminder. But periodically, the violation warranted three, even four. I know this for a fact.

Our classroom was in the basement of the community's original 1923 school building. Echoing hardwood floors, glazed brick walls, and stair rails made of military thickness piping was the motif. The severe architecture matched the tough atmosphere of discipline. Anytime we left the classroom, be it for lunch, recess, music, art classes, or zoo day in the auditorium (I remember touching a three-toed sloth and a wallaby), we had to line up at the classroom door in an orderly fashion. One particular day, I really wanted to be up front. I don't remember the event or why it mattered so much to me that time, but

I decided to make an efficient beeline. The main obstacle to that plan was a row of desks. For some reason, I thought I could clear them hurdler style. As I tumbled amidst the erasers, pencils, books, and rulers, I heard from Mrs. Sims for the first time personally, "Jim, let's go out in the hall!"

Corporal punishment at school was well thought through. The presiding teacher was required to get another teacher to witness the spanking. The target was precisely identified between the lower buttocks and upper thighs. (We had even heard of kids being crippled from spinal injuries…at other schools, of course.) I'm not sure, but I think this first occurrence was only a two swatter. It stung and I was duly notified of my mischief. Being the textbook teacher that she was, upon returning to the classroom of blank faces, Mrs. Sims insisted that I pick up every scattered thing and apologize to the students whose desks I had violated. And I ended up last in line. Crime didn't pay. Or *did* it?

The second time I was ordered "out in the hall", I made an important observation. Mrs. Sims didn't just bark the command and trust you to find your own way outside. She walked over to you, took you by the hand, and personally escorted you there. Once the ordeal was over and the witnessing teacher-comrade was dismissed to his or her classroom, Mrs. Sims would *again* take you by the hand and walk you back into the classroom. This was just her personal style, I'm sure, but it was *huge*. I had held hands with Mrs. Sims! Twice. And not just any hands. Hers were of a kind so unlike hands I had experienced before. *Now* I knew why she was constantly slathering them throughout the day with seemingly endless bottles of Jergens hand cream. That moisturizing lotion truly did miracles. Her palms and fingers were like a combination of wrinkled bathtub feet and the silk trim of a baby blanket. They were heavenly. My hand seemed to melt into hers. As I relayed this discovery to a few of my buddies, being boys, and young ones at that, a competition was birthed. We would see who could get the most swats that year. The prize was in the process. The winner got to hold Mrs. Sims's hand more times than anyone else.

Accidental Life

In all candidness, although this competition did actually exist, none of us were seriously *trying* to get swats. It hurt some, and we were still afraid and embarrassed during each episode that school year. But the competition did serve a purpose of which I'm sure none of us were consciously aware when we created it together. It provided a reinvention of what took place, allowing us to save face...and even gain some manly esteem. We were being boys and did what boys are prone to do in preparation to be men – put a spin on life's embarrassing, painful moments to make them seem purposeful, if not heroic. Buy back the moment. Being able to brag about holding Mrs. Sims's hand redeemed the shame and transformed it into fame. We were able to pretend we didn't see each other's tears that sometimes overflowed uninvited and were streaking our faces when we re-entered the classroom. Let the games begin, and a few of us were already spotted a few swat points.

Our teacher's Christmas gift to us that year literally backfired in my face. Each of us was presented with three colored

5th grade, perfect Mrs. Sims, 3rd row far left

pens – blue, red, and green. These were a big treat in contrast to the compulsory Number 2 pencils for all official assignments. We were only allowed to use these chromatic ballpoints for special projects and in our spare time. The pens were long, thin, and had little white stripes along the whole length. They also had a hole at the top necessary for airflow. However, as was often the case when I was entranced in a drawing, my writing utensil ended up in my mouth to be chewed on, or apparently in this case, sucked on. The bitter taste of blue ink was my first warning that something was amiss. The laughs and pointing by my peers was the second signal of trouble. Mrs. Sims was a true teacher, using my blue mouth, lips, and fingers as a pedagogical illustration, warning the rest of the students to "make sure you keep your pens out of your mouths so this doesn't happen again." She was also a reasonable lady, only verbally reprimanding me...this time. But later that week, when green was the color of the day as my mid-project mouthwash, the scene escalated to "Alright, Jim, let's go out in the hall." More swats, more points...and those hands.

I'm not sure of the exact order of infractions, but somewhere stuck in the course of the year was the glue incident. Amidst our arsenal of personal effects in our desks was a small bottle of Elmer's glue. Just before classes commenced each fall was an exciting tradition I always looked forward to. Shopping for school supplies. Each student was given a list of required items that went in his or her desk. There were boring, standard items to be sure, but even those graduated with progressive years. Sausage-fat pencils slimmed down to normal size by first or second grade. Blunt scissors gave way to pointed ones somewhere around third grade...which opened up all kinds of possibilities and problems. As the years increased, the spaces between the lines on writing paper decreased. Erasers, rulers, French curves, and notepads allowed for a little flexibility and choice during the purchasing. But by far, the most exhilarating particular that permitted creative expression was the lunch box. Although in retrospect the variety wasn't nearly what it is today, a kid's choices went way beyond the former basic black or Scottish plaid. One could express his inner hero or villain through Popeye, the Lone Ranger, G.I. Joe, the Flintstones, Batman and Robin, or even the quirky Munsters. My decision narrowed quickly to my two TV favorites, but *The Wild Wild West* eventually lost to *The Man from U.N.C.L.E.* Spies had shot down cowboys. But back to the sticky episode with the glue.

In my defense, the fascination with Elmer's glue was not my own invention. Another student first demonstrated its properties to me. You take the white paste and smear an area in your palm. Then you stash the bottle and hold your hand under your desk where it's out of sight while it dries. Once it's dry, but still flexible, you *slowly* peel it off. You don't rush this peeling stage because it's probably the most satisfying moment in the procedure. When removed, you are left with a wad of flexible putty embossed with your personal palm print to play with. Rolling it in a ball is one of the more common techniques. And of course, boys can find endless things to do with balls. That's when I got caught...the first time. Just like the pen debacle, I was given a warning and made an object lesson. We were not to play with the glue because "it's wasteful, can make a mess, and that's *not* what it's for." But it *was* for a number of us.

Despite the sensible lecture and threat that we'd be disciplined (since several kids had been caught white-handed), a few of us had already developed a habit. We *had* to try it again and often got away with it. We were white glue junkies. For me, there may have been something subliminal between the white glue in my palm and the Jergens hand cream, but I don't think so. Mrs. Sims did strongly resemble "I Dream of Genie", a similarly perfect blond vision from a bottle...of hand cream? It was probably coincidence. Nevertheless, the net effect was a union of the two milky images. When Mrs. Sims asked me to pull my hand out from under my desk and saw the not-yet-dry two-inch circle of paste, she took my hand...and wiped it on my face. She then told me to go to the bathroom to wash up, and "I'll meet you in the hallway."

The swat tally was mounting and I was in the lead, with back-row-Ricky a close contender. Ricky was probably a worse kid than me, but he had a cocky charm and could talk his way out of things, sometimes even swats. It didn't hurt that he was already nearly the teacher's height. She was probably a little scared of him - I know the rest of us guys were. In many ways, I was actually a good kid. I'm sure that was one confusing inconsistency for both my teacher and my parents.

I would bring home a report card that was consistently As, maybe a couple Bs, but the lowest possible score of 3 in "Conduct" (or "Comportment", as my grandkids' upscale private school now calls it. I know this because my one "fellow middle kid" grandson seems to have the same grades-behavior conflict as I did. I love him!). The scoring went something like: 1 – never an uncooperative moment; 2 – normal with moments; 3 – numerous repeated moments. I'm sure Ricky got lots of 3s in conduct also, but one way or another, I was winning the swats race.

When it all shook out at the end of the year, I had scored a staggering 14 swats and took home the intangible prize - the memory of *those oh so soft hands....*

Love of beauty in the female variety and my hard headedness got me into a different kind of mess the next year, in sixth grade. My ardent adoration for Mrs. Sims was quickly and fickly transferred to Debby, a classmate who stood a whole head taller than me. At least this time the focus of my affection was on someone my own age. But the more significant change was in teachers. For the first time in my schooling career, I had a male teacher. He would interject a needed element of discipline to my learning experience.

Mr. Saunders and I were entrenched in a friendly combat from the start, whether *he* knew it or not. He was Napoleon Solo and I was Illya Kuryakin – the men from U.N.C.L.E. (Fifty years later, I don't even have to hesitate in order to rattle off "United Network Command for Law and Enforcement.") Mr. Saunders was a pretty boy just like Napoleon. His dark hair was perfectly parted on the side and immovable with Brylcreem (the male version of hairspray, and precursor to hair gels). His clothes meticulously hung in straight lines down his lean, stiff torso. His shoes were as shiny as the finish on his Corvette, a pretty boy's ride. In short, he was perfect - the Mrs. Sims in guy form. I was his necessary counterpart, Illya. Semi-unruly blond hair, always taking a back seat to the leading man, Solo, but a *whole lot cooler* in my estimation. Illya was edgier as a Soviet counterspy, more rugged and laidback. Plus, he had some of the best sharp-tongued comebacks! In the mind of a budding eleven year old, Saunders and I were cast as sparring partners in Room 207 for the duration of sixth grade, the last year before complete maturity...Junior High.

My insubordinate, witty comeback ability was about to be tested against the top-billed superior, Saunders. We had begun a new approach to reading that year. In place of a uniform program in which everyone read the same books at the same pace, all of a sudden, independent study was encouraged. Groupings of short booklets were arranged by jacket colors, and you could move up from green to brown to blue, and so forth. Not only were we each on our own schedule, but we didn't have to stay in our seats. We could go anywhere in the room to read. What liberty! It was in that wild, wandering context that I made my tragic trip of the tongue.

I had finished one booklet and walked to the front of the classroom to advance to another color. As I was making the exchange, I was leaning casually on the row of encyclopedias. It was important to look relaxed and nonchalant (like Illya *would*) because Debby was right there a few feet away sitting in her front row seat. We locked eyes. I'm not sure exactly what got under her skin, but I'm conjecturing it was that tendency of boys and girls that age to pester one another to show affection. Debby slipped up beside me, shoved my arm, and was back in her seat as the Encyclopedia Britannicas dominoed off the shelf and around my feet.

Saunders, helping another student in a side aisle seat, looked up and made the reasonable assumption - "Pick them up, McCracken." I was being attacked from *two* sides now. Debby's smug grin on one side and Saunders' perfect dominance on the other. But he was wrong this time. Justice must be served (a big theme in my persona that I would learn about in years to come). I began my repartee with "But I didn't knock them down." I was already on shaky ground by omitting appropriate words like "Yes, Sir" and "Mr. Saunders." "You're the only one up there, Jim. Just pick them up." Decision time. But in my momentary insanity, it was dilemma time: *If I give in to Saunders... Illya has lost the joust with Napoleon, and in front of the femme fatale. But, if I give away Debby's complicity, that romance is over for sure.* He's waiting.... *It's time for a show of manhood in front of that sly vixen spy... it's time for a Kuryakin comeback.* "If you want them picked up, pick them up yourself."

I had never before and, to my recollection, have never since been that boldly impudent to an authority figure. Even if it fit my espionage alter ego, it was *way* out of character for this pipsqueak pupil. And I knew it as soon as it escaped my trap. What happened next was, in my retro-estimation, an accident. Mr. Saunders was as hot as one might expect. He came to me, grabbed me by both arms, and began to hustle me down the aisle toward the door. Somehow, whether on purpose or not, in manhandling me down the cramped aisle, he slammed my head against the blackboard. I went to the floor. I think the ringing of my bell and the corresponding *crack* echoing in the classroom served as a sober schooling bell to Mr. Saunders. Instead of taking me out in the hall or to the Principal, he put me in my seat and told us all to get to work at our own desks. Shaken and mortified, I put my head in my hands and looked down to hide the tears that were already puddling on my desktop, and tried to think what to do next. Some of the girls began to cry also. My fingers could feel a huge goose egg rising through my messy waves of hair. My guess now is that there was a much bigger egg being laid *inside* poor Mr. Saunders' head as he also tried to figure out what to do next.

That might have been the end of it, but it's a truism that your sins will find you out. It just so happened in the grand, overseen thing called life, that *that* day was haircut day. Whereas I usually rode the bus both ways, about once every two months I would walk home via the barbershop to get a "Regular Boy's Haircut." That was number two of three choices. "Buzz Cut", "Regular Boy's Haircut", or "Flat Top" were the posted options. The illustration for the Flat Top was a tiny man with a lawn mower walking across a guy's scalp, which at the time I thought was pretty creative. I had graduated from the buzz and only once later did my brother and I try the flat top along with it's requisite orange gel to make it stay "up." But it proved to be too much hassle and cost an extra buck. Anyway, on those rare haircut days, I walked home and Mom expected me later than usual.

As I walked toward the barbershop, the knot on my noggin began to worry me. The barber would certainly notice and ask me, "What happened here?" There's no way I could tell him without everyone finding out. In the exaggerated and self-fixated world of a young boy, I was already sure that every school employee and parent of my fellow students knew the whole ugly story by this time. Telling a barber was to spread it to the whole town. Plus, if I did somehow make it through the haircut without being scandalized, a "Regular Boy's" was short enough to expose the bump for sure at home. I always got the "look over" and compliments by Mom and Dad: "Good haircut... which barber did it this time?" There were only two – but no matter, it mattered. Just maybe keeping my mop for even a day or so would hide the offending mountain and give it time to level out before I had to go to the barber. So, when I reached the barbershop, I passed it and kept walking toward home. *I'll just tell Mom that I forgot about getting a haircut.* I'm sure I rehearsed that lie and visualized how to deliver it convincingly non-stop as I walked. I would be ready. At home, I opened the front door and casually (always important) walked in the kitchen as if nothing was unusual. And the question came just as anticipated. "Why didn't you get a haircut?" *Hesitate a bit...sound a little surprised and even disappointed with yourself...*"Oh, I forgot it was haircut day." I was ready and had delivered the line perfectly. "Then how did you remember to walk home instead of take the bus like usual?" Panic! I hadn't thought of that. A memorized and rehearsed lie was one ill-gotten skill, but an adlib, extemporaneous one was quite another level of talent. I couldn't pull it off. Mom was able to elicit the whole truth and nothing but the truth, so help me Dad when he gets home. I was busted, and I knew this was only the beginning.

Dad and Mom's response demonstrated the generally thoughtful and principled home in which I grew up. First off, Dad gathered all the facts he could from me. Second, he called Mr. Saunders and heard his side. Once off the phone, the conclusion and reprimand was pronounced: I had absolutely been disrespectful and way out of line saying what I did. There was no excuse or justification for that kind of behavior. At the same time, Mr. Saunders should have used proper measures of swats or taken me to the Principal instead of what he did. My teacher had agreed with Dad that such was the case. Tomorrow, I would initiate a formal apology to Mr. Saunders. In turn, he would apologize to me for his response. Both were wrong, but mine instigated it, so I needed to speak first. Additionally, the teacher was an authority figure and I was a kid. Mr. Saunders' mistake was understandable, but not justified. Finally in the discipline scenario, my goose egg and embarrassment in class would, this time, be sufficient punishment. But it had better *never* happen again. Case closed after tomorrow's recess!

I was hugely relieved and surprised to not be grounded until college. And as I'm sure was intended by my folks, I dreaded that little one-minute conversation throughout that entire night and next morning.

6th grade, perfect Mr. Saunders, top row far right

At first recess the next day, I walked to his desk and made the confession and apology with fitting fear and trembling. Mr. Saunders seemed contrite in his apology, yet remained firm in his authoritative role. From that day on, we were no longer Napoleon and Illya. We were appropriately Mr. Saunders, adult and schoolteacher; Jim, child and student. All was right in the world again.

I remember the particulars of that juvenile correction process clearly to this day, which shows the lesson did make it somewhere inside my thick cranium. Would the wisdom of my parents' approach have any long-lasting impact or practical consequences for me down the road? I'd like to think it has and still is. An interesting addendum to the story might indicate so, and that there was additionally an element of mystical guidance behind the scenes. You might even call it a thing of *beauty*. A mere five years later, at age seventeen, I was hired as a summer lifeguard at our municipal swimming pool. One evening, during a large kids' party called "Kiddy Night", I had to rescue a boy who was drowning on the bottom of the deep end. When I dragged him onto the deck and pumped out several gushes of pool water, my boss was standing right there watching. When we made out the report and explained the incident to the parents, my boss backed up my story and commended my actions. The lesson isn't lost on me, just how meaning-filled that vote of confidence and support was from my boss...Mr. Saunders, the swimming pool manager that summer.

street cruisers

The whole idea of St. Francis was that the Little Brothers should be like little fishes who could go freely in and out of the net. They could do so precisely because they were small fishes and in that sense slippery fishes.
– St. Francis of Assisi by G. K. Chesterton

When you live in a small town and have a need for adventure, you create it. As a boy, that usually meant adding risk to what seemed an otherwise safe and mundane life. My buddies and I typically fabricated it by venturing further from the permissible confines of time and space. Daytime was the acceptable time to be out and about, so we often chose the night. Home was the conventional space to stay within earshot and putting eyeballs on, so we stretched beyond the boundaries further with every year of age.

We weren't hoodlums and never entertained the supposed thrill of theft or even vandalism. We were merely living out G-rated fantasies, play-acting we were something we weren't - namely, cool, brave, and men. As we got into junior high school, some of our fictions wandered into the PG-13 category, but in spite of our passion to find excitement, we were a pretty tame bunch. As an example, when I went to see *Grease*, even though I knew I was supposed to be impressed and cheering when Sandra Dee showed up at the fair in black, skin-tight leather singing, "You're the one that I want", I confess that inside I was saying, "No, no...she was so much cuter wearing a white cotton nightgown singing, "Fool, forget him." We were pretenders.

Some earliest cruising began when we were finally old enough to leave Tallman Street, our street. Between the interruptions of breakfast and lunch, then lunch and supper, we had been set loose to wander on foot or bicycle the far reaches of two blocks further east into our old established neighborhood and two blocks west into the newly constructed housing development. Which reminds me of one subterranean adventure we concocted.

When the new housing area was being built behind our property in what used to be my dad's hunting grounds, they started construction with the underground stuff of course. Unlike our street, the newer development had curbs, sidewalks, and…storm sewers. The latter we soon discovered offered an alluring labyrinth of three to five feet high concrete tunnels. They ran through the entire neighborhood, popping up here and there at steel-lidded manholes. When the work crews departed, evenings and weekends left the underground world to us. We fought wars, searched out hidden domains, slimed through the entrails of gigantic beasts, and even lost my brother for a while in this submerged vascular system. If our parents had known, they'd have certainly warned us of potential flash floods on a dry summer day and forbidden us from ever crawling down there. But that was the point – the forbidden.

Above ground there was also adventure to be had. Rocky's Trail was our most common "go to." We were kids on stingray style bikes with banana seats. Rocky was a post-high school motorcyclist who literally paved the way for us. In a yet undeveloped sprawling field at the furthest corner of our allowed territory, Rocky wound and jumped his road bike through the same field until he'd created a motocross-like track. It was perfect. Two roughly parallel courses started at the street pavement corner of Madison and South Streets, twisted through weeds and over numerous humps of land we called "whoop-de-doos", converging at the last moment at "the big hill", a severe five-foot incline that tested one's endurance and ended the race. Whoever reached the trail fork first got to choose which route he'd take. The trailing bike had to take the other path. In a close race, there was always the exciting potential of reaching the big hill at the same time, which threatened and actually saw some terrific collisions. The top of the big hill (I'm not sure why we didn't ever think to give it a cool name) also became the natural convening spot for many meetings, stories, discoveries about life facts, and formulating the next quest to be had. It's location was high enough to see anyone coming for some distance (always important...like the cowboys sitting in the saloon with their face toward the swinging doors), and it was just far enough officially out of bounds to feel daring.

Becoming paperboys opened up an even greater sphere of excursions. I didn't have a route, but my two closest buddies, Rick and Keith, did. They couldn't help it that the available routes were in neighborhoods in other parts of town. *Yes!* I went along to assist deliveries and the exploration of adventures. A particular exploit stands out in my memory. One of Keith's customers lived in a spooky-looking house set back a bit at the end of a street. With wild gardens all around it, the far left side of it bordered a country road. We had to get off the bikes to hand-deliver the paper, winding through the layers of rose hedges, stone paths, and trellises hung with who-knew-what. While wandering back toward the porch, we happened to notice something dead in the road. Closer survey revealed a sizeable groundhog. That's when Keith came up with a brainchild. "What if we set this M-80 firecracker under it? I wonder how high it would blow." M-80s were restricted at that time because they had the sufficient gunpowder to blow a hand off. Truth be told, we were looking for someplace to use it and this seemed like a fortuitous encounter.

The plan developed into a little more elaborate scheme as a car approached, forcing us to leave the road-kill and act as though we were doing something else. Once it passed and was out of sight, we decided it would be a whole lot more interesting to set it off *when* another car was coming. In preparation, we realized a lengthened fuse would be necessary to give us enough time to see the oncoming car, light it, run, and hide. Keith, the more accomplished pyromaniac, twisted together several commandeered fuses from less worthy, regular Black Cat firecrackers. All was ready and here came our unsuspecting audience around the far bend. We lit the fuse and headed for the cover of some bushes in the customer's yard. Better than we could have possibly hoped (although, our expectations were pretty stoked), the explosive went off when the car was precisely close enough to appreciate the sight. Having placed the M-80 under the edge of the furry carcass, when it went off, it tossed the entire animal up and sideways off the road, giving the appearance of some kind of live, leaping creature! The driver braked, swerved, and kept on going with what I'm sure was bewilderment at what kind of animal could do that. Keith and I were ecstatic and enthusiastically congratulating each other...until Mrs. Newspaper yelled at us, "You two, get over here!" Not being hoodlums, we did what she said and slinked over to her. She warned us both what kind of accident that could have caused. She even threatened to call the police on us for trespassing. Keith got us out of that jam by reminding her that he was her paperboy and *that* is why we were in her yard. Just when I thought we were about to get away scot-free, she turned to me and asked who I was. Void of real street smarts, absurdly I answered in full, "Jim McCracken." Keith was probably thinking, *Why not give her your address and allowance money while you're at it?* The lady hesitated a fraction, then asked, "Is your mother Beulah, who writes the local newspaper column?" And again, not so savvy at giving outright lies, I responded in the affirmative. Then she proceeded to prove what I always knew was one of the reasons I'd never become a real bad kid. There were eyes everywhere in our hometown. Eyes that knew me or my folks. "I've known your mother for a lot of years, and I don't think she'd approve if she knew you were up to this kind of mischief, do you? I might have to talk to her...." That was all it took to set me on the straight and narrow. Well, at least for a week or so until I realized she hadn't phoned my mom and I was still a free man.

"What kind of things can you do only at night that you can't do during the day?" That was one of my dad's repeated rhetorical (and the closest he ever came to homiletic) questions, to which he answered himself, "Only trouble." Despite knowing he was right concerning

cruisers, Jim & Rick, small town life

the great majority of specific things that came to my mind, I still really wanted to get out there and try some of them anyway. As the proverb astutely strips down, "Foolishness is bound up in the heart of a child." Fittingly, my dad had a general curfew for me that conveniently matched my year in high school. Nine o'clock as a freshman incrementally progressing to midnight when I reached my senior year. If I wanted to be out beyond that hour, I had better have a good reason and permission.

Our town also had a curfew back in those conservative days. If you were under eighteen, you were off the streets at 11:00 p.m. or could be cited and fined if caught otherwise. Therein posed a not-so-lethal challenge to young guys looking for adventure. The consequences weren't quite enough to deter my buddy, Rick, and me from sneaking out in the middle of the night.

Rick's parents were sound sleepers and seemed to have very few suspicions. He could easily slip out of the house and never looked back. My folks, especially my mom, were raised with a good dose of guilt and skepticism, which I inherited. That meant getting out the house for me was a big deal. The meeting spot between our two houses was only about five minutes away, but I usually needed a good ten minutes to make it from the bedroom and out the back door, cringing at every creek in the floor and squeak of the door. Remarkably, I never got caught in our several outings.

We rendezvoused where Groveport Pike became Main Street and headed in town for most of our nocturnal cruises. At first we tried walking the railroad tracks to our destination, but that was actually hard going, always spacing our steps road tie to road tie without twisting an ankle. And it ran mostly through woods and fields that offered very little interest and a little creep factor, too. Consequently, our subsequent walks went right through town. Not in ordinary street clothes, however. This was clandestine business. We wore dark jeans, black sweatshirts, hats and gloves. We weren't amateurs.

We knew every block, every street named after a tree: south to north - Cherry, Hickory, Elm, Maple; west to east - Walnut, Oak. The in-town section was just a means to an end most nights. The girl of our mutual interest lived out in the country on a lonely road about five miles if we took a fairly direct route, which we rarely did. Any approaching car or house with a light on often made us change our course a bit to avoid being seen. Even though we knew they were easier for us to see in their lighted houses than we were in our surreptitious gear, we were still pretty anxious about being detected or, more importantly, prevented from our mission. We were going to try by some means to wake up our damsel locked in her upstairs bedroom at the risk of encountering her gigantic, red-headed Italian dad who would certainly run us off, if not worse. I'd seen him whack in the head with a hammer a bunch of unwanted kittens overtaking his barn. In my imagination, he'd shoot first and ask questions later.

Once out of town, the long stretch of country road (on which I would a couple years later have my run-in with the oak tree) provided almost unhindered time to talk and laugh as loud as we wanted. It had its creep factor too, as some of it bordered a peat bog and we'd both seen *The Creature from the Black Lagoon* numerous times on Friday night's *Chiller Theater*. Instead of "whistle a happy tune", our antidote for fear was humor. We laughed our way through the eerie portions of the trek.

The big left curve with the Stevenson farm at the top of the highest hill around always seemed like a hallmark along the route. We'd been on hayrides there and worked hard to find someone to hold hands with under the cloak of darkness and hay. And we'd been successful a few times. But honestly, most of those straw man dates had ended in corncob fights and itchy underwear as opposed to romantic encounters. Nevertheless, we were now boldly making the journey on foot and would certainly soon be rewarded with something worth it all. Even the German Shepherd that chased us into a corn field wasn't able to make us turn back. We decided to split up in different directions in order to confuse him. It seemed to work in that after a few minutes of crashing and being slashed by cornhusks, I couldn't hear the dog barking anymore. I also couldn't hear Rick anymore. Of course, we did find each other and congratulated ourselves on such a deft solution to the dog attack. Now to find the road again. Fortunately, this particular night contributed some significant moonlight. It was a perfect night for the adventure and the romance.

Reaching her house cast a different light on our plans. The old and slightly dilapidated two-story brick farmhouse looked quaint during the daylight. Andrew Wyeth would have been happy to paint it and our downhome female prize sitting somewhere in the surrounding fields. But at night and with the specter of her protective father, the house looked more like the homestead beside the Bates Motel in *Psycho* - another *Chiller Theater* regular feature. The simple formula of tossing a few small stones at her window started to sound way too cliché. Out here in the quiet country air, the *tic...tic...tic* against her windowpane would surely sound like a jackhammer to her vigilant dad's ears. So, after standing in the yard for several awkward minutes, we humiliatingly abandoned all thoughts of two Romeos and one Juliet, an absurd idea to begin with.

With our morale and guards down, we reversed our route and were entering town by crossing in the amber light of the train tracks and grain elevators on Front Street when we realized the car that just went through the intersection downtown was a police cruiser. "Do you think he saw us?" Our shared question was quickly answered when we saw him stop, back up, and then turn in our direction. When we heard his engine climb the scale of acceleration and the hum of his tires on the historic brick pavers of Front Street, all doubt was muted. Now we had a real dilemma that offered only a few seconds to be resolved. We had the peat bog to our left and no cover around the grain elevators to our right. Behind was open road and fields. The only reasonable option was *toward* the cop car. Mr. Officer Sir was 6 blocks south of Walnut Street and building up speed. We were half a football field north of Walnut Street and on foot. I don't remember which, but one of us yelled, "Run for Walnut Street!" and in a moment were both sprinting straight at the oncoming arm of the law.

A hard right onto Walnut and several panting strides brought us to a hedgerow that ran along the street and then bent perpendicular to it down the far side. We barely made the turn around the far corner of shrubbery when the cruiser wheeled onto the street. He slowed and began to scan our side of the street with his ultra-white searchlight. We had to crawl on hands and knees along the hedges in hopes of making it past the end before he reached us. In what seems much too fortunate for two inexperienced lawbreakers, we perfectly scurried around the backside as the squad car made the end of the street-side row and poured his light down the edge we'd just exited. We laid on our stomachs and hid the only white part of us, our faces, until he'd made a couple more passes and gave up.

Our circuitous round-trip of at least 12 miles brought us to our respective homes right at daybreak. Comparing notes later, we'd both gotten back in our beds, sweaty and thoroughly satisfied, only moments before our parents got up to an ordinary, quiet morning.

In spite of being less than jaded fugitives or successful Don Juans, we weren't bad schemers and quickly realized one way to half our risk of

football homecoming court – that 70s look, 2nd from right

getting caught. If one of us would spend the night with the other, only one set of parents had to be eluded, since the other assumed we were under good supervision. To make our escape odds even higher, tent camping in the backyard made it a breeze. Once the hosting parents went to bed, we knew they weren't likely to bother getting on shoes or risk stepping in dog poop to come check on us. They would think sleeping outdoors was enough of an adventure to keep us satisfied. But once we hit high school, the tent was merely a cover for bigger escapades.

My house was particularly well-positioned to pull off one of our riskiest endeavors. Rick and I spent most of our summer days at the local municipal pool. In addition to being on the AAU swim team every summer, we had risen to the coveted status of lifeguards. We didn't have keys to the gates (although had we been real bandits, we could have easily taken them to the local hardware and made copies since we locked up some evenings), however we did know every slippery chink in the property's chain link armor. And only a couple hundred yards separated the pool and my backyard camping site.

We knew the security lights would be on, and directly across the street was an apartment complex, but we were determined to do the preposterous – skinny-dip. It wasn't enough to simply swim during the forbidden hours, but the event needed some real edginess to make it unique. We'd already heard that my older brother and his buds had snuck in just as we were about to do. Being guys, we had to up the ante.

Slipping under chain link is actually quite simple, but does require some coordination and willingness to come out with a few scratches and maybe a dose of chigger bites. One culprit pulls the bottom up while the other slinks under like a salamander hoping he doesn't lose part of his tail. Then the roles are reversed as number two goes low. Once inside, we ran bent over like all the TV villains did, as if two guys in gym shorts running across an open field of grass and cement are less visible when uncomfortably bent in half. Our first layover was in the men's changing room where we could watch for a few minutes to see if we'd raised any alarm, and to catch our breath – more fear than exertion. A few minutes later, we decided to take off our shorts after entering the water. That way, if anyone should show up, we'd have the opportunity to pull them back on and deny such a perverse act.

We tried to make as few ripples in the water as possible in case any late-night duty cruisers driving by would have their suspicions raised. It didn't take long before slowly swimming around naked felt just like...slowly swimming around naked. Something was missing besides our shorts. We needed some excitement. "I bet you won't go off the high board" was the challenge that came off my tongue way too quickly. I should have known the back-and-forth rivalry Rick and I'd had for years would end up where it did - namely, taking up the dare. Rick was out of the pool, up the turquoise painted steps that always looked like dinosaur dorsal scales to me, and off the board with a horrendous splash. *What an idiot! That was great!* Now it was my turn to man-up. What do you do when someone calls your bluff? You raise the stakes. Up, out, up the 14 steps (how many hundreds of times had I counted them since I was a little tike?), and it was "gainer time!" A reverse full flip backwards would certainly win the competition. *Oh, yes I did!*

The exhilaration got the better of both of us. Soon we were going for number two, number three, and might never have stopped if one of us hadn't seen the police squad car turning at the intersection onto the pool's road! Like the skinks we'd become, we both instinctively slithered under the low diving board, which hovered only a couple feet off the water. Good cover, but that didn't settle the waves. And worse yet, it didn't recover our shorts laying in the gutter on the other side of the pool...in plain sight.

No siren and lights flashing was a good sign. But when he pulled in the parking lot, we were pretty sure our goose was cooked...in water. "Maybe he's only making his usual rounds and checking things out... stay still" was our mutual wishful thinking. Over the pool edge and under the board, we could see the officer's car creeping slowly along the sidewalk and pausing as it reached the diving area. I'm sure Rick's chest was thumping at race pace like mine. And then, the cruiser kept on moving and left the parking lot. Back to his monotonous, small town laps.

It didn't take any debate or further macho challenges to decide we'd had enough excitement for the night. We were both shivering and stuttering with cold and nerves as we made our way back through the field to the tent. But it didn't stop us from chattering it up all the way. "I can't believe we did that." "Did you see how close his car was to us?" "Man, can you imagine if he'd have seen those shorts?" "I thought we were going to have mug shots taken in the buff!" That's the stuff of homemade adventure. And the retelling is maybe better than the event itself.

KO'd in Detroit

...like bridges burned...
from the song "Lessons Learned"
by Dan Fogelberg (my favorite singer-songwriter)

Not only was I somewhat accident-prone, unduly romantic, and hard-headed as a youth, I was at times somewhat stupid-prone. In many things, I'd eventually learn the lesson. But, *unlike* the song "Lessons Learned", in which Fogelberg uses the metaphor of burnt bridges and suggests a single crossing is enough, sometimes I crossed Stupid Bridge multiple times before I learned to torch it. Such was the wobbly bridge of inebriation and, in particular, one dark, rainy night in Detroit.

I was an athlete. Athletes don't drink. At least they weren't supposed to if they wanted to stay on teams back when I was in high school. There was a zero-tolerance drinking rule...often enforced even against star players. Of course there were those who'd sneak around and get away with it, but at least you had to sneak around in those days.

And there were those who *hadn't* gotten away with it. If nothing else got my thick-headed attention, one of my heroes fallen should have. As a junior higher, I had two fair-haired heroes ahead of me in high school - Mike and Robin. In my eyes, they had it all. Wearing numbers 81 and 44, they were stars on the football field. Strumming 6 and 12-string guitars, they had a strong, classic 60s folk harmony. And I wanted to be just like them. Not only would I cheer their every highlight under Friday night lights, I also had a backstage pass to their musical talents. My folks and Mike's parents were good friends. Often when they'd get together, Mike & Robin would be hanging out and offer an impromptu concert, channeling Simon and Garfunkel, the Beatles, and Peter, Paul and Mary. I would sit as close as I could to watch their cording and feel like I was somehow part of the act. Sometimes they'd show me a few licks to try on my guitar at home. In retrospect, I know I was just a scrawny, fawning fan, but they treated me like I was somebody.

And then came Friday night, January 22, 1971. It was basketball season and I was sitting in the bleachers with a horde of my junior high buddies watching the varsity guys play. Through the end doors of the gymnasium, I saw my heroes enter with a few friends wearing their red, black and white varsity letter jackets. Who cared about the game - I wanted to see them, be seen by them, talk to them. As they walked in front of the bleachers, they started to pick their way up through the crowd right toward us. I was hopeful they'd see me, but also a little afraid they might ignore me in this public setting. But it happened. When they saw me, they not only smiled, but with enthusiasm, said something like, "Hey, Jim, what's up? How you doin'?" They leaned over to give me five. And then they moved on to sit with their gang. All my buddies were duly impressed. "Wow, you know those guys?" It may as well have been Simon and Garfunkel themselves, identifying with me. I was about to bust with pride.

I remember that ache of awe as I watched them leave the game that night. I also remember that ache of emptiness and despair I felt the next morning when I heard that Robin had been ejected from the car and killed, having gone drinking after the game. As I remember it, Mike decided to not join in or to leave early. But Robin was gone. *How can it be?* I had just seen him. He had seen me, and talked to me, and gave me five. As my mom would miserably repeat many times over the years, "That beautiful boy with such a gorgeous voice...gone." I wanted to throw up. I cried. I punched things in anger that he could do such a thing. *But Robin was a good guy!* How could I forget such a powerful moment? But I could.

Just four years later, you'd think I'd never known the sadness for my fallen hero. For the most part, my parents' vigilance and the tight community in our smallish Ohio town kept me on the straight and narrow. But when given a chance to be out from under that tattle-tale eye, I became one of those sneaks a few times. I seemed to get away with it. But Detroit proved to be out of my league!

The track coach, Mr. Butts (yes, that really was his name), decided to take a bunch of his athletes to watch the college National Indoor Track and Field Championships at Cobo Hall (now Cobo Center) in Detroit. It was meant to inspire us to greatness. A great idea and motive on his part, sadly squandered by my best buddy, Rusty, and me. Somewhere we had learned that hard liquor could be bought in Michigan at age eighteen. Not that we were eighteen yet, but at seventeen we had been able to purchase fake drivers licenses for five bucks at school (this was the era when a license was just a piece of white card stock without a photo on it, easily forged with a typewriter and skillful placement on the roller). So, we planned our foolishness in advance.

The pre-lim events were Friday evening. The finals started Saturday morning. We would go with the team that evening to Cobo. Once everyone was settled and caught-up in the races, I would sneak out to a liquor store we had seen near the hotel on the way into the city. It was dark and rainy, but it was only a few blocks away in downtown Detroit. *I'm a track star. I can run fast. What could go wrong?* Rusty would stay there as a distraction to the coach. Everyone knew Rusty and I were inseparable, so if Rusty was there, Jim must be there somewhere also. Brilliant! I'd buy the booze, run it back to the hotel, put it in the back of the toilet to both hide it and keep it cool, run back to Cobo, and never be missed by the coach. Only one problem. It worked.

After the evening events were over, we all walked back to the thirty-one-story, formerly luxurious Cadillac Hotel. Once back safe and sound on our twenty-second floor, the coach reminded us of the rules (no one leaves the building, stay in the rooms and not in the halls, etc.). And warned that he would be checking on us later! That should have deterred us, but sadly it didn't. We not only had the momentum of paid-for booze (a bottle of Southern Comfort), but two female statisticians from another high school had invited us to join them in their room, adding thrust to our stupid trajectory. Unlike our somewhat sleepy Erie Canal village school, these girls' school, WRHS (name abbreviated to protect the guilty), was known for its wild girls and partying. So our engines were revved and visions of craziness raced in our heads. The girls had learned of our purchase and added that we could bring the booze, of course, if we wanted. Perfect. We even had the foresight to tell a freshman teammate, Joe, where we were if the coach should come checking rooms. Joe could call down to the girls' room to give us a heads-up and we'd hightail it to the room. Yet another problem. It was all still working.

As the saying kind-of goes, "to make a long story presentable", everything went as planned minus any real romantic encounters. The girls, as it turned out, had invited the other statisticians and a few athletes, so we ended up being a party of about eight crammed into one room. Hardly romantic and nothing remotely wild. Rusty and I did our damage with the Southern Comfort, and just as the alcohol's effects were really setting in, the plan began to come unraveled.

Faithful Joe called down to let us know that the coach was making rounds and we'd better get to our room now. We left the bottle and set some kind of two-floor-stairway-door-key-indoor-track record! After about half an hour of waiting for Coach Butts, we finally learned that faithful Joe and friends had scammed us, and thought our break-neck return was hilarious.

Then came the critical moment when I decided to make one more crossing over Stupid Bridge. Rusty was bleary-eyed, ready to give up hopes of wild times, and went to bed. Cock-eyed optimist Jim thought there still might be some partying left and headed back for the girls' room...alone this time.

Important context: Meanwhile back at the girls' room, much had transpired, unknown to our foolish and persistent hero, me. The party had dissolved, leaving the two girls alone in their room. While Rusty and I were needlessly faking being good boys back in the room, some bona fide bad, drunk college boys had seen these two girls and had tried to get in their room. They had been loud, obnoxious, and scared the girls. What to do? Enter Cueball.

Cueball was a large, shaven-headed (not typical back then), powerful discus and shot-put thrower for WRHS. He was also, how shall I put it, a simple guy with an appropriate nickname. The girls had called Cueball to come sit in their room just in case the rowdy college guys should come knocking again. They didn't. But I did.

Not knowing this perfectly unscripted scene of potential mistaken identity was all set for action, I knocked on the door. I knocked loudly assuming the party was still going on. No answer. Adding the fact that I was not in a mental state of good judgment, I knocked even louder and said something obnoxious and terribly creative like, "Hey, come on, let me in!" Surprisingly, the door opened quickly. And there was Cueball's right fist coming with a mighty uppercut.

The next thing I remembered, as I came-to, was lying on my back in the hallway with Cueball and the two girls bent over me. They were profusely apologizing and explaining to me Cueball's innocent mistake. Stupid Bridge was falling down, falling down, falling down...

I don't think Coach Butts fully believed my story the next day. In fact, I'm pretty sure he didn't. He was a good man. (He's since passed away and I have respect for him as a teacher, coach, and informal personal mentor.) At breakfast I explained my black-and-blue, dislocated jaw and missing front cap (Remember my dog-dentist accident?) with the whole mistaken identity story...deftly deleting the partying and Southern Comfort. I don't think my parents bought the whole revised story either when I got home from the trip. They were not naive parents, and were also wise enough to let whatever really happened work its own consequences in my jaw and my conscience. It worked... eventually.

I can't say I never crossed Stupid Bridge again. I did. But lessons were being learned from this amazingly directed "accident" of scene changes and character switches that left an impression on me. I didn't like the kind of guy who would deceive a good coach and mentor. I didn't respect someone who would make a liquor store run on the rainy, sordid streets of Detroit. I dreaded trying to remember and cover my edited story lines. This was no accident - neither getting KO'd, nor once again escaping a foolish and dangerous scene relatively whole. I would *not* be a bad person. I *would* be a good person. I wouldn't end up like Robin. I wasn't sure how, but I knew it would happen.

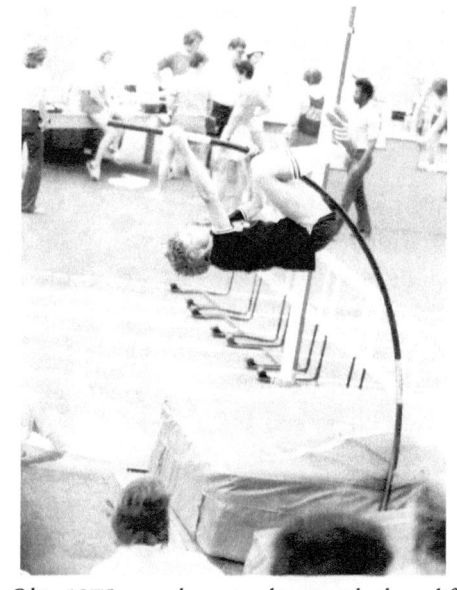

Later that year as I stood on the runway of the pole vault at the Ohio State Track and Field Championships, focusing and steeling my mind for the next jump, it slowly dawned on me that someone was calling my last name. I looked up to see the friendly, innocent grin of Cueball yelling at me, "Hey, McCracken, remember me?"

Ohio 1975 state championship, upside-down life

It was a hundred degrees out, but I remember initially shuddering. How could I forget? Somehow, the drunken, stupid guy that Cueball cold-cocked at the Cadillac Hotel had made it to this respectable event. Coach Butts was there and proud of me. My parents were there and proud of me. I wouldn't forget. I *would* be a good person.

second fiddle's fine

Knock knock.
Who's there?
The guy that finished second.
The guy that finished second, who?
Exactly.

Silver medals, red ribbons, the bridesmaid, back-up quarterback, leading man's understudy, vice-president, runner-up, the little dipper, co-pilot, substitute teacher, Tanto (The Lone Ranger's), alternate juror, sous chef, spare tire, B-level anything, assistant anything, minor anything, a bogey, a heart transplant, consolation prizes, magna cum laude, Miss Congeniality, second string, second chair, second class citizen, secondhand, second base, kissing your sister...

Now *there's* an odd saying, but it illustrates my point somewhat. Years ago I was trying to describe something to my wife that was very unfulfilling, and I used a simile she'd never heard before. I described the situation with the unsavory idiom, "It was like kissing your sister"... to which she shockingly replied, "When did you kiss my sister? And which one?" She missed my point (and didn't really care for the saying even after I explained it!). The point is that coming in right behind the best, even though it means being second and ahead of everybody else thereafter, can be frustrating, unsatisfying, discouraging, and sometimes maddening. Especially when it seems to happen with regularity.

I'll be vulnerable. I have to a degree habitually felt like I play the role of all those second-tier descriptives above. Now, I realize there's actually nothing wrong with or intrinsically negative about any of those things. It's quite commendable and meaningful to be employed as a vice-president, living with someone else's heart in your chest, or only getting to second base. But when that sort of "second best" seems to be the repeated norm, it can leave one wondering why he or she can't be the president, keep an original functioning ticker, or have been the one who hit the bases-loaded homerun. And that's how I've felt many times over the years. It's like...kissing *one's* sister – not very satisfying, nor what *one* was going for.

For example, I played the French horn for five years, but I was always second chair. Susie was first, I was second, and Barbie was third. I had to sit between two blonds everyday in band, but that's not the point. There were only three French horns. It wasn't like I chose to play the popular trumpet with tens of competitors, especially knowing that first chair would go to the band director's son, Little Wally. (Caveat: Little Wally genuinely deserved to be first chair. He could blow!) I never moved up or down. Second chair.

Football and basketball were the biggy sports in our neck of the cornfields, and provided another arena in which I could semi-excel. In basketball you had to try out and actually make the team. Football weeded people out by letting them get beat up and quit on their own accord. Two football drills in particular terrified me, and I'm convinced were intended to. One was the circle drill. You got called into the center of the circle, given a ball to *not* fumble, told to start chopping your feet (that means run in place real fast), and random other players' names were yelled out by the coach. That player would charge at you full bore and you were supposed to stay on your feet. Ah, but from what direction was he coming? That was the real thriller. If you did well and survived a few attacks, then you were rewarded with *two* names at a time being yelled out. Oh joy!

The second terrifying drill was called the "triple butt tackle." Once again, you were given a ball to hug to your belly like a precious treasure and warned to "Start chopping those feet!" If you had any hope of *keeping* your feet, you'd better. Directly across from you was another guy, the tackler, whose hands were free, by the way. The first two times the coach blew his whistle, the tackler was going to run at you, hit, and wrap. This was just a painful warm-up and taste of things to come. The third whistle (hence, "triple butt") gave him permission to run at you, hit, wrap, *and* take you down on your back. You were not allowed to duck a shoulder, dodge or do anything evasive. You just had to take it like a man. If you did do something as sane as lower a shoulder or turn sideways, you got to do it over again until you got it right. My first experience at being the triple butt dummy put me up against Garrett. I was a 145-pound defensive halfback. *Why do I need to be carrying the ball anyway?* Garrett was a 190-pound linebacker. *He's feared by dogs in the area!* First whistle – I absorb much of the shock with my faceguard...and it bends partway to my face. Second whistle – my faceguard makes it all the way against my face along with a good supply of Garrett's sweat. Third whistle – I'm on my back instantly and Garrett bends over me, smiling on his way off me, just to make sure I know how much he loves this drill. And how much he hates me...because I'm second string.

One interesting addendum. Garrett was in jail or prison last time I heard about him. No joke.

Next, to basketball season. After sweating-out the overnight sleep-robbing wait to

second-string halfback & wide receiver

see if my name made the team roster or if I got humiliatingly cut, there I was on the list of just twelve names. But unsurprisingly, the twelfth name. Rusty, my conjoined twin, was eleventh. Just to make the situation clear, coach "Be-bop" Miller called Rusty and me into his office. "I want you guys to know where you stand. Most practice scrimmages obviously require ten players. You guys will be standing by and just watching some of the time. We need you though, especially if a teammate can't make practice or gets hurt, then you're in. You probably won't see much play-time in games (that was a grand understatement). If you don't want to stay on these terms, say so now. Otherwise, congratulations, you're on the squad." All I really heard was the last part. I was so jacked to have made the team again! But why? First string would play most of the game. Second string would play some of the game. Rusty and I made up the absurd duo of third string, and would never play. Nevertheless, we stuck out the whole season of practices and games.

I got to play in two games. Both times we were so far ahead Coach figured I couldn't hurt anything. The second of those games, I decided to make the most of my total 48 seconds before the final buzzer. We were playing man-to-man defense (who knows why when we were ahead by an untouchable point lead). I was determined – *My man will not score.* I think I set a school record of committing three fouls in 48 seconds. In my overly-enthusiastic moment on the court, I almost fouled-out in less than a minute, earning from my teammates the fitting moniker, Hackin' McCracken. But…my man never scored. Only because he missed every foul shot I so profusely provided him. Why? Because he was second or third string too!

And then there was the nastiest of personal fouls. Rusty and I were tolerated by a few of the players, but for some reason despised by a few seniors. Bruce, the 6 foot 5 inch center, was one who never made a civil comment to us. In the hours before a particularly big game, the school held a pep rally on the front lawn to pump-up the team toward a win. Unintentionally, I ended up standing beside Bruce, who had obviously snuck out earlier that day to McDonald's since he was drinking from one of their Coke cups. Out of the corner of my eye, I could see him glance sideways at me, but then he did the unexpected. He held the cup out to me offering a drink. *What's this... an act of friendship?* I normally wouldn't drink after someone else, but how could I turn down this unique gesture? I took a good-size swig through the straw. In an instant, I was coughing and spewing, doing all I could to not throw up the rest of whatever I'd eaten that day. Bruce was spurting laughter. *Call a technical foul, Ref!* Bruce hadn't been drinking. He'd been chewing tobacco.

Rusty and I tried to get our revenge for having sat the bench all year long...and *almost* did. Our unspoken, designated place on the bench during games was, of course, at the very end furthest from the coach. We were certain that most games he was totally unaware that we existed. As we approached the last home game of the season, a plan was hatched to catapult us into the halls of yearbook fame. A friend and yearbook photographer, Gary, was to bring his magnetic chess board to the game, set it on the bench between Rusty and me, get down low and catch an action shot of Rusty and me leaning over the board, intently pondering chess moves...with the game going on in the background. What a great idea! What a great photo it was, too. But, like Rusty's and my basketball fame, that classic photo got "benched" for fear of consequences. It never made the yearbook cut. Even our attempt at a sporting "fail" didn't have game.

Even back then I knew sports was not everything. Academics and that nebulous thing called "our future" were a lot bigger. When a rare elective course in aeronautics was offered, I saw big possibilities. Not only would the course prepare one to take the Federal Aviation Administration's exam, which gave the flying equivalence of a temporary driver's license, those who passed the FAA Written would be in the running for a scholarship that would result in a Private Pilots License. I could potentially be a pilot as a junior in High School.

The course was taught by our science teacher, Col. Moore, a retired officer in the Air Force with over 20,000 hours of flight time. That's over 2¼ *years* in the air. He was a pilot in the Korean War and afterwards flew KC-135 Stratotanker refuelers - a flying gas station for suped-up jets. And he was a good friend of my Dad through Lions Club and other venues. This was a real possibility.

I took the course. I loved it. We got to fly several times with the Colonel. I got to take the controls from the co-pilot seat and began to get a feel for coordinating ailerons, elevators, and rudder. Just for the fun of it, we did hammerhead stalls in a Cessna 150 and 172. That's kind of a half-turn, half-flip, nose-down spiral toward earth until the Colonel reversed controls and pulled it out. It made you want to vomit, but it was exhilarating! We got to hear all kinds of flying stories in class and while flying. The ones in the classroom were interesting, but tamed (there were girls in the class and the Colonel held his generation's standards). The ones in the air with just us guys were edgy, heroic, and sometimes vulgar. After all, the Colonel had flown refuelers...that meant he "passed gas" for a living. And that wasn't remotely the spiciest of the stories either.

Near the end of the year, we all sat for the FAA Written. Only three in a class of twenty or so passed it. I was one, along with two good friends, Steve and Mark. In order to determine which of us would get the scholarship and become a Private Pilot, we would write an essay stating why we wanted and deserved the opportunity, each would interview with the school principal and the airport director, and our exam grade would factor in (mine was the lowest of the three). I did my best, but I felt a familiar premonition. I wasn't self-confident like Steve. I wasn't self-promoting like Steve. I couldn't even handle a motorcycle like Steve, who already competed on a motor cross team. I was part of his pit crew a few times. *Oh, no, there's that second-tier, background position again!* Steve was Buzz Lightyear with unfolding wings; I was Woody with a pull string. I felt it coming and wasn't wrong. Steve got the scholarship, took flying lessons, soloed, became a pilot, and flew Cessnas. I was second or third place, and drove my parents' Buicks.

My perspective on this has radically changed since then, but for many years, it sure seemed to me that I was fated with some kind of chronic "second place" curse. It was as if my accomplishment engine had one of those old truck governors that kept it from going too fast. It seemed true in large and small things. For instance, my wardrobe always appeared to me to be one style behind hip or one brand away from the coolest. I found out about the weekend party the next Monday morning at school. I had chosen sissy French horn instead of macho trumpet.

I developed a negative expectation in daily events and opportunities. I might have just purchased Board Walk, be cruising the next lap past Short Line Railroad with momentary, excited anticipation of hitting Park Place...only to land one lousy square short on Chance and read, "Go to jail, go directly to jail, do not pass 'Go', do not collect $200." I expected to come up a day late and dollar short. I started believing Murphy's Law was the greatest force on earth, at least for the likes of me.

It was an emerging perspective, and a rotten one at that. I was becoming a person I didn't want to be. A complainer. A glass-half-empty guy. But, I believe Hope and Good were at work behind the scenes. New perspective was slowly germinating in an invisible cultivation process.

This fresh perspective surprised me at the end of my senior year. Even knowing sports weren't the biggest thing in life, our small-town culture often made it seem they were. A big end of the school year event was the annual Sports Banquet. Jocks of all brands would be paraded across the platform

Ohio 1975 state championship, 4th place

to receive accolades, building a crescendo to the final grand honor – the Mac Sims award! I don't even remember who or what the original Mac Sims was or did, but his fame and name went to the "best all-around athlete" of the graduating class. We all had our earlier guesses as to who it might be that year, but now the anticipation had built, and the suspense was electric.

Just before the Mac Sims climax, one other award was to be handed out. It was the Agonis Award, which went to the scholar-athlete of the year. The actual plaque would be presented by a state senator in a special award ceremony a few weeks later. As they began to describe the characteristics necessary in the recipient, my mind heard my Dad's comments in previous years: "I think the best award is the Agonis instead of the Mac Sims. It shows balance of academics and athletics. Look at the kind of guys that have gotten it the previous two years, Robby and Ken. That's the award I'd be most proud to get." As that remembered conversation was tumbling around simultaneously with what Coach Starr (yes, that was his real name) was saying, I heard, "And this year's Agonis Scholar-Athlete Award goes to Jim McCracken."

Agonis scholar-athlete award

My Mom was there at the banquet that night, but Dad wasn't. Once again, he was in Australia selling underground mining machines. He actually had patents on some of the designs. But Mom knew this award would really please him and she "rung him up", as the Aussies would say it. She said, "Jim has some news for you" and handed me the phone. How great was this? I wasn't confessing a wrecked car or reporting a torn-off finger! "Hey, Dad, guess what..."

And while John (the Baptist) was completing his course, he kept saying, "What do you suppose that I am? I am not He. But behold, one is coming after me the sandals of whose feet I am not worthy to untie."
– Acts 13:25

the college experiment

Hence it came about that I concealed my pleasures; and that when I reached years of reflection, and began to look round me, and take stock of my progress and position in the world, I stood already committed to a profound duplicity of life.
– from Jekyll's letter to Utterson in *The Strange Case of Dr. Jekyll and Mr. Hyde* (Robert Louis Stevenson)

To me, college these days seems less a verified solution and more a questionable experiment. For every byte of empirical data and logical lecturing going on in American undergraduate institutions, there are terabytes of, shall we say, *un*empirical information and *il*logical learning going on. That's a generous way of putting it.

The way I personally decided on the university I would attend was in itself less than rational. Despite a few partial scholarship possibilities at some upscale Ohio schools like Case Western Reserve and Otterbein, I knew I would be going to a State university given our family's financial priorities. That helped limit my choices - an appealing thing to my avoidance of research. With that starting point, I ruled out schools I didn't like for a variety of nonsensical and unsubstantiated reasons: Cincinnati U. - because I didn't like the city (which city, ironically, I would move to 40 years later and find very pleasant). Ohio U. – because that's where all the party-hardies go (which is exactly what I became from the first night at the school I did choose). Kent State U. – because they had that famous campus shooting there (as if that typified campus life). Ohio State U. – because it's too large and too close to home (I would have to still live in my parents' house under watchful eye, so "no"). You get the idea. There was not an erudite set of criteria guiding my decision-making process.

On top of my deficient scientific methodology was a no more impressive effort quotient. I glanced through a few catalogues on the State schools and asked my friends where they were going. That pretty much entails my "research" on the matter. Then, somewhere during the summer before I was to enroll, my dad asked me if I'd decided where I was going. He was under the assumption I had given it a lot more thought and investigation than I had. Dad was clearly hoping to hear some evidence of forethought and decisiveness...so I gave it to him. "I'm pretty sure I'm going to Bowling Green." How had I come to that on-the-spot confident conclusion? For starters, I was on the spot! And there were actually a few factors that had previously tripped through my brain. Number 1: I didn't know anyone else from my high school going there and that had a positive appeal to me. Namely, don't go with the flow. Number 2: That's the school the track star, Dave Wottle, of Olympic gold medal infamy went to (He's the runner who forgot to take his trademark hat off during the medal ceremony and had his Gold revoked until a later review board reinstated it). *Therefore, they must have a good track and field program.* I was correct, but my logic was deplorable. One hero does not make an army. Number 3: I was sure it was far enough away from home to have to live on campus. So, "Bowling Green" my mouth said confidently.

Dad looked duly surprised and encouraged. He suggested we take a trip there, see the campus, and we could maybe go fishing at Lake Erie from there. *Aha...Bowling Green must be north of here!* It really wasn't much more elaborate a plan than that, but it changed the course of my life in profound ways, as any major move and college decision will. I had chosen my educational direction almost by...accident. The result would frame my life. But that's getting ahead of things.

I got my roommates by accident also. Tim and Larry were assigned to me. We were definitely an unlikely admixture. My parents and I met Tim as we first keyed into my Rodgers Quadrangle dorm room.

Sitting cross-legged, with black hair parted in the middle and down to his shoulders, playing an electric bass guitar, there was Tim in the middle of blue shag carpet. My parents admitted later that their initial thought was "Oh no!" When his answer to their friendly inquiry "Tim, where are you from?" came back "Hawaii. I went to high school and surfed there", their seed fears must have shot down some deep roots. On the other hand, Tim was the son of an Army Colonel, stood to his feet in greeting them, looked them in the eye as he spoke, and consistently used "Yes, Mam" and "Yes, Sir." This quelled enough anxiety to not take me back home immediately. Tim was in Army ROTC and would shave his head military style in only a few days. He and I would become great buddies that year. Tim's the one who came up with a way for me to finger guitar chords with my available three fingers. I bought my first car from him - a lemon yellow 1968 Renault R10 that didn't run. For all of $50.

Then there was Larry, whom I hate to admit I didn't get to know better. Larry was a shy, conservative, studious, black guy who wasn't ready for or fitted to the likes of Tim and me. We were friendly with each other, but had little in common. He didn't party or drink. Well, not until months later when Tim and I left him some beer in the fridge and told him to help himself while we were out. We came home later that night to find him studying at his desk, having downed several...over ice...through a straw. A silly, dazed grin let us know he wasn't really getting much studying done. Larry found another roommate for the second quarter, leaving Tim and me the whole 11' X 13' puke-infused blue shag carpet room to ourselves.

To say that in college I was a walking contradiction might be a little over-dramatic. At the least, I was certainly inconsistent in character, conflicted in morals, often lived at variance with my values, and even qualified as a hypocrite at times. Yeah, I was a walking contradiction. And the duplicity bothered me deep inside.

I always went to class, did my assignments (minus some reading when I knew I could get through just on class notes), turned in papers on time, participated in class discussion, actually used the library, often made the Dean's List, and graduated on schedule. I never missed track practice or weight-room workouts, earned increasing financial scholarships, and was awarded "Most Improved Athlete" on the track team my senior year. I joined a barbershop quartet and chorus, submitted articles to the school newspaper, and chose a roommate my sophomore year because his dad died and he needed a friend (and he became a great friend to me). I ate a balanced diet, did my own laundry regularly (except bed sheets; I am a guy), showered twice daily (athletics, not hypochondria), and kept my car maintenanced.

What's so fraudulent about that list of things? Nothing, that's just the good stuff. At the same time that those things defined me...

I abused my brain and body by excessively drinking, smoking dope, sometime cigarettes, and popping No-Doz to pull all-nighters cramming for exams or writing the long-procrastinated term paper. When I say I over-drank and smoked pot, I don't mean I got tipsy or tried it a few times. I awoke in places having no idea how I got there. I awoke to faces I just met or barely knew. I staggered miles in snow and rain, ill-clad, getting bronchitis and pneumonia. I threw fruit at automobiles from the fourth floor thinking it was funny to make drivers slam the brakes and rage. I streaked the girls' dorm, twice on one snowy night. I drove and rode with others way over the legal alcohol blood levels. I drank strawberry-scented shampoo somehow thinking it might be good. I bowed numerous times to the porcelain god, trashcan, bush, whatever was immediately available. I switched girlfriends like a day trader. I risked reputation, health, scholarships, invested credit hours, others' lives, and my own life...for no sane reason at all. I did things for which I could or should have been greatly ashamed, justifiably kicked out of school or thrown in jail, severely maimed, or unquestionably dead. My college experiment looked a lot more like a mad scientist tossing every possible chemical into a beaker, all the while hoping it wouldn't blow up, poison someone or eat away the beaker!

Now, some might not regard that second list of behaviors to be heinous or disgustingly incompatible with the first list, but I did. And it was an acid eating away at my conscience.

dorm hall guys, seated row 3rd from left

Like many of my fellow collegians, I was experimenting with life, and the added input of my mid-1970s professors was only creating confusion. My very first Sociology 101 class should have clued me in. A classroom full of fresh, green freshmen waited to meet our instructor and be enlightened. After ten minutes of waiting on him, one overly-zealous student pointed out that the university handbook said (*Some people actually read those?*) that if an instructor is more than ten minutes late, the students can leave and not be held as absent. His implication was that we skip our first college class. Although a few feigned ready to enact such boldness, no one left. And, on cue, our professor entered. His perfectly tardy entrance was prophetic of his overall crappy attitude and message. Imagine the following being your introduction to college lectures.

First, the visual cues. A lumbering, thirty-something male in torn jeans, un-tucked flannel shirt, hair and beard down to mid-torso, carries a vending machine cup of coffee in one hand and a pack of Carltons in the other. Class notes are appropriately tucked in their second-tier priority location, under his armpit. Prof pulls a chair up behind the table-top podium and sits on the back of the chair, hiking boot shod feet on the seat, and casually deposits his paraphernalia on the table. Leisurely lighting his cigarette and sipping his coffee, his eyes scan us, his malleable clay, letting the scrutiny have its purposeful, unnerving impact. Then comes the verbal evidence of his rotten attitude and message.

"So, freshman, huh? All primed to learn. Well, before we get into Sociology, let me share a little with you about higher education, since that's what you're ultimately here for.

"IF, after four years of studying hours and hours through blood, sweat, and tears, and spending thousands of dollars to do so...should you succeed in getting your much-anticipated Bachelors diploma... then (at this point he turned, reached a piece of white chalk, and scribbled 76% on the blackboard) you will have a 76-percent chance of getting a job in your related field of study. Not too bad.

"However, if you're real smart, you'll decide to go on and get a Masters degree. And you'll spend two or three more of your precious years studying hours and hours through blood, sweat, and tears, and spending thousands more dollars to do so. Should you succeed in getting your prized Masters mantle...then (and once again, he scratched on the blackboard) you will now have a 58% chance of getting a job in your related field of study. Hmmm?

"Now, if you are really sharp and ambitious like me, you'll decide to continue toward the auspicious Doctoral degree. And you'll invest another who-knows-how-many years of studying hours and hours through blood, sweat, and tears, and spending thousands more dollars to do so. Should you finish your dissertation and survive your comprehensives, and finally become Doctor So-and-So...then (chalk noise communicating frustration behind the strokes) you will now have a 34% chance of getting a job in your related field of study. THAT, my esteemed friends, is 'higher education.'"

As he went through the syllabus and began talking about social constructs, mores, and models, all I could think was, *And I'm here for this?* - his intended counter-productive response, I'm sure. I did good work in his class that quarter. He gave me a C. I went to see him about it. He didn't like my attitude!

My health class Prof, the golf team coach, wasn't any more motivational or constructive in guiding me on to more lofty heights. His first "lecture" included tossing out the most vulgar, trashy, and crude words in the unofficial English language in order to ask the question, "Does it bother you to hear that from a professor? Why? They're just words. Words aren't anything. They're only symbols and representations. Loosen up! Come on, let's do an exercise together. Let's say together out-loud '_ _ _ _'...release the bomb. Don't be shy, bellow it out - '_ _ _ _!'" As if I needed a professor for that. I could just go back to the locker room or dorm, and smoke dope with friends to do that. *And what does this have to do with Health?*

Certaintly, the bulk of classroom information was more the meat and potatoes of macro and micro economics, differential and integral calculus, environmental biology, managerial accounting, and the dreaded Western Civilization. But there was a lot of flavoring and spice mixed in that sounded a lot more like the additives of processed food labels – Butylated Hydroxytoluene, Sodium Benzoate, Acesulfame-K, Olestra, Monosodium Glutamate, Red Dye #3, etc. There's a good reason those latter words sound more like they ought to be additives for your 1975 Ford Mustang. The educational additives I was collecting were probably about equally as humanly nutritious and socially healthy.

It wasn't the in-class learning that most effectively exposed my Jekyll & Hyde proclivities, but rather the extra curricular stuff of daily (and nightly) campus life. I was an accident looking for a place to happen, and the university scene provided me plenty of crash sites. Dr. Jekyll was basically holding it together on the academic and athletic fronts, but nothing to write home about (which my parents could confirm I rarely did). Mr. Hyde was coming undone at the seams on the character and social fronts (nothing I would have dared write home about). The flip-flopping was increasingly disquieting to me. My religious upbringing had given me some good moral bearings, at least to know what was on track and what was off track. I knew I was derailing. But the real *want to* and *how to* get back on track was another thing. I needed some kind of catalyst. I needed some relief.

That catalyst and relief came in ways I wouldn't have expected or chosen, but the redirection was profound and lasting. Thankfully, when it came, I recognized it for what it was. My mad-scientist approach to semi-adult life was a personal re-enactment of that climactic scene from *Dr. Jekyll and Mr. Hyde* in which he's desperately looking up, then down, then up, then down...anguishing over his topsy-turvy inner conflict. The events of the next couple of years would offer me the formula I would need to come back "upright" from living life "upside down."

All the real argument about religion turns on the question of whether a man who was born upside down can tell when he comes right way up.
   – G. K. Chesterton, *Orthodoxy*

a thundering velvet hand

He earned his love through discipline...
Dan Fogelberg (about his father in "Leader of the Band")

My dad, in exasperation at some bone-headed event in my young life, asked me, "Why does it take getting kicked in the head just to get your attention before some sense can get in?" An insightful and fair question, and spoken in what I know now to have been real love.

Maybe a new venue and new people would be the answer? At the end of my experimental freshman year at BGSU, my dad had taken a new Vice President position in Pittsburgh, Pennsylvania. I had yet another new place and adventure ahead, which I welcomed. All I needed now was a summer job and hopefully some friends. Coincidentally, Mark's dad had also just moved them from New York to the house directly across the street. We became partners in stupidity right from our first meeting. Mark had secured a big house-painting job, so he brought me in on the deal as his painting associate. I had a car that didn't run, so I brought him on as my assistant mechanic, rebuilding it on the floor of my folks' garage every night after work. We both knew very little about car mechanics, but a retired mechanical engineer neighbor and my dad offered to consult us. Now that we were mechanics, of course we had to start smoking like fiends. Two packs a day. It was part of my upside-down track and field off-season training. Yeah, more bone-headedness.

We did learn a lot about car engines, and by the end of the summer I had a purring little Renault that would get me 40 mpg. My dad and mom would get their garage back, along with some nice oil stains on the cement floor. Mark and I would finish the three-story, 5,000-square-foot, wood exterior house...all hand scraped and painted with brushes. We didn't even have any big accidents using 40-foot ladders. We saved our accidents for off-hour escapades.

One particular time, we decided to check out an all-night record sale in downtown Pittsburgh. Naturally, it wouldn't be any fun unless we went at the insane hour of 3:00 or 4:00 a.m. Our chosen fuel for the outing was some weed I'd bought by simply walking up to a strange kid in South Hills Village Mall and asking if he knew where I could get some. He made a call, gave me an address, and said we could take the cash there. As one might guess, the address wasn't in a nice part of town, but the business exchange went down without a hitch. Lucky?

By the time we arrived at the record store in Mark's dad's Fiat, we realized this was particularly strong pot. I'd previously experienced the usual effects of elation, delusions of grandeur, and munchies. But I had never known paranoia like what this produced. I was unnerved the entire time in the shop thinking everyone was watching me. I was sure that I was loudly broadcasting my inebriation in some bizarre manner and the police were going to come busting in the door any second. I finally convinced Mark and his friend who came along that we needed to get out of there.

Mark drove, I rode shotgun, and his high schooler friend was in the back seat. For context, it is an understatement to say that Pittsburgh is a confusing city in which to drive. Nothing resembles a logical block system. One-way streets don't alternate directions. There are exit ramps with no re-entering ones, scads of hills, three rivers, and over 400 bridges. (According to one recent article: "All together, a total of 446 bridges are in the city of Pittsburgh, officially the city with the most bridges in the world, three more than former world leader Venice, Italy.") All that should be enough substantiation - Pittsburgh is a driving challenge even in the best of mental states. We got lost, of course. Being the oldest, riding in the navigator's seat, and a paranoid control freak at the moment, I lied and said I knew how to get us home. "Just follow my directions." I knew I was bluffing, but somehow it felt safer than putting myself in either of their hands. We flew by the seat of my too-big pants through a series of lefts and rights until something finally seemed familiar to me. Why a sign with the word "wharf" on it looked familiar to me, I have no idea. I guess it seemed logical since I knew we had to go over one of the big bridges in order to get through one of the Liberty Tubes back to Upper Saint Clair. Trust me, that is *not* enough info or clarity for driving in Pittsburgh. Nevertheless, I insisted we take the wharf.

The next thing I knew, the kid in the back seat was screaming, "Stop, Stop!" at the top of his pot-filled lungs, waking me out of my half-observant stupor and throwing me into an over-attentive panic. The yelling, fortunately, threw Mark's feet to the clutch and brakes. Now intensely alert, as I took stock of my surroundings outside the car, I came as close as I've ever been to hysteria. Off to at least one side and ahead of us was water, dark churning water. To my remembrance and perception at the time (neither one trustworthy), we had driven onto some pier or discontinued bridge, and nearly into one of Pittsburgh's great rivers or some side water, in the dark, in a cramped Fiat - something three stoned kids would never have survived.

I remember Mark backing up fast, but the remainder of the drive was mostly a blur to me. It was in that time of panic that I did what many people have done for ages, I suppose. Feeling like a football player who'd just used up his last time-out and had one second left on the clock of life…I tossed up a "Hail Mary" prayer. *God, if you'll get me out of here and home, I will never do this kind of stupid thing again.* The next thing I do clearly remember was walking from Mark's driveway across the street to my parents' house on very shaky legs. I was home and immediately cognizant of my super-charged prayer and promise. I thanked this God I rarely ever talked to, told him I would follow through…and then I got real honest. *I have no idea how to do it. I need help.* Maybe the most honest prayer I'd ever prayed.

The summer ended and it was time for me to go back to Bowling Green. Although I had a new roommate whom I hoped might be a good influence on me, I was afraid. I was going back to the same hall with a lot of the same guys I'd partied with the year before. How could I refuse to do all the dumb stuff I'd previously done, and not look like a wuss to them? How could I resist jumping right back into the same enticements I'd always given in to? I knew me. It wouldn't take much prodding for me to say, "What the heck...."

Two weeks into school I was hanging on by nine fingernails. I got ribbed a bit for not joining in, but most of the guys were oblivious to my changed behavior. It was as if they were more interested in themselves than me! As the saying goes, "You wouldn't worry so much what people think about you if you knew how little they actually do." Nevertheless, my resistance was already wearing thin. I wanted to join-in pretty badly.

camping & carousing with buddy Mark

"*Knock, knock, knock*" on my room door. It was a guy named Tom from down the hall looking for my roommate, Phil. Phil took over and I went back to whatever I was doing. Curious, I overheard Tom invite Phil to join a Bible study with guys on the floor. Phil didn't sound interested, but I immediately connected this encounter with my "Hail Mary" in Pittsburgh - *I have no idea how to do it. I need help.* I probably shocked Tom as I forced my way into the conversation, enrolled myself, nudged Phil into joining, and actually agreed to let them meet in our room! Tom was no dummy - if the study met in my room, I had to show up. I didn't care. This was *my* answer. Yes it was.

It wasn't quite that simple though. For an entire school year I did what I call the "spiritual splits." Much like what I'd seen cheerleaders and gymnasts do, I had planted one foot firmly in my old world and the other foot firmly on this otherworldly plane. As those two foundations insistently slid further apart, the "stretching" got really uncomfortable. It became painfully clear that I was going to have to step one way or the other. The duplicitous life still didn't work, but at least the momentum was finally stronger in the direction of sanity. And, of huge significance, I had a corps of spiritual marines who weren't going to let me slip back.

Tom and the guys in this group were the hardcore Special Forces of college Christians. It wasn't at all that they were stuffy, mean, legalistic or even pushy. These guys were a strange combination of joy and determination, which I'd never encountered before. Tough while tender. And it was attractive. I wanted to be like them.

When I say "Bible study group", don't picture soft, milky-skinned boys sitting knees together in hard chairs, sipping weak tea while discussing how to be Good Samaritans to old ladies and little children. These young men were average students of varied physical description, social backgrounds, and educational pursuits. But these ordinary guys came each week with Bibles that looked like the ragged, well-used military field manuals they were. We laughed uproariously at times, but also held each other's feet to the fire concerning right living. They had an unwritten code of ethics about coming prepared to participate. I got a big shock when I admitted to the study leader (some months later at a discussion in his apartment) that I had not finished my study prep. In a very friendly but matter-of-fact way, he said I could go in the back bedroom and finish preparing while they continued talking. If I finished before they were done, I could come back in and join the discussion. We were here to serve each other, not just ourselves. *Ouch!* As I numbly retreated to the back room, I was livid. *How dare he! This is voluntary, not a mandatory activity, not a college required course! Who does he think he is? Why should I put up with this?* Then...I found myself working feverishly to finish. I hated missing a single minute with these guys and what would be discussed. I was hooked. And it was a good thing. I would be like them. I *would* be a good person.

I didn't have these poetic words for it at the time, but it felt like... *thunder*...and...*velvet*.

In addition to coming prepared for study discussions, I learned that "How about breakfast together tomorrow at 6:00 a.m.?" didn't always mean just a nice Old Timer Breakfast and regular coffee in order to shoot the breeze. It sometimes meant, "You're in for some loving kick-butt, Bro. I've noticed _____ in your life, and I'd like to help you boot it out." I hated those breakfasts. I felt embarrassed and never wanted to sit for that kind of spiritual strip-down again. I hated it every time it happened...and I kept coming back for more. The junk and crud I *really hated* in my life started disappearing. And I liked the freedom from being an idiot at times. I knew this was good even though the process hurt. It was like...*thunder...velvet*.

God's warriors, college Navigators ministry, top row far right

A whole sophomore year of inner wrestling ended, but my faith and resolve was increasingly getting stronger. I had memorized dozens of Scriptures and they were working on me. But now I was heading off to yet another summer in a new place, Ashland, Kentucky, away from these comrades in arms. My dad had accepted a new position and moved us to a large house on a lonely mountain cul de sac. It was so remote, he was sometimes picked up and dropped off by company helicopter. My Fred McMurray-type, mild-mannered, engineer dad was the James Bond among our few hilltop neighbors! The kids ran to watch Mr. McCracken swoop in and out. I was proud of him. A man of much velvet and just a little thunder.

My self-designed job that summer was to build office furniture for Dad in our garage-turned-shop. That and lifting weights by myself in a local YMCA was it for the summer. No friends, no social life. So when the invitation came from Tom to attend a weekend Christian camp, as much as I resisted in my gut and failed to commit in advance, I ended up driving several hours to sleep with a bunch of guys in rows of old, musty cabin bunk beds. Why was I doing this? I *hated* big group sleeping. But other arrangements were in the works, with purposes much deeper than I could have imagined.

All the guys and gals did sleep in big group rooms with rows of bunk beds...except for four of us. We had our own little cozy corner room. In retrospect, I selfishly believe this arrangement was premeditated specifically with me in mind. I think my roommates were designed to humble and thrill and challenge and rip away at my soul all weekend long. I knew the Bible's message. I was drawn to it. But I needed something concrete that would put me over the edge to being "all in." I needed something that combined all the things I *hoped* were part of the Truth, but wasn't absolutely convinced really existed. Until I met and roomed with the "dream team!"

Sonny was my perfect jock. Matt was my perfect brain. Frank was my perfect invalid.

Sonny was handsome, blond, built like an Adonis, had played some minor league pro baseball, and was full of enthusiasm and optimism. He had the whole ten-talent package. I quickly idolized him. And he had a cool name. Sonny.

Matt was friendly, considerate, mature acting, was some kind of science student at a prestigious university, and had a clear mind that made me want to pick it for all it was worth. He had the intellectual package my starving brain craved. I respected him.

Frank. Frank had the broken package. Something I never wanted and was even afraid of. Frank lived mostly in his wheelchair. Every night at bedtime, I watched him deal with his colostomy bag and all the gyrations necessary to just get into bed. Frank had been an athlete and wrecked his bike missing a tight, downhill turn at 40 mph. He'd hit a porch post across his back and was now a paraplegic. I was repulsed by his condition. I wanted to run the other way. And...I was powerfully attracted to him. He was full of determination, peacefulness, and solid character. I chose to be his "lift" at every meeting and meal, up and down every hill and set of stairs. I wanted to serve him. I wanted to be around him.

All three of these guys talked about God with a comfortable strength that was irresistible. And then, there was me. What was I doing as the fourth person in this special dream team corner chamber? What did I bring to the team? For maybe the first time in my life, I realized I wasn't the one bringing something. I was the one needing something. I was the receiver. I needed what *they* had. And it was clear that with all their differences, they had one thing in common. They attributed it to Jesus in them. And He was real. He was tough and tender. He was love and justice. He was God and man. He was...*thunder*...and...*velvet*. He had spilt...blood and water mingled. There it was again, but now glorious! I had been studying Him all year long and it was all coming into focus, embodied in these three guys. I needed Him. I found real faith that weekend. I confirmed it in a simple vertical conversation while sitting on a big boulder in the woods one afternoon. Just God and I were there. I told Him I finally got it and wanted to be "all in". He let me know He heard me. It was silent, but forceful. It was frightening and thrilling.

The last two years of college couldn't have looked more different than the previous two. But certainly not less exciting and rewarding. A domino effect of fortuitous occurrences tumbled in my path. They were no accidents.

Why was I in the School of Business Administration? I was a junior and felt like I had just woken up and found myself in the nightmare that was Operation Systems 340. I had no interest or ambition in any of the things I was studying. But now I was so far down the road with so many credits in business, it would be crazy to start over. If I changed, I'd never finish in four years. And if I could switch course, what to change to?

In desperation, I resorted to the university's publications, searching for something I could genuinely sink my academic teeth into and still come out with a degree in two years' time. Well, what do you know - the College of Arts and Sciences had a major in Business Administration that required me to only take three more classes my whole senior year. But I would have to add a minor. As much as I tried to find a program both interesting and workable as a minor...nothing. Then I saw it: "Self-Designed Majors and Minors." Could I design my own minor and actually have it be approved? It was worth a try.

A few weeks later, all prayed-up and with proposal in hand, I walked in the office of the Dean of Arts and Sciences. I had successfully switched to his College, but now to convince the man himself concerning my idea of a minor. The Dean was a big man, both in stature and in respectability. Just what you'd expect of someone in his position. I was intimidated, but plowed through the defense of my minor - a combination of classes in communication, history and theology with a view to cross-cultural transmission. I forget exactly what I titled it, but it made sense in my head. The Dean seemed to listen attentively and followed with a few questions. He wasn't overly personable, but I liked him. He said he'd give it consideration and let me know. It was a Friday.

The next Monday, I arrived at my 8:00 a.m. class, picked up the *BG News*, and to my interest, saw a distinguished photo of the Dean's face as the cover story. *Hmmm, wonder what he did?* He had unexpectedly died that weekend. *Oh my gosh. What a tragedy.* And then, *Oh no! What about my proposal? Will I have to go through that whole thing again with a new Dean? Or maybe he had decided....*

As it turned out, before he left the office that Friday, he had signed-off on my proposal with a condition-free "Approved." Obviously, it wasn't all about me. The Dean's life and death was a much bigger matter. But I was aware that I had prayed and something significant had gone my way. Academically, I had a positive track to run on the next two years. And the Dean had played a role in it as one of his last acts on earth.

Speaking of "a positive track to run on" (yes, a pretty cheesy segue for someone with a self-designed minor in Communications. But here goes anyway...), another providential surprise took place for me on the athletic track. It would serve as a highlight of my senior year and a powerful, personal revelation of God's intimate and generous involvement in my life.

Pole vaulting was paying for about half my college education, and taking almost that percentage of my time. With afternoon practices, evening weight training, and often weekend-devouring travel to other universities to compete, I had invested a lot of my time and concentration. However, unlike my sky-rocketing high school career, I had not progressed like I'd expected as a vaulter in an NCAA Division 1-A environment. I often won and placed in meets, but my 14 feet record in high school had only improved to 15 feet in college. As I entered my senior year, I didn't anticipate a stellar final season, and was accordingly getting frustrated and bored. I briefly considered quitting, but my spiritual mentor and now roommate, Tom, once again was instrumental in encouraging me to finish strong. I resolved to continue competing, but I certainly needed something to make it exciting again.

Early in the outdoor season, after formal practice had ended one day, I walked over to the high jump area to hang out with those attempting lower altitudes of propulsion (track guys' "smack talk"). They were still jumping, so I joined in. My older brother had been a pretty successful high jumper in high school and college, and had taught me to do the Fosbury Flop. (It's what everyone does today, having completely debunked the old scissors or roll techniques that had been standard for decades.) I started clearing my head-height, which equaled my best ever. After a while, I saw the coach approaching and clearly coming toward me personally. My anticipation was that of getting chewed out for risking injury in an event not mine or for hampering the real high jumpers' practice. Instead, he asked, "How high was that?" I replied, "Six feet." After a quick chew on the corner of his mouth (a habit of his when thinking), he continued, "I didn't know you could high jump. I know you can do middle distance. Can you hurdle?" I said, "Yes." It was a bit of an exaggeration in a university context, but I'd played around with it some. I was still clueless where this conversation was going, and was trying to just not be in trouble. Then Coach Wright gave me the biggest athletic boost I'd had in years. "Why don't you get with Joe and start training for decathlon." Joe was our only decathlete. I agreed and that was that.

I cannot describe what a new energy and purpose came into not only my workouts, but my days and weeks on the whole. I am the proverbial "Jack of all trades, master of none", but had not thought of applying it in this arena. Ten different events. It fit. I knew it and I loved it. (Later that year, I even got to meet and run with Bruce Jenner, then Olympic decathlon gold medalist, the greatest athlete in the world! But now these days, I'm not so sure I should mention that. Makes me sad.)

After several weeks of practicing the other nine events, I was entered in my first decathlon. My performance wasn't good enough to place, but it wasn't a wipeout either. It proved a great introduction to the whole experience of doing ten events in two days. Exhilarating as it was exhausting. The best part about that particular competition, the Akron Relays, was that my dad and mom were there to cheer me on. That was a rarity in my collegiate years. I'm

decathlon shot put, Akron Relays 1979

not sure who was more excited about this new twist, my dad or me. He walked around the infield snapping photos of me in the various events.

When the year-end Mid-American Conference championships came around, the coach entered me along with Joe. I was thrilled. But admittedly, my hope of placing was negligible. Despite there being six scoring places, most schools would have a couple of experienced decathletes, meaning as many as twenty competitors. And I was the newbie. This would be my last college competition, so I geared-up to make a strong performance. I wanted to do well, whether I placed or not. To place and contribute points to the team effort was, candidly, not even a realistic blip on my radar.

Day one of the decathlon consists of five events in this order: 100 meter dash, long jump, shot put, high jump, 400 meter dash. Day two incorporates the other five events: 110 meter high hurdles, discus, pole vault, javelin, 1500 meter run. The second day included more of my stronger events. Nevertheless, at the end of the first day, I had personal bests in 4 of 5 events. I was pleased with my scoring but, unsurprisingly, I was not in the running for a top six finish to medal and score team points.

Day two wouldn't go anything like I expected, but will always stick in my memory as one of God's odd gifts to me. I loved running high hurdles and achieved another personal best time. Discus went fair, near the top of my average. Then came the pole vault, my specialty. It was a high scoring event and I was confident I could make up some points there. Disappointingly, I jumped well below my previous best. Still, I scored high respective to the group. I was gaining ground on the field of competitors. Then came the javelin, an event that could make or break any chances I had of placing.

Why do really strange accidents happen - like ripping a finger off while water skiing? I can't say I know for sure, but I don't believe in chance or fate. I do believe God is in control of the great and the small things of life. I sure don't believe life's events revolve around me. But on that particular day, with one particular javelin throw, things got really weird!

Accidental Life

There's a tight set of etiquette for competitors rotating turns in the javelin competition, for obvious reasons. Eight-and-a-half foot long metal, pointed spears are being thrown hundreds of feet in the vicinity of human beings. Simply explained, the etiquette goes as follows: After athlete A throws his javelin into a pie-wedge-shaped field called the "sector", athlete A then walks outside the right sideline keeping watch as athlete B is throwing. Once athlete B throws and his javelin lands, athlete A retrieves his own javelin from inside the sector, athlete B begins walking outside the sector, and now athlete C waits until athlete A is outside the sector before he throws. Once C throws and begins walking, B retrieves his javelin, D waits, and so on and so on. The point (no pun intended) is that *no athlete* is inside the sector when a javelin is thrown.

It was warm-ups. Etiquette applies to warm-ups, again for obvious reasons. I was athlete C on deck waiting for my turn to come. Ken was athlete A, had thrown, and started walking. Dave was athlete B on the runway in the process of his run up to throw. Ken (A) got distracted and began walking into the sector to get his javelin *before* Dave (B) had thrown. A huge mistake was happening and I saw it unfolding. I yelled for Dave to wait, but he had run past me and couldn't hear me. He released his javelin. I began screaming at Ken, "Watch out, Ken. Watch out!" Once Dave saw Ken in the sector, he too began to scream at Ken. Ken finally heard the warnings while the javelin was in the air, turned toward it to look, and seeing it coming, quickly turned away just in time to miss a frontal hit...but not in time to avoid an impact. The javelin hit him full force in the upper back and neck area, impaling him in the trapezius muscle, but not exiting his chest. It was grotesque.

Most importantly, Ken would be okay. Those who came to Ken's aid were able to hold him still and have presence of mind to not remove the javelin. When the paramedics arrived on the field, they used the Jaws of Life (motorized metal cutters) to cut the javelin off about a foot outside his body and wrap the wound with the javelin tip still inside his shoulder area. Although the javelin pierced about

4 inches deep, amazingly, no bones were broken, arteries severed or internal organs injured. He was released from the hospital that day.

Dave was a mess. As soon as he saw Ken hit, he crumpled to the ground and began crying, thinking he may have killed or seriously wounded him. I held Dave down, reassuring him Ken was apparently alert and he was being tended to. But Dave was so shaken, he would not finish the competition. Frankly, even after the ambulance left and things settled down, it wasn't easy for the rest of us to pick up our javelins and make that first throw. In the competition, I threw well enough to move up a notch or two.

All that was left was the grueling metric mile. After two days and nine events of intense competition, four laps of the track feels daunting. It just plain hurts to run that last event. As I stood at the starting line, I was so repulsed by the thought, I felt like I wished someone would offer me $5 to drop out, and I'd take it. Then *bang* smoked from the starter's gun, and the adrenaline kicked in. Our teammates were fantastic, positioning themselves at different places around the track to cheer us on with all the usual prods: "You can do it, keep your pace." "Go hard, you've got more!" "He's catching you, pick it up!" "This is it, now kick, kick, kick!" And it was over.

Hearing my race time of 4:38 gave me the first indication that something extraordinary was happening - it was much better than I expected, by far a personal record. I knew that I'd had personal bests in three events that day. Then came the final tally, and I couldn't help but laugh when I heard it. I *would have* taken seventh place, which was good in light of my newness to the decathlon, and better than I anticipated. But...because javelin-catcher, Ken, had been ahead of me in points and couldn't finish, I had medaled in sixth place and scored a point for the team. *Incredible.*

There are times when you just know there's more going on than meets the eye. Once again an accident had entered the drama of my life, but in yet another unique, personal way. I knew this was a gift to me from a good God. What good thing God intended in Ken's life - that wasn't mine to know - but I'd bet my left ring finger God had one!

Accidental Life

on track

The past accidents and inadequacies of my youth made some sense. They were preparations. I hadn't arranged the seemingly negative events and people over the years. I hadn't wanted to sit the bench four years in basketball, hadn't planned to meet Cueball, certainly hadn't calculated ripping a finger off, hadn't enjoyed being facedown hurling into toilets, hadn't really wanted to go to that musty-bunked weekend camp.

Accidents. *Thunder.*

On the other hand, I know I had also experienced a lot of good things in those short years. And I hadn't arranged the clearly positive events and people in that era of life either. I hadn't chosen the faithful parents, hadn't gentled that car into a tree or stopped another one short of deadly waters, hadn't convinced the scholarship award boards, hadn't organized exciting family vacations, flying planes, singing on stage, designing my own college coursework, or competing in the decathlon. I hadn't placed all those good people in my path.

Life. *Velvet.*

I had been carved and polished with the tough and tender love of God throughout those formative years. The Sculptor of Souls. And now, fittingly, I started loving God back. What was ahead? I didn't know it, but the real adventures hadn't even begun. "Accidental Life" was just getting rolling!

part two: more serious times

The greatest thrill is not in the bleachers. – 70s poster

hitchhiking and hijacked

And I've seen by the highways on a million exit ramps
Those two-legged memorials to the laws of happenstance
Waiting for four-wheeled messiahs to take them home again
  - from "Here in America" by Rich Mullins

Not too many people have the inauspicious privilege of saying they've been a victim in a hijacking incident. I can. I even had a second row seat for the ordeal. In fact, now that I think about it, "shared travel" has provided me with more than a few intriguing, if not harrowing, experiences. Some were just plain amusing...so I'll start there and eventually arrive at the hijacking.

Ever since I was a youngster, I'd always heard, "Hitchhiking is dangerous." Once I reached the age that I was going places apart from family, my parents made it clear that I was never to get in anybody else's car without their permission. They wanted to know who was behind the wheel of any vehicle in which I might ride. That pretty much limited me to...no one, at first. I graduated from no one, to other family members, to certain friends' parents, to a select few friends with drivers licenses. But something as crazy as hitchhiking was expressly forbidden. "Don't *ever* do it. It's stupid. You never know what kind of person might choose to pick you up. They might be drunk. That guy might be a _____...." Anyway, I believed it and basically never had the occasion or desire to do it. That is until I was stuck at college one weekend. I wanted to see my girlfriend back home, but didn't have a car and couldn't find any students offering to share rides via tear-off tabs on bulletin boards around campus. This informal shared taxi system didn't emerge because students back then were magnanimous or concerned about the ecological footprint of a single driver. It was economics. An extra rider would help share gas expense that had skyrocketed from 30 to 60 cents per gallon...in the 20 years since we'd been born. In addition to not finding a posted ride that weekend, I hadn't thought enough in advance to put up my own "I need a ride to Columbus this Friday" advertisement. The option of being a "ride searcher" was also within the non-existent rules of practice. In any event, being in love and desperate, I decided I was old enough and independent enough to risk thumbing a lift. My parents wouldn't care, because they'd never know, because I wouldn't tell them.

My first experience went well. In fact, it went great. I had no sooner reached the bottom of the highway onramp when an eighteen-wheeler pulled to the berm and waited for me. *That's not what I anticipated.* I expected some boring, bored guy or sweet, old couple would have mercy on me. But here was a hardened road warrior air-breaking his big rig off pace to pick me up. Although it did run through my mind that this could be "that guy" that I'd been warned about, I was committed now. I ran up to catch my first hitch. Just as one might expect in the 1970s, a middle-aged flannel shirt with flared sideburns smiled and said, "Climb on up." The cab wasn't anything glamorous, but what a great view. Within a few miles, I quickly realized how clearly truck drivers can see down into average passenger car compartments, and logged that in my head for the future. I don't even remember what very normal and friendly exchanges the driver and I passed for the next half hour to the Findlay cloverleaf, but at that junction, I needed to divert to Route 23 toward Columbus, and Sideburns was continuing on I-75 to Dayton. So I expressed my thanks and jumped down from my first high-seated ride in a semi cab. Not a bad start.

To continue my good fortune in this new world of thumbs-up, I hadn't even finished my clockwise lap on the cloverleaf when a sporty sedan pulled over right in front of me and waved me in. *This is too easy.* He wasn't a familiar face, but asked right off, "You go to Groveport High?" Although I was a freshman in college, I had worn my old high school letter jacket thinking it was still cool and, more importantly, that it communicated respectability to prospective chauffeurs. Proudly, I made it known that I had already graduated and was now an impressive college student. As it turned out, this guy was a new teacher at my alma mater's vocational school and saw an opportunity to do a good deed for a fellow Cruiser.

Cruiser wasn't your typical mascot name. In those days, almost every school claimed some variation of an imposing animal or military patriot. A large majority of high school clashes involved Wildcats chewing up Eagles or Raiders stabbing Cadets. Since cigar-smoking dads and scarf-shrouded moms sitting on cold aluminum football bleachers hadn't yet learned to worry about the politically incorrectness of American Indian tribe names, lots of Cowboys were still having skirmishes with Redskins, Apaches, and Comanches. An occasional mysterious Blue Demon would swoop down upon a relatively helpless Lumberjack, but that's about as non-traditional as it got. I've since learned that Ohio has expanded its repertoire to oddities such as the Ceramics and the Potters (*Do they throw their competition in the kiln?*), the Executives (*Cleats and neckties?*), and Madhatters (*They'll drive you crazy down the field!*). I actually like the contemporary breakaway idea of being creative and not making the focus of all that is high school always the jocks and their carnivorous battle on the field of sport. *Good* for Ohio's modern mascots – the Electrics, Presidents, Lawyers, and Zeps! I'm not sure about other states with their Hoboes, Halfbreeds, Hillbillies, Maniacs, Cheesemakers, Midgets, Awesome Blossoms, Ladies and Gentlemen, Imps, Millionaires, and yes, even the Criminals. And maybe worst of all, the town of Hooker, OK has its Horny Toads. Oh my.... But personally, I must stay nostalgically loyal to the Cruisers.

Cruiser was the name of a horse, but not just any old horse. It was renowned in 1850s' England as the fiercest horse, unable to be tamed or trained. John Rarey of Groveport, Ohio, also famous internationally for his training of wild horses, was issued a public challenge from Cruiser's owner, the Earl of Dorchester. Rarey not only won Cruiser's trust, but in the process of breaking him, maintained the feisty spirit of the creature. He also became the horse's new owner. Rarey and Cruiser starred in shows, even obtaining the praise of Queen Victoria. Once Stateside in Groveport, this rare black stallion was eventually buried on the old Rarey family farm, which became the high school football field. Cruiser's hallowed bones lie under our gridiron. Now, my friends, *that* is a mascot!

Anyway, my black and red jacket had gotten me a second ride. Robert was young and super friendly. He was headed to a hotel in Columbus for a meeting, and would take me the rest of the way. Once again, other than relaxed, lively conversation and several, "Oh, you know _____, well he....", there was nothing noteworthy about the trip itself. Arriving and meeting up with my girlfriend, Robert insisted on buying us a drink in the hotel bar before we parted. My maiden pair of free rides had been a wave-free cruise, refreshments included.

I'll bet I only resorted to hitchhiking a few other times, and that locally. But my experiences were so positive, I decided once I had my own car to return the favor and began to make a habit of picking up hitchhikers anytime I possibly could. It became a benevolent conviction of mine for a couple of years. That personally adopted rule of the road ended up beckoning quite a different set of experiences than I anticipated.

All people have quirks. Some people are quirky. I think a lot of the latter decide to hitchhike. Certainly not every stranger who slid onto the front seat of my car displayed manifest issues. Unremarkable encounters with folks simply needing to get from point A to point B rolled by with predictable conversations and deboarded with appreciative cordiality. And yet, a few others have stuck in my recall as more stimulating.

Woodstock had been history eight years or so, but maybe this guy had been wandering lost since then. He was a mass of hair and rugged accouterments. Hearing a car approach, he seamlessly rotated his body, lifted his thumb, and began backpedaling...like he'd done it the thousands of times that I later learned he had. Dumping his huge backpack be-dangled roundabout with various straps, lanyards, bags, tools, and trinkets, this pre-Star Wars Chewbacca comfortably settled into the front passenger seat as if it was his easy chair at home. In essence, it was.

We exchanged the usual greetings and pleasantries about weather and road conditions. Wendell had been in many cars with many people over many years, so his interest in me resembled nothing of mine in him. I'm not sure he ever really turned his head to look at me or allow our eyes to meet. He wasn't unfriendly and didn't avoid conversation, but he was clearly a loner, used to long periods of silence. He was a man of few words. I'm sure I appeared an overly curious chatterbox to him. In asking how far he was going, his answer was something along the lines of "however far you want to take me." Without me prying too much, Wendell was comfortable divulging that he wasn't going anywhere in particular, but just going. That's what he does – he wanders. A rudimentary bearing mostly tied with season, climate, and whim was about all the direction there was to his life agenda. I knew at that point that I had a travel partner for the remaining couple hours of my drive.

During one of the painful extended silences, without asking or explaining what he was doing (*Why should he? Why would anything he wants to do matter to anyone else?*), Wendell twisted toward me, contorted his massive upper torso over the seat, and detached a small, army-green, canvas bag clinging to the outside of the larger host pack. Having already learned that he was a Vietnam vet, I immediately envisioned his hand emerging from the pouch with a grenade, gun or bayonet. To make my heart thump even harder, it was a knife! The knife was casually laid on his thigh and a neatly folded chamois cloth was then placed front and center on his lap. Very methodically and slowly, he splayed out the loose cloth leaves to reveal a piece of bone. I don't know if Wendell was toying with my emotions or just oblivious to his actions' effects on me, but either way, I was beyond intrigue and rapidly moving toward inner convulsions. I'm sure it was only seconds before my eyes and brain put together the reality that it wasn't actually bone, but antler. And that the antler had some carving done on one end...quite beautiful carving, in fact. I breathed.

It turned out that this is what Wendell did for a living. This is how he funded his wandering lifestyle. The particular piece in his lap was going to be a pipe when finished. I asked to see it and he let me inspect it by alternate glances from the artwork to the highway ahead. I commented on what detail it had. He said, "That's nothing", and again dug into the army daypack in front of him. One by one he displayed an array of bracelets, rings, earrings, pipes, cigarette holders, paperweights, and miniature sculptures, all in some kind of ivory-like substance. They were truly marvelous in design and handiwork. One ring in particular caught my attention by its tiny, complex, knotty features. It looked convincingly like Celtic braided cords.

"As I'm hiking, especially on country roads, I sometimes stumble across animal antlers. If I see an abandoned barn or shed, I'll check it out. I've found lots of great pieces like that. Sometimes I'll ask a farmer if he has any. Only a couple of times somebody's given me a piece of real ivory to work with. That's really a treat. If you see anything you like, let me know and I'll make you a deal." I asked about a few pieces, but quickly learned they didn't fit my budget. Not many extras did in those days. He didn't offer any reduced prices, and to my surprise, explained that he was able to usually get his asking price and had supported himself for years doing it.

Wendell carved the remainder of our trip, catching the cream-colored shavings on his chamois. Before we parted, he meticulously wrapped-up his wares and stowed them. Like the rest of our conversation, his "good bye" was without flare or gush. My guess is that very few situations make much of an impression on a guy who's lived through gorilla warfare and navigated America's twisted roadways. He probably forgot me as soon as he wheeled about to implore the next passing vehicle on his journey. But his visage and craftsmanship has stayed in my mind's eye for decades.

One observation I gleaned from the composite of experiences I had picking up hitchhikers was the inability or lack of desire of some hitchers to relate. More than a handful I'd picked up were content to mutter a greeting of some kind, manage a one or two-word answer to my attempts to engage them in conversation, and then remain completely detached the rest of the ride. Several guys sat like they were lobotomized escapees from the asylum, staring straight ahead as if there was something interesting about monotonous approaching pavement. It is seriously baffling to me to meet someone willing to get out there on the road, voluntarily choose to get in other peoples' confined personal space...and then expect to basically not communicate. That may be, to me, the *weirdest* thing of all in the world of hitchhikers.

I have to say, however, I can only remember one female doing that. I think she was simply young and shy. And quite attractive. I took her all the way to her house even though it was a little out of my way en route to my job, frankly, fearing for her vulnerability with someone else. I told her so when I dropped her off, charging her like a big brother to think twice about car-hopping again. Her eyes widened, but she still didn't say anything, making me think she may have gotten the point. I hoped so.

In contrast, there was also one loquacious brunette I decided *needed* to be shut down, not necessarily verbally, but relationally. Suffice it for me to say, it wasn't difficult eliciting interaction with her. It became clear to me that she was more than happy to engage. I quickly thought of a stop I needed to make and apologized to her for not going any further. Yes, there's a double meaning in that. Back to the gender observation...the rest of the speechless ones were guys. I guess that's another insight I gained - the general tendencies of the genders in terms of verbalization. I'll say no more on that.

Nevertheless, I will say that I've only scraped the surface of my strangest pre-Uber conveyances. There were a few that were just outright weird!

He had to be the most unconventional hitchhiker I'd seen, wearing a jacket and tie, nice slacks, dress shoes, and carrying a briefcase. A bit of a dandy. His appearance threw me off so much that I almost passed him up. He looked too well-dressed to need a ride; but then again, with his professional neatness, I figured he had a good reason for thumbing. And he did.

"Thanks a lot for stopping. I appreciate it greatly. That was a relatively short wait this time. How are you this afternoon?" This preppy traveler's demeanor, smile, and educated vocabulary happily fit his apparel. *Oh good, I get to talk with someone normal and well-spoken this time.* Of course, my first query was to find out, "What's a nice guy like you doing on the side of the highway?" Turned out he'd had a business engagement up in Wisconsin and was on the way to visit his mother when he experienced car problems. He'd left the car with a mechanic and decided to hoof it since it was nice weather. His mother lived in a town just another ten miles past mine, so I could get him most of the way.

This time I didn't have to carry the weight of the conversation. My guest started asking about me, even showing genuine interest with follow-up questions. *How nice is this?* Once we'd covered my person and place in the scheme of history, I also wanted to hear about him. "Where were you in Wisconsin and what kind of work do you do?"

His response was *not* what I expected...not in a light year! "Ladies and Gentlemen, Madison, Wisconsin is burning! The stage is the toy department of human life. And that's where I've chosen to hang my hat. What do you make of that, my southern sidekick?" Pause... *Oh crap...I've got a stark-raving loony in my car!* Not only did the words not make any sense to me, but his voice and New Yorker accent were completely different than previously. Before I could process this new flood of disorienting input, things got even worse. He answered himself in yet *another* voice and accent. "Well, hang my stirrups on another poke's hook! I ain't never been on a stage and my cowboy boots ain't light enough for that line o' work. You tryin' to knock this boy off his pony?" This time, the answer was in an unmistakable Texas cowboy twang. *This guy's schizophrenic...multiple personalities! Should I pull the car over? Is he harmless or about to do something dangerous?*

And yet, there was something in what and how he said those things that was vaguely familiar to me. *Wait a minute...I know those voices...that's...* But before I could completely formulate the answer, yet another voice emerged from someone new sitting beside me. As both his hands raised in a pair of peace signs and his jowls shook in denial, he emphatically stated, "I would not deceive you, my friends. The American people need to know...I am not a crook. I've earned everything I've gotten." *Oh, what a relief! It's only Richard Nixon sitting in my passenger seat, making his appeal to the American people.* And before that, I was just putting together the first pair of voices – the familiar Monday night NFL football repartee between the famous broadcaster, Howard Cossell, and color commentator, "Dandy" Don Meredith. *But still...what are they doing in my car?*

Perceiving my confusion and possibly the discomfort, laughing lightly he said, "That's what I do. I'm an entertainer, an impressionist. I just did a gig up in Madison. I do about 60 different people."

Now that I could laugh along with him and the butterflies in my abdomen were landing, I was primed for more. I asked if he'd do some others and he was glad to oblige. The balance of the drive proved to be a wonderful barter arrangement. He entertained me well and I agreed to drive the extra miles to his mother's house just for the show. He did all the old standbys – John Wayne, Jimmy Stewart, W.C. Fields, Jonathan Winters, Kirk Douglas, Paul Lynde, Jack Benny, and a bunch more. Who'd have thought? Wish I could remember his name. I'll just remember him as "Dandy"...my first impression, and his second.

In glaring contrast to my preppy entertainer, a disheveled, wild-eyed young man climbing on all fours over the road embankment couldn't have been much different. He didn't lift the traditional thumb, but frantically crisscrossed both arms like he was waving down a train. I couldn't *not* stop, he looked so desperate. Out of breath, covered with morning dew, and nervous as a spooked hare, he attached himself to my passenger seat. It was about 7:15 Monday morning, and I was in commute on I-75 heading north to Toledo for my weekly 8:00 staff meeting at Connecticut Mutual. Reporting my sales activity and getting a pep talk was on my mind, not dealing with a scruffy, damp nomad, but it was my self-imposed conviction to pick him up. "You alright?" seemed the obvious opening question. "Maybe. I think so. Can you get me to my house? I just need to get home."

The story that unfolded to me over the next half hour was genuinely traumatic, if not confusing. The reason this 19-year-young man was so rumpled and wet was that he'd just been dumped on the side of the road by an abductor. As best as I could get it from his shocked and shaky delivery, his ordeal started the night before in a mall parking lot. He had hitched a ride from a guy who pulled a gun on him and demanded he give him his money. This poor fellow only had a little cash, so the man told him to withdraw some at a bank machine, but that ended up a "no go." The captor was apparently wired out on some 70's recreational drug and drove him around the city all night long, badgering him to think of somebody who could give him money. I little before daylight, my companion thought of a family friend who was a wealthy doctor. Somehow, he was able to get $70 cash from the doctor, gave it to the guy, and was driven down I-75 to be dumped out on a barren stretch. He'd hidden beneath an overpass until dawn and started walking. That's when I came into the narrative.

The pieces of the young man's story wasn't exactly fitting together for me in a reasonable depiction. I asked if he'd rather me take him to the police station, but he was insistent on just getting home. So that's what we did. He shook and stared blankly through the rest of the in-town residential streets, except to periodically say, "go through the intersection", "next street go right".... He thanked me, but barely said "good bye" as he slammed the door and ran up the sidewalk of his house. With that he was gone, and I drove numbly to my meeting. Probably should have sold him some life insurance.

songs of the road

That strange encounter still wasn't my most unnerving on-the-road incident. I've finally come to the hijacking episode of my youthful travel series. The evening didn't start on a pleasant note. I had been home from college for the weekend, but was about to return on a Greyhound bus. Before leaving for the terminal that Sunday sundown, I needed to say farewell to the family dog, Candy. She was fourteen, mostly blind, deaf as a post, and becoming a pitiable creature, stumbling around the yard, bumping into things, but as sweet a girl as ever. My Mom would be taking her to the vet to have her mercifully put down the next morning.

I went to the backyard and called her name one last time. Actually, several last times before she heard me and came lumbering. I sat in the grass with her panting her familiar canine bad breath in my face. I didn't mind this time. I remembered the first time I saw her at the dog pound with my dad and brother. A litter of black and white Heinz 57s was brought into the room. As the other siblings sniffed around the floor, she made a waggly beeline for us, and spun in circles around our legs until we finally picked her up. It was an easy choice. Black as licorice, she became Candy. I was 5 then and 19 now. Old enough to not cry easily, but not this time. I talked to her, praised her, thanked her, rumpled her tangled mane, and squeezed her while the burning puddles overflowed my eyelids. I left her feeling loved and totally unaware of tomorrow's fate. I felt like a traitor.

All that to say, when I took my window seat two rows behind the driver, I was in a somber mood already that dark dusk. A very nondescript, nice-enough coed from my university was my seatmate on the aisle. Although we talked some during the scheduled three-hour journey over flat, boring, peat-black farmland, I didn't tell her about Candy, because I knew I'd probably get choked up. I wanted to tell somebody and would have welcomed the sympathy, but it wasn't worth the risk. I was still of the macho mindset that it's girls who cry publicly, not guys.

Somewhere mid-trip in the middle of rural nowhere, amidst the dull bus noises of engine, wind, and tires, I realized someone further back in the bus was talking more loudly than usual. At first I thought it was just somebody relating a story in an animated voice. As his volume increased, I began to distinguish an irritated tone, but couldn't make out any words. A few miles and minutes later, I began to make out snippets of sentences, which caused a tightening in my gut. "You people don't know... I seen lots of things... not gonna put one over on me... the corruption in this world... think twice about it...." There were times when the man's words were more mumbling to himself, but then he'd lift his voice and start addressing someone or all of us on the bus. And he wasn't happy. He was clearly a disturbed man.

I looked at the girl beside me and raised my eyebrows while she tightened her neck muscles to a grimace that said, "This is uncomfortable and creepy." It became clear after a while that no one was interacting with the troubled fellow. I began to watch the driver's eyes lift to his big rear-of-the-bus-view mirror as the man's monologue intermittently swelled to a crescendo, then trailed to a pianissimo muttering. When it was obvious the bus was slowing and pulling to the side of the road, a silent tension among its population could be palpably felt. As our driver rose from his seat and started down the aisle, I turned to venture my first look backwards. A twenty-something black man with an untidy afro sat on an aisle seat, but stared at the floor and was quietly murmuring. Everyone around him, though still in their seats, was leaning stiffly away from him. The driver asked him if there was a problem. He shook his head, but kept on whispering to the floor. The driver then asked him if he was going to behave himself and quiet down. He nodded and persisted in his downward drone. The driver gave him a clear warning that he would either be quiet and act right, or he'd be removed from the bus. The authority figure waited a few seconds to let it sink in, exchanged reassuring looks with the folks around the mumbler, and came back to his pilot's seat.

A different murmur could be heard among the rest of us as our chauffeur released the brakes and pulled back on the highway into the dark nothing of northwest Ohio. Our transient community of strangers was already beginning to coalesce around the shared need to be safe, be known, not be alone. My seat partner and I joined in with what I can only imagine was the common buzz. "I wonder what's wrong with him...He's clearly not right in the head...You think he'll stay quiet?...Wonder what the driver will do if not...." It didn't take long to find out the answer to that last question.

We hadn't made it more than a few miles down the road before what we all hoped wouldn't happen happened. The inarticulate built to amplified ravings understandable to all. This poor man was full of anger at someone and felt the need to express it for some reason here and now. His words attacked society, an unspecified "you", and "the man" of course (this *was* the 70s), as he made all kinds of claims of insight into right and wrong, and the need to do something about it.

His volume and invectives eventually brought him to his feet. With the scene clearly intensifying, the bus driver was looking for a place to do whatever he was going to do. I had noticed that we passed a State Highway Patrol station a few miles back, and was pretty sure the driver had also. When he turned our hotbox on wheels around, I knew where he was headed. His attempt to loudly tell the man to "Sit down right now!" went unheeded, if not unnoticed in the man's tirade. The riot of one decided to take to the streets, pacing the aisle from back to front, and began directing his vitriol left and right at the passengers. He railed at our government over injustice, made slanderous racial epithets toward whites, even threatened individual women that he was going to rape them, being explicit enough that a number of the women were trembling and crying. And yet, it was still all just words at this point.

By the time we reached the police parking lot, everyone onboard was wound tight, but none of us took any action against the man. A few had tried to talk him down, but to no effect. Our driver appeared confident and assertive. Personally, although I had a number of scenarios running through my head as to what I might or should do, I had more trust in the driver's knowledge of what to do on a bus full of people. So I sat and waited with the others. At least this wild man hadn't gotten physical or violent...yet. To my surprise, once the bus fully stopped, the driver opened the door and headed for the station! *What? You're leaving us with him?* Just as I considered making for the door with my seatmate, the crazed man ran toward us in the front, tried to close the bus doors...but failed (the bus driver apparently locked them open), and jumped in the driver's seat. The bus was still running.

Looking back on this moment, I can't believe how quickly it all unraveled and that I couldn't find a confident, wise action that would thrust me out of my seat. That would have been more in keeping with my personality in a crisis. But I knew the police were right outside and assumed the driver was doing as trained.

The distraught man was looking all around the dashboard and grabbing frantically at the door lever, gear shift, and steering wheel, but it seemed obvious he didn't know how to operate it and that the driver had prepared the system to lock us down. Then it really heated up. "I'm takin' over this bus! We're gettin' out of here. I'm in charge now." *No he's not...but if he does get this thing in gear, I've got to jump...I've got to go for him...but wait...wait....wait....* At this point, in his thwarted and truly crazed state, he stood up on the driver's seat and faced us all. He began to scream without words, holding the two support bars behind the seat in each hand, looking like a wild beast caged in the zoo, banging his head on the ceiling over and over again...screaming in obvious anger and frustrated rage in his foiled attempt to hijack us out of there.

As two uniformed officers approached the bus with the driver, I noticed...curiously from my vantage point...they were walking instead of running, and without weapons drawn. By the time they reached the bus steps, our disturbed would-be hijacker had dismounted the driver's seat, hurried to the back, and was in his seat with his head on his knees, wailing and cowering like a different kind of animal. A terrified one.

The police approached him calmly and *asked* him to "Please, come with us. Let's go. Let's go outside and we'll work this out. Come on, it'll be alright. Let's go." Without handcuffs or any need to manhandle him, the officers flanked him and peacefully led him toward the front door. The man was a withered, sobbing mess as he walked the aisle past us, and slinked off the bus.

The scene that played out inside the bus was nothing like one might see in the movies. No huge dramatic "take down." Our newly formed rows of brotherhood didn't burst into a roar of applause once we were rescued. It was largely quiet with only a smattering of weeping and sniffling and subdued consoling comments. The girl beside me had her face buried in her hands, and I was surprised to realize my hand was on her back, and had been for some time, patting her reassuringly.

The bus driver returned, apologized for our horrific experience, commended us for not panicking, and told us he'd thanked the police on behalf of us all. He was sorry we'd be a little late into our destination, but he'd get us there safely and directly. Then, a growing ripple of clapping for him did take place, but it was short-lived and melted into a stunned hush again.

The ordeal was over. I hadn't leapt into action. I hadn't done anything heroic...or stupid. I had felt fear and compassion toward this pitiful man. I was shaky and could feel myself relaxing as I patted my neighbor's back. At least I didn't cry.

What's my retrospective takeaway from these varied and questionable shared travel experiences? Never hitchhike again? Never pick up a stranger? Never take a cross-country bus again? No, not much at all along those lines. As so many before me have observed, written, sung, and philosophized...Life *is* a road, and we are all travelers. It's not a question of traveling or not. It's a question of *how well* we learn to travel. That's the hitch.

presidents and pygmies

Nothing about God is small.
– Charles Haddon Spurgeon

An insurance agent making $10,200 a year isn't a very exciting or remarkable start out of college. I even knew it was about $4,000 below the average salary for graduates those days, but it's what I thought I needed to be doing. By the time I graduated I was resolute about pursuing a life in foreign missionary work. I pictured myself in some exotic place, probably a jungle. Wherever it was hardest to go, that's where I wanted to go. Why, then, an insurance office in Toledo, Ohio?

I had heard a sermon in which the speaker said that lots of pastors and missionaries don't understand and relate well to their congregation and hearers because they haven't lived in the work-a-day world of real life. That made sense to me, so I decided to give at least a couple years to secular work. It was a thoughtful, planned decision (kind of a new thing for me), but I had no idea what abundant training and rewards it would yield. Including a wife! (But that's for another chapter.)

Connecticut Mutual's office had some intriguing characters. My supervisor, Sam,

newbie "life" agent

was a loud, fidgety, gregarious Jewish guy who loved doo-wop music and sports (my inroad - he'd seen me pole vaulting while recruiting me). Bob, the General Agent, was a confident, robust, glad-handing, salesman par excellence, and the absolute captain of this ship. I think nearly everybody in his family worked in the office. Don, my aged trainer, was the nicest guy and called me "Jimmy." Only my mom and siblings got away with that. He had a bit of a "habit" that involved stopping at a little watering hole around the corner each evening after work, but I liked him a lot. And he called me Jimmy. John was the other new agent in training with me. Going to lunch together one day, he decided to demonstrate the acceleration of his '79 Porsche's turbo. Fourth to fifth gear meant 90 to 140 mph in a few seconds on the newly opened outer belt. I asked him to never do that again, and returned to my '75 AMC Hornet, a horrid orange box with plaid interior on skate wheels. Kay was my big sister, giving friendly advice and hugs. Susan was my little sister, needing advice and hugs.

There were go-getters, plodders, neat-nicks, curmudgeons, inspirers, grouches, sweethearts, sad sacks, heart-throbs, cronies, lots of jocks (competitors make good salesmen), winners, losers, skirt-chasers, and of course, skirts. In our office of forty-some agents plus management and staff, there was plenty of "real life" to be experienced.

Real life is another way of saying "people." Stuff is just stuff, but people make life interesting. In addition to the office menagerie, my clients provided a regular influx of twists, even in my short two-year career. My first sale was to a synagogue cantor, whose name I got from a Welcome Wagon list. Being spiritually geared-up, I was intrigued from the start with this man of a different cloth and pictured our first appointment as a mixture of sales presentation and religious discussion. Cantor Israel let me in the door, sat down, and told me, "Go ahead." I tried a little small talk, but elicited only the barest of conversation from him. I assumed the worst – he felt trapped by a salesman, wanted it over with, and I'd never get a follow-up appointment, let alone a sale. I gave my presentation while he sat head down, hand half-covering his face, and silent. I wasn't sure he was awake at times. I thought he might have a migraine. When it came time to broach an outright request for commitment, he simply said, "Sure, let's do it." I was shocked and fumbled around trying to remember just how to write up the contract. Then it was over, and much too easy. My first appointment, my first sale. Exciting and flat all in one.

And there was the dicey *almost* love triangle. I had contacted a young mother who, I learned, was in the midst of a divorce. She wanted to prepare to be a single mom and life insurance seemed like a sensible step. Somewhat unconfident and visibly sad, she alluded to her ex-to-be in ways that implied a hot-tempered, if not physically rough, guy. I felt concerned for her and wished I could make life a little easier for her. I determined I would sell her only what she needed – a conservative policy for her and a small rider policy for the child. A few weeks later, when the Home Office application approval came through, there was just a final document delivery appointment to look forward to. These were genuinely fun – briefly reviewing the coverage and congratulating the newly insured on their brilliant decision. No pressure. It was more like delivering a Christmas present than doing sales. When that evening came, it only took a few minutes to explain the policy to my new client and the official business was done. She had been nice enough to offer coffee and had put the baby to bed. I would leave momentarily. But before I could drain my cup, the not-yet-divorcee husband walked in the front door to find his still-married wife sitting, having coffee alone with a similarly-aged guy nicely dressed in a coat and tie. The jealousy and rage was immediately apparent as he started across the room toward me, "the other man", barking the insinuation, "And who is *this*?" She and I both reacted like boot camp privates called to inspection! She jumped up between us, nervously firing out words like "insurance, independence, responsibility, single mother".... I snatched the policy from the end table, presenting it to him like an excited kindergartener showing his first finger painting...emphasizing phrases like "just helping, basic coverage, baby's future, just leaving." And I did, just as quickly as I could.

Referrals are gold in the sales business. How much better to be able to say, "Kevin suggested I give you a call" than, "Hi, my name is... I'm with... the reason...I'd like the opportunity to...." One of my referrals was more tannish than gold. No reflection on the referring party, but this prospect was, shall we say, less than serious. She was downright dingy! I arrived at the afternoon appointment in coat and tie despite the heat. It was an invitingly hot day and I'd have much rather been playing tennis or running several miles, but referrals are gold. Usually. Miss Dingy met me at the door and said, "You don't mind if we meet outside, do you?" I agreed and began following her toward the middle of a large, community sunning area before it registered what was happening. Without the least indication of sensing impropriety, Dingy asked me to help her spread out the large blanket, dropped her long over-shirt, and began to apply suntan lotion. I managed to formulate an abbreviated version of my sales presentation. I wanted out of there. Not only was it awkward talking to a bikini with tens of people observing, but I was sweating profusely. Removing the sports jacket, loosening my tie and rolling up my sleeves was all I was willing to do, and I was still Sponge Bob under my square outfit. How much of the sweating was sun-related I didn't know, but I needed this to end. To top it all off, her questions and answers revealed not only a total blank when it came to insurance (which I typically welcomed, loving to teach people), but uncovered in her some deficiency in things like common sense, basic logic, the English language, and maybe left and right. But gold...she had it going on head to toe! Nothing was sold or bought that day. I went running.

Sales forces don't just try to motivate buyers, they have to motivate themselves at times to get out there and sell. Our agency came up with an entertaining and rewarding way to inspire production. An agent auction. Each of the youngest agents (about seven of us) was given an equal sum of Monopoly money with which to bid on the other more senior agents. The auction took place with everyone crammed into the conference room. Somebody lamely tried an auctioneer's rapid-fire call, "Hey-bdbdb-do-I-hear-a-bdbd-bid-for-a-hundred-dbdb-dollars-for-the-man-in-the-pdpd-purple-jacket?", but he couldn't keep it up. As would be expected, the known big producers went for more money, and I decided to bid for quality over quantity. Once every agent was bought and the teams established, the competition began in genuine. At the end of that month, whichever team sold the most premiums (nice word for "*your* cost") would win an all expense paid trip to Mackinac Island (pronounced "*MAK-in-aw*") – a delightful resort island in Lake Huron with no cars, and only bikes, horses, and people's feet for conveyance.

As the youngest agent, beginner's luck had landed me a superb team, as well as some of my favorite folks in the agency. Married sweethearts and business associates, Bill and Kay, were among them. So was my boss, Sam. And so was Bruce, leader of annual sales in recent years. Bruce cost a chunk of orange $500s, but emerged as reliable a ringer as I'd hoped. Each team member proved their mettle that month with ample sales. I had one of my best months and the end result was the jackpot – we were off to Mackinac Island!

When I say "we", I must elaborate in order to explain the only hesitancy I faced concerning this good fortune. "We" were all married, *sans* me. And each agent was expected to bring his or her spouse, or in my case, a significant other. For the first time since I was about fifteen, I didn't have a girlfriend. I was consciously embracing singleness for a season in order to take any potential relationships more seriously. But at this juncture, I was momentarily questioning that resolution. It struck me that I would be the unenviable fifth wheel at all meals, outings or events the whole weekend. It would be five couples...and me. The more I pictured it, the less this felt like a grand prize and the more it felt like a booby prize – with me the boob at the end of the table nodding and smiling stupidly. I could visualize it: The couples would sympathetically break their happy repartee in order to include me, saying things like, "So, Jim, and what do you like to do in your spare time?" *No thanks.* But, I *had* to go. It was my team after all. So, when the General Agent's secretary asked me the name of the "friend" I'd be bringing, I blushed and said, "I'm coming alone." She managed a forged smile and gave me a reassuring, motherly speechette about what a nice time it would be *anyway*...that I'd find lots of fun things to do *nonetheless*. *Ouch* – it was starting already.

Eventually reconciling myself with my lone bachelor's role for that weekend, I accepted an invitation from Bill and Kay who welcomed me to ride to the island ferry with them. They ended up being comfortably engaging during the drive. Bill asked if I wanted to run the seven-mile circumference of the island with him. Sure! Kay didn't treat me like a charity case to be patronized. Being single was no pariah. All was going to be okay. We arrived and I found myself in a beautiful setting with plenty to do – run, swim, horseback ride, hike, explore. Being alone might actually be an advantage.

"Jim, I don't think you've met my daughter, Mary. I thought you might enjoy a dinner partner this weekend." Curveball! Maybe a sinker. It was a thoughtful effort on the boss's part to bring along his college-age daughter, but it made for an initial shock and mental adjustment to the whole weekend. She appeared as unsure of this arrangement as I was. We survived the gawky introductions, and now it was time for me to limply smile, not display discomposure, and say, "So, what kind of things do you like to do in your spare time?"

It was true that we hadn't met, but I did recognize her. While at the university, I went periodically to music venues at The Coffee House (that name hadn't yet become genericized like Jell-O and ChapStick). Sometimes during the music I'd seen an artsy, eccentric girl go down front and perform an impromptu interpretive dance, usually in avant-garde flowing gauze. The dancer was Mary, my date. And what would be the first event after dinner? Live music where some of the guests were dancing. As we sat and listened, I knew she wanted me to ask her to dance, but I was not going to show off my ineptness with a professional. We wallflowered as I injected forced topics into the conversation, begging to find something mutually interesting. The pressure to dance was building with every new *clack clack clack* intro of the drummer's sticks, so I offered a counterbeat of "Want to go for a walk?" Walking was safer than dancing.

Things got better and Mary turned out to be a pleasant companion for the weekend. We swam in the lake a couple of times. We talked in the lounge over drinks. And we went horseback riding, which is where my ego got a deserved kick.

At the rental barn they asked about our riding ability – a progression something along the lines of : never before, novice, comfortable, proficient, expert. She said "comfortable" (accurate), so I one-upped with "proficient" (inaccurate). They assigned horses accordingly. As the handler gave me the reigns to Jack and watched me mount, he looked a little incredulous and asked me one more time if I was sure I could handle him. "Jack's pretty strong-willed and needs to be controlled." Too late now, I'd signed the disclaimer and Mary was clip-clopping out of the barn on Brownie, or some tame name like that. I answered the handler with a sham affirmative and followed Brownie.

We were told of a large, grassy park area in which to walk or trot them, so we plotted that course. As long as we were heading away from the barn on the paths and Jack was behind or beside Brownie, the horses were content to amble along. Interpretation: They were lazy, tired of tourists, and tolerant at best. We looped paths and occasionally inspired a brief lope or trot from the beasts, but it was definitely a geriatric pace. Then we reached the park. That's when Mary showed her "comfortable" spunk, kicking Brownie into a canter diagonally across the middle of the field. A slight kick and Jack was on her tail. We reached the other side of the green intact. *Well, that was more fun!* "Let's go again", suggested phony "proficient" Jim.

Had I truly been proficient, I might have known that there's a big difference between an unwilling horse heading *away* from the barn, and a very willing one heading *toward* the barn. There were hay and stalls and rest in the latter direction. Mary jumped first and that was all the cue Jack needed. He moved quickly through the lower gears and reached a full gallop by the other side of the field. With no hesitation, and me barely hanging on, he hit the blacktop path en route for the barn. I could feel his metal shoes sliding outward on the asphalt pavement as he leaned into a curve in the woods. I was already tensing every sinew I had, but went into full cramps when we rounded the trees. There, spread out across the path, was a nice family out for a peaceful walk! Astoundingly, with the combination of the pedestrian humans' survival reflexes and the horse's innate ability to coordinate four legs, we wove through the middle as family members fled left and right. I was seriously alarmed by this time.

We had already passed Brownie and Mary. The sound of Jack's shoes as he approached the rental barn was announcing our arrival. As I looked ahead, I saw handler Eastwood heatedly waving both extended arms downward in an effort to signal me to rein Jack in. I had been *trying* that since the park! And it was obvious to all that I was out of control. Mary's horse had followed suit and wasn't far behind, receiving the same icy-warm welcome back at the ranch. We were clearly in hot doo-doo, and I was busted. Eastwood called my bluff as a rider and gave me a good chewing out as he took Jack into the barn.

As we walked away, I was red-faced with embarrassment and expected Mary to be equally chagrined or, worse yet, fuming at me. I got up the courage to look at her, and to my surprise and relief, she looked exhilarated and humored. Then with an ornery grin, she snickered, "Did you see that family scatter?"

Another jackpot event extended this time to the whole agency. Our Toledo office had won the President's Award for the blue chip company nationwide. The president would be coming from Hartford, Connecticut to put on a big black tie gala for us. The main banquet had all the glitz and glamorous gastronomy typical of corporate success. Everyone from secretaries to the top dogs was present. It was an honor to have played a part in earning it. The event has been a memory-worthy one over the years. Yet still, a brief conversation the evening before that climactic event stands out as much more significant in my recall.

A more intimate soiree was given the night before, to which only the agents and managers were invited. After a full-bodied meal in a party room at a swanky Italian restaurant, we kicked back for a lighthearted skit (mocking one of our competitors' TV show, "Wild Kingdom") and a pep talk from the President. Per usual, an open bar was available and being frequented by some more than others. At the end of the night as I was walking toward the cloakroom to leave, boss Bob and Mr. President were chatting privately. Seeing me passing by, Bob waved me over. One of his statements to me in that brief exchange sat like an uncomfortable, slow-burning ember in my head, until I could pluck it out for fitting use in a later conversation. The gist of the first talk went like this:

"Here, I want you to meet one of our rising stars!" Right away I recognized that generous, warm-hearted, syrupy sentimentality common when one has had just enough to drink to make everything and everyone seem *won-der-ful*. At this stage of relaxed, euphoric optimism, lesser men often opt for the sloppy cliché, "I love you, man!" But Bob said, "Jim here, is a first year agent and has done a bang-up job so far. He's found a niche market among pastors that's really bringing in the business. It's a natural fit for Jim. See, he's still involved in a campus ministry at the university and has even talked about the possibility of missionary work in the future." And then came the burning coal. "But you know what I say, Jim? You've got too much going for you to run off into the jungle. You've started a promising career and shouldn't waste it going to some pygmies."

Wow! I knew some of that was the Chivas Regal speaking, some of it the satisfaction of reaching a corporate milestone for him, and some was probably a sincere desire to encourage me. But I felt it jab like a punch in my spiritual gut. As the months following reinforced my resolve to enter vocational missionary work, Bob's comment continued to simmer inside until just the right moment.

Nearing two years with the agency, the nervous moment came for me to sit down with Bob and tell him I was resigning. I knew he'd be disappointed. Looking across his desk at him, I finally choked out the news that I was tendering my resignation in order to go to seminary for ministry training. Lifting his eyebrows and leaning back in his leather chair, Bob proceeded to offer me another reminder that I displayed a promising future in the insurance business. I thanked him for the vote of confidence, but sensed I had another calling. Then he surprised me a little with comments about how much they had invested in me and the cost involved in dispersing my clients among other agents, etc. I knew that multi-billion dollar company would continue to receive my residuals and would be just fine, so when he asked his final question, the answer came easily to me. "So what are your plans? Where are you headed?" The time was right to extract that burning lump. I reminded him of our conversation with the President. "I'm going to the pygmies."

Nothing about God is small. – Charles Haddon Spurgeon

family planning
"Three Times a Lady" - Lionel Richie

Hands down, the best thing I ever did accidentally was to get married. Not that there wasn't some forethought to it, or that I just woke up one day and found myself unwittingly hitched. No, nothing like that. Yet there was certainly the element of results exceeding plans. I thought I knew what I wanted and needed in a wife, but as the song goes, I got "once, twice, three times" the lady I thought I was getting.

In making my move from Ohio insurance agent to Texas seminary student, I *didn't* make my move asking, "Will you marry me?" until 1,200 miles and four months later. Deb was the secretary of my former insurance supervisor, Sam. During my last months there, an office romance had bloomed. I thought I was in love, but felt like some distance and time would either confirm that affection...or not. In my thinking, it was a very mature and adult-like approach. And as if half a continent was not a big enough test, in order to make the conviction either way more confident, I added the suggestion after I was settled in Dallas that Deb and I not even call or write each other. *We need to be as objective as possible.* That sounded so reasonable as it ricocheted around in my head. Back in Ohio in Deb's head it sounded like, "Dear John...." Imagine that!

Chip was a friend, fellow student, and mentor to me. In Deb's absence, I was dating him and his wife...another very responsible, cognitive invention - I would observe happily married couples.

Waiting for him at his house one day, his wife, Theresa, gently probed me about Deb with "How are things going?" In answering her, I explained my very cerebral, well-paced, strategic approach. Theresa insightfully asked several more questions...not about my approach, but about Deb. Being a guy, I thought we were just having a casual conversation, but I must have unknowingly slipped right into her feminine entrapments. The next thing I knew, I had chattered on about Deb so much that Theresa finally turned from fixing a tuna sandwich to face me and blurted out, "Oh, you know you love her. You need to ask her to marry you. And you need to do it *now*. She's sitting there in Ohio thinking you've dumped her. Get on the phone and ask her to marry you!"

How in the world did she get to *that* outrageous conclusion in such a short conversation? What kind of advice is *that* from my mentor's wife?

Deb literally dropped the phone when I proposed that evening by long distance (for any young readers, that's what we called a non-local phone call that cost money to make). Now, thirty-five extraordinarily wonderful years later, she still insists she said, "Yes" before dropping the receiver. Amidst my brain-fog at the time, I don't remember that. Serves me right. Yep, it sure does. It serves me right.

Several months later it was Chip's turn. We were casually volleying on the tennis court and he was characteristically making the most of the time by asking me questions about my newly married state. Not being a light-weight hitter,

honeymoon flex for my bride

Chip asked what our plans were as far as kids. Amid back-hands and foot shuffling, I very spiritually conjoined the phrases "leaving it in God's hands" and "rhythm method." Chip went to the ground. He wasn't injured, but he was rolling on the court surface...laughing. *Not nice.* When he caught his breath, he basically toasted Deb and me saying, "Congratulations on the baby this year!" *Not funny.*

Somewhere around...ten or eleven months later, Chip was present at the hospital to celebrate and pray with us and Ellie, our firstborn. I don't remember him slipping in even the smallest "I told you so." But then, there are lots of details I don't remember about those years.

About 15 years before Deb and I began life together, psychiatrists Thomas Holmes and Richard Rahe came up with their Stress Scale that measured 43 specific, normal life events that typically add stress to one's life. These life events they called "Life Change Units", or LCUs, and each was assigned a "weight" reflecting the amount of stress it added. For instance, things like marriage and pregnancy were heavier, adding 50 and 40 LCUs, respectively. Lighter weight stresses like changes in eating and sleeping habits registered lower weights of 15 and 16 LCUs, respectively. Mid-range stressers included "change to a different kind of work" (36), "begin or end school/college" (26), "change in living conditions" (25), "change in residence" (20) and so on. The point of the test was to tally up your LCUs in a given two years, and if your total was over 150, "you have a moderate to high chance of becoming ill in the near future." If over 300 points, "a high or very high risk." Deb and I had multiples of those and more. In our first two years together, we were *both* in the 600 LCU range, with a whopping combined marital total of over 1,200! Like I said, there are a lot of details I don't remember during those early years of family life.

What I *do* remember is having absolutely loved being surrounded by a bunch of squealing, cuddling, giggling girls. Once, twice, three times – a little lady. Despite the rough and rowdy boy's life I'd lived, I had always pictured myself with a passel of girls. Deb's and my "let 'em come as they will" family planning produced three beauties in two and a half years. And that poker-like approach couldn't have dealt me a better hand.

They were all girls, but the personalities that manifested over the years were, of course, as different as Charlie's Angels. Or maybe I should say as different as Madam Curry, Amelia Earhart, and Barbara Streisand. But that's a bit of an over-the-top, braggadocio comparison. So, humor me as I take one more stab at it. One time, in trying to describe the girls to our family and friends who lived at a distance, the following images came to mind, and I wrote:

What one thinks or sees when she looks in a mirror can reveal something about her character. Here's a description of our girls by what they might likely think while looking in a mirror:

Ellie (age 8) – Is my hair clean and neat? Should I be looking in the mirror or doing something more important? I wonder how a mirror works.

Kate (age 6) – Isn't my hair beautiful? Mirror, mirror on the wall.... I wonder if I should be Snow White or Ariel the Mermaid today.

Sarah (age 7) – What hair? Wow, what a face when I suck in my cheeks and put my fingers up my nose.... isn't life great? What mirror?

three times a lady, Sarah, Ellie, Kate

Our estrogen-dominant gaggle has managed to bring a little testosterone balance into the family equation by attracting three more men, evening out the numbers. So, what's a guy who likes being surrounded by girls going to do? Just wait. To date, these three prolific couples have followed our "just let 'em come as they will" lead, and have produced a dozen perfect grandbabies...seventy-five percent of which happen to be of the squealing, cuddling, giggling variety.

Now *that's* what I call family planning!

Acapulco gold

The center of every man's existence is a dream.
– from *Twelve Types* by G. K. Chesterton

It was a New Years resolution. Actually, more of an epiphany. *Why not take Deb on a special trip?* In instantaneous response to the proposition in my head, a few very good reasons *why not* popped up, waving arms in the front row to give the no-brainer answers: *You're in your last do-or-die semester of a six-year struggle (I was cramming a four-year Masters program into six years), you have three toddlers, and you have no money.* That alone should have settled the matter and stalled my audacious idea before it ever got traction. But it didn't. I couldn't get the idea out of my head and decided right then, at the hope-filled start of 1987, to ask God to do it...for Deb.

To say that Deb deserved a break is, in my heart, a colossal understatement. We were both on empty, but I was about to get a diploma, more letters behind my name, congratulations for a milestone reached, and the relief of writing that final check to Dallas Theological Seminary. Deb would be thrilled right along with and for me, but I knew she had earned a post-graduate degree in perseverance. Let me try to write her *curriculum vitae*.

Deb worked our first year of marriage as secretary to a vice president of Baylor University Medical Center. Although we both had jobs, she carried the lioness's share of our financial burdens. Once Ellie was born, she cheerfully let that rewarding job go in order to stay home, but it was a sacrifice - her boss loved her work and made staying a tempting offer.

Deb was also *my* administrative assistant. It was before the days of personal computers, so a clackity typewriter had to be employed for my many and technically demanding papers. When I wasn't ahead of the game with hand-written drafts (let's just say it happened more than once), Deb would sit up late nights taking in shorthand the content from my dictation (she was clocked for speeding at 130 words per minute in one Dallas job interview), falling asleep during my "Uhhs" and "Umms." When it came to typing from her stenography or my notes, she would sometimes have to adjust for me to insert hand-written Greek or Hebrew. No small hindrance to her 100-plus typing speed. She was also my sounding board for all kinds of theological quandaries. These school-related tasks were all after-hour extras on top of the kids and home.

The home was Deb's arena. It was her fitted niche, which was a good thing because she was *stuck* there. We had one car and it conveyed me to school and work, leaving her with our lesser vehicle – a Radio Flyer Little Red Wagon. She eventually became proficient at "driving" three kids and groceries to and from the Brookshire's about half a mile away. It wouldn't have been easy for a "full size" wife, but she was only five feet tall and ninety-five pounds. The Little Red Wagon got great gas mileage, but as I intimated, Deb's tank had been drained to fumes quite a few times over the years.

With each of the three children, we moved from one duplex to a little larger one on the same street - three moves in three years. Home being Texas, we had air conditioning, but...we couldn't afford to run it. So Deb opened windows and did everything with a glistening bead of perspiration. Disposable diapers were becoming readily available, but that too was cost prohibitive. We calculated that in the heyday of three not-yet-potty-trained kids, Deb washed about 200 cloth diapers a week.

And then came the challenge of putting together healthy meals for five when the meager grocery budget habitually ran out several days before the next paycheck. Deb baked her own bread, mashed into being some of the baby food, and lived by her second Bible, "More with Less", a cookbook teaching how to make whole proteins and the like. One memorable time, the pantry was depleted to some potatoes, Saltines, and a few canned veggies, and we had another four or five days before payday. During dinner that evening, a knock at the door was made by a thoughtful couple in our church. They explained that they had just gotten a cow slaughtered and wanted to share some with us. They dropped it off, and Deb and I excitedly dove into the bag, finding several packages of hamburger, various cuts, even steaks! Our little family got its protein those next several days.

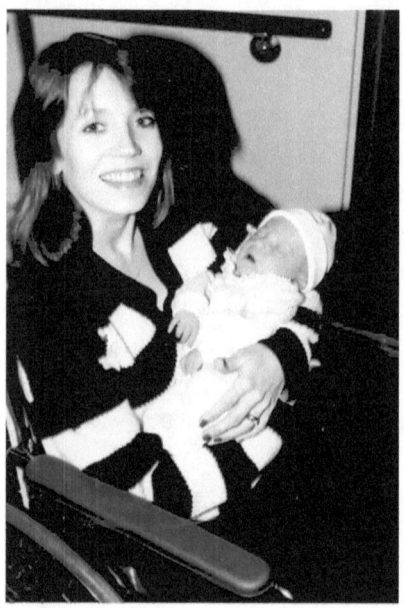
#3 arrives and heads home

From my perspective, Deb had earned some kind of major reward, and a relaxing get-away in some beautiful spot was the trophy that I was locked in on. Spring break from classes in four months was my deadline, and I dared to ask God to provide for it by then. I knew I couldn't come up with it. There was no time for extra jobs and we never had money left over. So I prayed boldly and connived a few little means of my own.

Since the whole thing was a big, uncertain test of faith, and because I love to arrange surprises, Deb never had a hint of anything being in the works. First off, I began to starve our already emaciated food budget of five or ten dollars here and there. At one point, Deb dejectedly mentioned that things seemed even tighter than usual, causing me both guilty pain and seeded anticipation! I also made a stealthy business deal with a neighborhood kid, right under Deb's nose. He told me his Dad was going to start taking him hunting that year, but he had to get a shotgun first. *Ding!* My first gun from when I was his age was only hunting dust-bunnies under our bed. I sold it to his dad for $45.

I got excited every time I went to the top-secret envelope taped under my office desk drawer at work to slip in a few more greenbacks. Now it was getting fun. Then came some big shockers to my primed hopefulness.

I spun the familiar combination of my tarnished brass seminary postbox and pulled out a curious envelope. Only my name was typed on the outside. I opened it to discover one hundred dollars in twenties! No note, no name, no nothing. Since I knew immediately what I'd use the money for, I felt as though someone must know my surreptitious scheme. But I had told no one at all. No one knew my plans because I wasn't completely sure it was going to materialize. And if it did, I wanted to know God had done it. Such an out-of-the-blue, anonymous gift had never happened to me before. This was significant. I wanted to thank whoever had done this, but it was clear they wanted no credit or thanks. As I walked across campus, I silently thanked the One who inspired them and asked Him to honor their humble generosity. The only bummer about this was not being able to share it with anyone, especially Deb. She was always the one who fielded all my news, the home runs and the strikeouts. But mum was still the word.

Sometime in the following few weeks, I was asked by a businessman in the church to go play racquetball at the downtown YMCA. I loved to play but rarely had the opportunity those days. Then the thought of the entrance fee hit me. *This isn't a season to be spending any money on extras.* (Now comes my confession from the dark side.) It also struck me pretty readily that AC (that's what he went by; I don't think most people knew his given names) was a wealthy and very generous man, and that as an Elder where I pastored, he knew my tiny income and he would certainly pay my way in. "Sure, I'll go."

AC and I met at the Y entrance, changed in the locker room, played several invigorating games, and headed back to the locker room. AC was a make-things-happen sort of guy, so it wasn't a surprise when he handed me the key to our shared locker and said, "Take your time showering, but I've got to hustle off to a business appointment." I think it was in the shower that it occurred to me (Some of my greatest revelations come to me as "shower thoughts.") – I hadn't paid when we came in and AC was gone. I was going to have to come up with the $3 on the way out. That was all I had in my wallet...all I had in expendable cash, period. *There goes some of my growing treasure trove.*

It may sound like a small amount of money, but it felt huge at the time because I was starting to believe this dream of surprising Deb was becoming reality. In my soul, this small setback forecast a dark cloud of doubt that started growing every minute on my vacation horizon. I finished showering, changed, and walked to the front desk to pay the weatherman. Opening my wallet, there, slipped-in beside my three wrinkled little Washingtons, was a crisp, pursed-lipped Ben Franklin. I was $97 flush! Somebody else was *also* good at clandestine giving tactics. *Well, God, bless AC and forgive my easily-doused faith.*

Despite never having been able to accumulate any kind of surplus during the skinny seminary years, within the first three months of this adventure, something in the range of $450 had been conjured up. From the beginning, the vision I had in mind for our get-away was a cabin somewhere in Colorado. If I couldn't swing that, maybe something closer like one in Oklahoma might do. I had no connections, so I decided to go to a travel agency to see what was available. The agent's initial response of "We don't have very much call for cabins..."

started feeling like another harbinger of overcast skies. Next came the sticker shock of the one place he did find – high rent and low amenities. More gloomy clouds. Then a ray of unexpected sunshine. "Right now we have some great package deals in Mexico. Some of the lowest rates in years. The dollar's strong against the peso these days." Before I put my umbrella away, it sounded to me like this agent had missed my hinting grimace, and was heading in the wrong financial direction, into an even higher class escape than my Colorado cabin hallucination.

But within a few minutes, the agent had Deb and me boarding a plane and lounging in the sunbeams of Acapulco - four days and three nights in a balconied room on the beach, for the amount of money I already had saved. All I would need was money for food, taxis, and any extras. As I walked out of the tourism agency with reservations in hand, I could hardly believe what was happening. Deb, who had made a silverware organizer out of a cardboard box and Scotch tape, was going on an exotic vacation to the tropics! I was grinning throughout the drive home. How was I ever going to keep her from asking, "What's wrong with you? Something's up." So, I put all my eager energies to planning the reveal.

The necessary additional $250 spending money did mysteriously trickle in to make a grand total of nearly $700. I got the time off from work and two families in the church were willing to split hosting the kids for those dates. It was all coming together, and I waited until three days before departure to let Deb in on it...but only partially. I love crafting surprises.

Deb was at an evening volleyball practice. *Where did she find energy for that? Ah, an evening away from the kids and house. Got it.* Once the girls were in dreamland, it was set-up time. I watched the clock to make sure everything was perfect when Deb drove up. Lights lowered, a bowl of Rocky Road ice cream, hot black coffee, a cryptic letter telling her to pack for a trip alone with me in three days, she might need a bathing suit, and there's a 45 RPM single cued on the stereo turntable that would explain why. It was Lee Greenwood's popular song "I.O.U." that so well communicated what I wanted to through this surprise trip. Deb felt like she was the one on the greater receiving end of our relationship, when I knew all along that I was the more indebted one! (Go on, be a romantic and give the song a listen.)

Unlike some anticipated highlights in life when the envisioned picture far exceeds the reality that follows, the trip to Mexico was nearly idyllic. The planned and the spontaneous elements satisfied our hopes for relaxation and adventure. The cheap hotel was actually pretty nice and our room faced the bay. All the typical vacation stuff of hot climes didn't seem hackneyed or cliché to us. We soaked it all in - the sun, beach, waves, pool, breezes over our balcony, fresh-squeezed orange juice. Glorious.

I showed off survival Spanish to my bride (this *was* the honeymoon we'd never had) by not just getting advice and directions from taxi drivers, but badgering them with broken conversational Spanglish about their family, the weather, did they like their job.... I was a bit ridiculous, but having a ball.

One of our first outings was the compulsory bullfight. I was jazzed, Deb was game for anything. We had been to rodeos, but this was a new twist in which the humans win and the animals lose. In contrast to our Yankee cultural sensitivities, they don't just compete against beasts. They don't even hunt them. As they put it in Spanish, they would be *killing* three bulls that day. We were genuinely intrigued by the pageantry, varying roles of *picadors*, *banderilleros* and *matadors*, and the impressive bullish determination of the brute animals. By the time the third and last bull was nearing his demise, we were nearing our threshold of blood and goring, but decided to stay to the finish. The surprisingly young, teenage matador deftly side-stepped, leapt, thrust, and made a clean kill. *Bravo!* In customary manner, he cut the ears from the bull and began circling the stadium, teasing his roaring fans, each one hoping to be the lucky recipient of a hairy, bloody triangle of yet-warm leather. The matador finally made his choice, flung the furry prize...which landed in the excited clutch of Deb's left-hand seatmate, a very enthusiastic little *amigo*! In his exhilaration, he just had to show it to Deb, waving it up close to her face. Yes, Deb got her *dinero*'s worth at the bullfights.

For a handful of *pesos* tip, we were serenaded by talented, but expressionless *Mariachis* at our outdoor dinner table under torch light. Delightful. We parasailed high over Acapulco Bay to land in the competent hands of bronzed beach boys. Breathtaking. Our last night, we perched with Cokes at a cliff-edge table to take in the 115 foot adrenaline splash of the world-famous La Quebrada Cliff Divers. Enthralling.

Deb parasailing, Acapulco Bay

It was finally time to fly home. Carefully calculating our last departing expenses down to the coin, I figured we could get a small trinket souvenir for each of our girls and a keepsake remembrance for Deb. As we hurriedly made a loop through the tourist trap shops, I almost lost those last *pesos* to the cutest little street beggar as she feigned a hug and skillfully went into my pocket. It was literally going to be this little girl or my three at home that was getting a gift, so sadly, she failed.

Our "three *amigas*" at home loved their brilliantly colored made-in-Mexico toys, and Deb had a woven basket that moved with us for many years before falling apart. The basket is long gone, but our golden days in the sun of Acapulco will never leave us.

home sweet hospital

If you have raced with men on foot, and they have wearied you,
how will you compete with horses?
And if in a safe land you fall down,
How will you do in the jungle of the Jordan?
Jeremiah 12:5 (RSV)

Answers to two closely related questions were often solicited from us by friends and acquaintances:
"Do you feel like Turkey is 'home' yet?"
"Does it seem strange to live in the Middle East?"

It had taken me eleven years of preparation and formal training to get to the foreign mission field from the time that Jeremiah's words charged me to "get ready." Turkey was now our new home in terms of residency, but not yet in familiarity or assimilation. Cross-cultural adaptation involves a lifetime of adjustments that require a lot of commitment, endurance, humility...and sense of humor. I knew those facts in theory before giving everything away and moving my family overseas. It's what I'd trained for. But actually encountering that jungle of challenges proved to be a lot more demanding.

The first month or two in the land of the Ottomans, we were consciously aware almost every moment, from the time we awoke until we put our hyper-alert brains on the pillow, that we were in a foreign place. Even after the initial culture shock, there was always a strange cognizance of not ever being completely relaxed.

"Do you feel like Turkey is 'home' yet?"
One way I've thought about trying to answer and describe the

feeling to someone who hasn't experienced living abroad is to use an analogy – a hospital visit. Let's say someone you know has been admitted to the hospital and you've decided to visit him or her. From the moment you walk through the automatic glass doors, you are arrested with a foreign culture. You are constantly aware of your surroundings – sterile surfaces, white noises, and pungent smells. The smells especially offend and repulse the senses. Some assaultingly foul, some too clean, but none "homey", warm, inviting.

And there's an intuition of permissible and impermissible spaces, expectations and rules...and an awareness that you don't know what they are! You don't know exactly where you are or need to go. You don't just enter anywhere you please. You don't touch certain things. And all this is before you even get to the person you came to visit.

Approaching the individual's room may be one of the most daunting moments due to the awkward situations potentially waiting beyond that windowless, wooden portal. A wide range of possible scenarios barrages your thoughts: *Am I waking much-needed sleep? What if she's "indecent" at this moment? Bedpans, needles, bathing, backless robes. Will there be something gross? Is there a roommate? If the doctor's in, should I leave? Does she want visitors right now?*

Even with the closest of friends, but especially with mere acquaintances, what to say or not say tosses in another whole intensity of eggshells to walk on. To talk about the sickness or injury may be exactly what the doctor orders – to let your friend share it and to know that you care. But maybe he's tired of discussing it or is embarrassed, and wants distracting conversation about the outside world. *Should I be serious or light-hearted? Stay long or short?* Once you *do* eventually leave, you wonder how it went and often rehearse the whole time in your mind, second-guessing innocent comments or questions.

Once it's all over, you feel a little tired from the tension and yet also relieved to have it over. After all, it's only *sick* people who like hospitals! You sense the rightness of making the effort, but it had some very real draining effect.

That...is what living in a foreign context feels like 24/7. So, does it feel like "home sweet home" yet? No, it feels like "home sweet hospital" much of the time. All the normal activities of a day – work, play, rest, conversations, incidentals – all have a generous layer of tension slathered on them. Quizzical letters and words on signs. Unfamiliar customs. Uncertain expectations. Unanticipated difficulties. Unnerving shocks. Humiliating *faux pas*. It's very tiring. And it's one of the richest experiences I believe a person can ever enter. I highly recommend it!

Six years in Turkey provided a regular array of intriguing experiences. Just going to the butcher for hamburger opened up one of our earliest adventures. Salim had some of the biggest hands I've ever seen. To watch him man-handle sides of beef and carve through gristle was like watching a caveman. His coarse, black hair exaggerated the impression – I'm talking about that on his forearms and neck. When I would enter his shop, upon seeing me, his one foreign customer, he would flash a big smile, drop his chops, wipe his hands on his bloody apron, and reach out warmly with his huge red hands, kissing me on each cheek, scratching his wire-brush bearded jaws on mine. I loved him.

And he loved us, even inviting us to attend his upcoming wedding to a girl from the Black Sea area. As is often the case, the couple had met only a few times through family arrangements. She was as dainty and fair as he was thick and dark. We were excited about the opportunity to observe a Turkish wedding.

Arriving with our three light-locked girls, we drew everyone's eye as we weaved through the crowded, dimly lit party room. As soon as we sat down, ladies in headscarves began bringing us food and the ubiquitous *chai* tea. We had no idea what was going on as different characters mounted and dismounted a stage, performing ceremonies and making speeches. We were glad to hide in the shadows and simply observe. At one point, however, it seemed apparent to Deb and me that the attention on the platform had turned from the couple to us.

Some applause went up and, perceiving we had been acknowledged as guests, we waved weakly. But that didn't suffice. Gestures by Salim and others seemed to imply that we should come forward. We stayed put. Then an emissary was sent to bring us, saying in broken but understandable English, "The couple asks you dance them."

My reticence to dance in front of people was not my biggest concern. I had studied Islam and the culture enough to know that I wasn't to touch another woman. How was this going to work? Deb was firing whispered questions at me, "What are we supposed to do? Jim, no, I can't go up there!" It was out of our control as we were led onto the stage, both flustered inside, not wanting to offend the couple or violate cultural taboos. As I glanced at Salim's bride, Salim stepped in front of me, faced me, raised his arms overhead and began snapping his fingers and gyrating as the music started screeching. Oh, what relief! *I don't have to worry about her. I'm dancing with him. Wait, I'm dancing with him?* As usual, Deb picked up the idea quicker than me, and in no time was mimicking their moves as she danced with the bride. Before long others were joining in the *halay*, a sort of Turkish conga line dance.

When we returned to our table and I told Deb that I had been mentally entertaining the question of how to dance with the bride, the look of horror on her face let me know what a slow learner I was in the enculturation process.

That wasn't my only cultural near-blunder. I had many of those, and some full-fledged gaffes, too. I have inadver-

doing the Halay at a Turkish wedding

tently ordered "naked chicken" at a restaurant and asked for feminine hygiene products at a hardware store. When asked how my business was going, meaning to jokingly say, "We're getting poorer everyday", I accidentally switched two syllables around and creatively responded, "We're becoming infidels more everyday." Not a Christian's best witnessing line. I've even flooded the eighth floor of an office building.

My office was on the top floor overlooking a prominent street in downtown Ankara, the capital city. Steve, a PhD geologist, and I were in the mining machinery sales and geological services business as our official means of being in this host country. We had just rented, painted, carpeted, and furnished our shared space. Turkey being nearly 100% Muslim, each office is equipped with a tiny sink for doing ritual ablutions. That means washing face, hands, inside the ears, snorting and spitting to cleanse the sinuses, and sticking ones feet in the sink...before praying. Steve and I washed our hands in ours.

At the end of one typical Friday workday, I left and locked up, descended the eight floors, caught the public transport *dolmush* (which fittingly translates "It's fullish"), and went home. Early Saturday morning, I received a panicky phone call from a fellow eighth floor businessman, repeatedly yelling in Turkish, "Jim, come quick...lots of water. Hurry!" Having no idea what was going on, I dressed, hailed a taxi and made it to *902 Mithatpasa Caddesi* in less than fifteen minutes. I tried the elevator, but it wasn't working. So I began running up the switchback stairs. My stomach lurched as I came across water cascading down the stairs on floor five! I splashed up the next three flights to find the eighth floor six inches deep in water. It was all coming out of my office door, which had just been kicked open by my neighbor not knowing I was seconds behind with my keys. Wading into my office, we found the little sink faucet pouring full-throttle.

Our building wasn't the newest and periodically had a water pressure problem. Apparently, at some point on Friday I had tried to use the sink, but no water came. I had left it "on" assuming water would come within a few seconds, which was *sometimes* the case. It obviously didn't that time. I evidently got distracted and forgot. I left that evening, and sometime during the night the water reached my sink. One other unfortunate detail – the rubber plug that sat on the sink back must have vibrated perfectly into the drain, allowing all the water to spill over for hours and hours. I felt sick.

In addition to verbose apologies to my neighboring attorney, architect, and accountant on the hallway, I made reparations for damages. I paid the architect for drawings that had to be redrawn – they had been lying on his floor. I paid two offices on the seventh floor to be repainted because of ceiling leaks. I paid the building landlord for extra water and, yes, for the elevator that wasn't working; water had run into the shaft and burned out an electrode. And of course, I paid to replace the kicked-in lock on my door. The foreigner had made his mark...a watermark.

For months to follow, numerous Turkish acquaintances would condescendingly tell me, "Tsk tsk tsk...We *never* leave the faucet on in such a case!" Some visitors would even walk me to my sink to demonstrate "left is on" and "right is off." You see, when one doesn't speak Turkish fluently, the native speaker often thinks the problem is basic knowledge, not language. I have been shown how to use a screw driver, tie my shoe, staple paper together, and plug in an appliance...simply because I didn't know a word and asked, "What is this?" Cross-cultural growth feels like being a three year old again. Very humbling. And that's a good thing, a potential gift of the enculturation process – humility.

Foreign living also offers many inconveniences and threats that test character flaws like impatience and insecurity. Who would have thought that getting packages in the mail from Hometown, USA would be an attitude tutor?

Accidental Life

As an American it seemed like a pretty straightforward thing to take the package slip in my mailbox to the post office and pick up the package. *Rookie!* The clerk at my local post office (five minutes walk away) informed me that foreign packages must be picked up at the central post office downtown (30 minutes each way using four public transports). *Thanks.*

Once arriving at the downtown mail hub, there is waiting a gauntlet of bureaucracy that truly bewilders the western mind. I would eventually learn that it would require between five and seven different "stops" within that building before I *might* be able to take home my precious care package from family or friends in the USA. Underpaid, bored, and reluctant clerks "greet" me at each station with slow-motion movements, painstakingly inspecting my slip as if it were written in hieroglyphics. The same information of name, address, slip number, etc. were recorded in at least three different ledgers. One guy adds his red rubber-stamped imprint and signature over it. Still another *sells* me a stick-on stamp, also needing his prized autograph over it.

Then comes the most amazing moment. Not receiving the package, but meeting the top officer of this institution for his personal signoff. Keep in mind, this is the Turkish equivalent of the American Postmaster General at the Washington D.C. main post office – just to get a package of kids' socks, crayons, and Gummy Bears! As I enter Mr. Mudur's office, I am struck by the emptiness of his desktop. There is only his glass of tea, an open newspaper, and his elbows propping the paper in reading position. Without a word, I lay the paperwork (a short novel by now) on his desk, step back, hold my hands in the soccer fig leaf position of submission (a learned cultural norm), and wait. To speak may short-circuit the whole process by raising issues or offending his supreme authority. I wait. Mr. Mudur looks it over, glances up at me ever so briefly, signs it, slides it almost within my reach, and says the magic word – *Buyrun.* "Here you are." Now, back to his very important newspaper and tea.

Only one more stop to receive the package from the final clerk. But not so quick.... There is still the mystery of which final scenario might play out.

Scenario One (my favorite): He takes the slip, disappears into the shelves for a few seconds, and emerges with the un-opened package, hands it to me and says, *Buyrun*.

Scenario Two (like kissing your sister): He takes the slip, disappears into the shelves for a few seconds, and emerges with the already-opened and rifled-through package. *Is everything there?* Who can be sure? (We did learn over time to have family include a written list of items inside as proof...as if that would make any difference at this point.) I leave wondering what pair of frilly socks might be on some clerk's daughter's feet...and feeling a little angry, too.

Scenario Three (like wanting to choke your sister): He takes the slip, disappears into the shelves for a few seconds, and emerges with the already-opened and rifled-through package. *And* then he informs me that the package included a video, which must be formally viewed by the authorities to make sure it has no propaganda or pornography. I tense. Not only was this threatening movie "Mary Poppins", but I will probably see "Mary Poppins" mysteriously start showing up in video stores...right beside the propaganda and pornography. Nevertheless, I will need to give them a month to "review" it, which means making the journey once again to retrieve it. I get to do this again. *Oh joy!*

I'm sure patience and perseverance was what I should have learned through the process, but I failed the test more often than I care to admit. It usually took the entire half-hour return trip on two buses for me to go from hard boil to simmer.

Throughout our years living in Ankara, there was a smattering of unnerving events in the area to make one jumpy. A prominent Turkish author, whose writings were unflattering to the establishment, was blown up in his car two streets uphill from us. The gas station we could see from our apartment had a Bonnie and Clyde style mow-down of a Turkish mafia player. The church we helped start and lead received its own little Molotov cocktail through the window. We weren't in Ohio anymore.

One of our earliest scares started about 4:30 a.m. as we still slept.

Something had awakened me, but I wasn't sure what it was. As I lie listening, something like the sound of a drum registered in my ears. The crescendo as it came up the hill toward our apartment building confirmed to me that it was, in fact, a drum cadence...which to my ears sounded military. By this time Deb was awake asking the same question I was entertaining – "What's that?" By the time it got right in front of our apartment, the beat echoing off cement buildings a few yards apart, was truly intense! Our hearts were pounding in kind. A coup? A madman? Military police coming to arrest the missionary? But it passed by and eventually faded in the distance around the corner.

That day, by asking around, we were informed that this was the *davulcu*, a traditional religious drummer during the month of *Ramazan*, which had just started that day. Muslims practice a month-long "fast" in which they are not to eat or drink anything during daylight hours. Some of the most religious claim to not even swallow their spit. It may seem extreme to "fast" for a whole month, and might elicit some sympathy from the outsider. But there's a reason I put the word "fast" in quotation marks.

Although most followers of Mohammed do desist from eating between sunup and sundown, they blunt the point by feasting in between. As the sun goes down each evening, families gather to eat elaborate meals. And in order to make it through the following day, they arise early in the morning before sunrise...say, about 4:30 a.m., to eat another large meal. The *davulcu* was the ancient *Ramazan* alarm clock for each neighborhood. Interesting statistic: Muslims typically consume more food during the month of the "fast" than they do during other months of the year.

So after thirty nights of being awakened by reverberating *bump-d-bump-bumps*, I was a bit caught off-guard when the young *davulcu* showed up at our door expecting a "thank you" and tip for his services that month. Thankfully, in this encounter, I simply informed him that we are not Muslims and wouldn't be contributing. He looked like he'd seen an alien! And he had.

As kids growing up in a foreign land, our three elementary school aged girls had their own set of enculturation experiences. There was one over-arching advantage that I'm sure undergirds their current, generally positive childhood memories of Turkey. We were somewhat rock stars. Turks are customarily friendly to foreigners. It's part of their religion to show hospitality to strangers. In addition to this, Americans in particular were at that time an interesting anomaly. People wanted to meet us and learn about *Amerika Birlesik Devletleri* (USA), the confusing land of plenty and infidels. Thus, the girls admittedly received a measure of special status and deference at school and elsewhere. One of the more humorous (to Deb and me) daily events at school was our girls' participation in the Turkish "Pledge of Allegiance." A different student each day would step to the microphone and lead phrase-by-phrase, "*Turkum, dogruyum, chaliskanim...*" – "I am a Turk, honest, and hardworking...." Our girls took their turns leading the whole school, ending in the paradoxical (for them) "*Ne mutlu Turkum diyene!*" – "How happy is the one who says, 'I am a Turk!'"

Another thing none of our girls avoided, unfortunately, was an emergency room trip. They each made their contribution to carrying on the tradition of their father by visiting the local hospital.

If you've ever been awakened in the middle of the night by your child's scream, you know the sick dread it brings. If you've been subsequently roused from your bed by your spouse's scream, you know real fear. If you've ever found your child not breathing in the middle of a gran mal seizure, you know how we felt at the onset of our youngest daughter's introduction to the medical world of Turkey. Without any prior occurrences or warning, Kate yelled out to us before she began fully seizing. The other four of us cried and rode it out with her until she fell into a deep, snoring sleep. She remembered nothing except the lead-up auras and severe tensing and twisting of arm and leg muscles beforehand.

The doctor we reached on the phone advised us to stay home unless another seizure should follow. Another did follow and we spent the next few days in the hospital and a specialist's office. To our great relief, we found a very compassionate and well-seasoned Turkish pediatric neurologist who spoke impeccable English. Kate was correctly diagnosed with a form of childhood epilepsy, which would be treated and effectively out-grown over the next six years.

Kate was a trooper and, in her stubborn little way, soaked up the attention of having wires and machines attached during repeated testing. She did have one complaint, however. When she learned from her sisters that "Dad cried" each time she had an episode, she was incredulous. "Man, and I missed it!"

Addendum: I have been faithful to supply Kate with numerous subsequent opportunities to see her dad cry. Compassionately, she doesn't take delight in those moments.

And then there was Ellie's turn. We were not and are not Christians who see the devil directly involved in every difficult event or crisis, but we also are "not unaware of his schemes", as the Scripture adjures us. In retrospect of Ellie's accident, however, we felt the incident was prefaced with a "recipe for an attack."

Some of the ingredients prepared in advance included encouraging progress in our ministry: Start with a generous portion of advancement in unity among the various local Christians. Mix in the gift of a Volkswagen van big enough to comfortably carry nine people. Sift in my increased responsibility as Field Leader and in assisting some cooperative efforts nationally. Combine the "first fruits" of three college students coming to the Faith through our efforts. Stir in new teammates on the field; a couple had just arrived this particular day to join the work as our teammates. Accompanying them for a short visit and observation of this newly opened field of Turkey, was a unique and special guest – the founder and president of our agency, Ted. (Ted's resume included leaving the prestigious and lucrative position as National Sales Manager of the Wall Street Journal in order to start a missions agency that paid him nothing financial, but everything eternal.) And finally, blend all ingredients into a smooth and rich celebration! It was time to "heat to 212 degrees Fahrenheit."

As Ted and our entire team finished our celebration dinner and Deb began to serve dessert, the enemy may have said to himself, "Enough of their progress and celebration." It was time for some heat. Our oldest daughter, Ellie, collided with Deb as she was exiting the kitchen with water for coffee. An entire mug of boiling water drenched Ellie's face, left shoulder, neck, chest, and right wrist. The result was second-degree burns on her face, and more severe ones in the areas where her blouse held the hot water against her longer.

What came out of this oven of testing?

As soon as our guests realized what the screams and commotion were about, they went to prayer for her. The battle began in the right realm. Ellie responded with amazing faith, especially for a child of age nine. Within seconds of the initial yell, she was praying for help and strength to cope with the pain. He gave her uncommon strength.

At the hospital emergency room where everything was taking place in Turkish, Ellie continued to call out to God, even praise Him...in Turkish. As they scrubbed the wounds and removed the blistered, loose skin, Ellie called out, *"Tanrim, bana yardim et, yardim et."* ("My God, help me, help me."). Again, she prayed out loud, "Thank you, Lord, that I'm a Christian. If I wasn't, I'd be screaming, but You're giving me strength." The doctors couldn't help but be impressed. Her mother and I looked at each other with our own admiration.

Ellie was a faith-filled one. The song she began to sing on the way to the hospital and the verse our daughter Sarah recited to Ted as they prayed – *All things work together for good for those who love God and are called according to His purpose* – was taking place in genuine.

All the ingredients were available. The enemy served up his course. What he intended to sour the stomach toward the Master Chef, was turned to a banquet of praise over the next several weeks. Great man of faith that he was, Ted would remind us throughout following years of what he witnessed that night at the hospital and what we translated to him throughout. A small part of his vision in forming this worldwide outreach was being fulfilled by a little girl.

Accidental Life

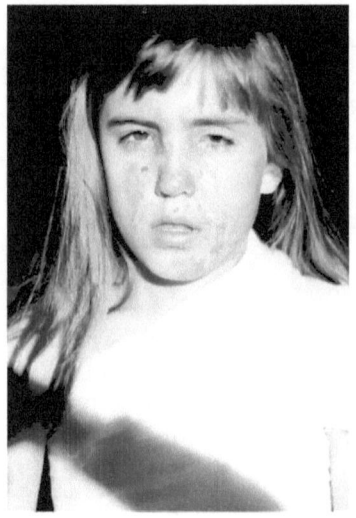
brave Ellie with burn bandages

Middle daughter, Sarah, had a much less dramatic accident, but the tiny event reveals yet another difference that existed between our two cultures. The girls were at school, Deb and I were home with "Ataturk's Revenge." Even after months of acclimation, every once in a while Turkish germs would invade our American guts. A phone call from the school informed us that Sarah and others had been playing in the building and a piece of glass fell out of a window, cutting her on the forehead, and she'd probably need stitches. Hesitating in my state of ill-repair, the teacher offered to have her brought home in a taxi. I accepted her offer, thinking it would give me time to change clothes and get her to the hospital as quickly as possible.

When the doorbell rang, I didn't expect to see Sarah and Ellie there with no teacher. Spokesperson Ellie explained. "The principal had me come with Sarah, but they're expecting me to come back for classes. Can I have some money to pay the taxi driver when I get there?" The school had sent two little girls (a second and first grader) by themselves in a taxi, albeit only a few blocks away. I paused to process this different approach to handling things, but in the end gave her money and sent my seven-year-old daughter back to school alone in a yellow cab.

I realize, to the modern American ear, that decision sounds outrageously dangerous and foolish. But at the time and in that setting, I knew that in the prevailing Turkish culture, rooted in its strange combination of honor, shame, protection of children, accountability to society's ever-watching eye, and the school's more culturally relevant judgment...I could take that step of faith. It was one more of many steps of assimilation into a bigger, different world than my own. I guess that foreign land was beginning to become somewhat "home" for us.

inner-city slaughter

When anything looks strange, you must look deeper.
Robert Falconer in *The Musician's Quest*, by George MacDonald

Tuesday, July 3rd, 1990 was not a typical day. Deb and I got up early to prepare our minds, souls, and stomachs for the morning ahead. Hearing and seeing our neighbor and good friend, Mehmet, going outside with his tray of knives, we hurried to get the kids up and dressed, grab the camera, and follow. We had been invited to observe.

Mehmet was wearing the same striped T-shirt and jeans he'd had on the previous evening as we visited informally over tea and some games of Okey, a Turkish version of Rummikub. But as we watched him that next morning, our minds were filled with other images – the Jewish priests' robes in Solomon's Temple, Abraham and Isaac ascending the mountain, Jesus facing Calvary....

Daughters Ellie, Sarah and Kate were curious, but quiet and tentative. "Can we watch the whole thing?" one piped up. "Once it's dead you can," was Dad's predetermined answer. They watched the beautiful, brown goat they had petted the day before walk by. Then the girls obediently stepped around the corner of our apartment building to wait for the next few minutes to pass. Deb and I proceeded to watch our first, real religious sacrifice.

Mehmet was a mechanical engineer and a member of the directing board of a large cement company. He and Reyhan, his wife, were our closest Turkish friends, living in the same building just one floor above us. We spent many evenings together like the prior one, doing the stuff of normal life. Throughout our first year in country, they patiently repeated sentences and waited as we stumbled through our baby-steps of Turkish. Friday nights together became a pretty regular event, watching old horror films on their TV or playing Okey. Evenings usually started around nine o'clock and went until we couldn't stand drinking any more tea, laughing, and making our brains and mouths form the different constructions and sounds of Turkish. That was often one or two in the morning.

Mehmet and Reyhan are devout Muslims who meticulously practice their faith, especially the five pillars of Islam. Despite living and relating in such close proximity with them, I never saw Reyhan's hair. Although Mehmet and I exchanged Turkish kisses every time we greeted and good-byed, I never even shook hands with Reyhan (and still haven't now some twenty-five years later). It's the law of Islam and they take it seriously. For instance, we might be having a picnic when the call to prayer sounded from a local mosque *minaret* tower. Without apology, and even with some pride, Mehmet would leave our blanket on the grass, pick up his rolled prayer carpet, find Mecca's east location on his pocket-ready compass, retreat to face a distraction-free bush or tree, and begin his *namaz*. About ten minutes later, we would resume our day in the sun without a hiccup.

This particular day of July in our apartment backyard is their religious practice of one of the five pillars, the annual sacrifice. Mehmet would be "cutting" (as it translates) two goats today. One to pay for his sins committed this past year, and one for his wife, Reyhan's. This isn't taking place in some ancient century or in some backward village in a remote corner of the Middle East. This is being performed in the suburb high-rise apartments of Turkey's modern capital city of the twentieth Century. And Mehmet is not alone in this practice. Neighbors on all sides of us are killing sheep, goats or cows this morning.

Mehmet leads the first goat to the prepared place, a foot-wide hole dug in our garden to catch the blood. All the while, he pats and speaks gently to the skittish creature. He then begins reciting Islamic scriptures and softly singing a song of worship to his god, Allah. Does he believe this re-enactment of Abraham with Ishmael (the Muslim interpretation on the biblical story of Abraham and Isaac) is taking away their sins? He has paid a hundred dollars for each goat. He regularly, evangelistically, tells us of the virtues of Allah, Mohammed, and Islam, knowing very well our differently held Christian beliefs. Yes, this is something in which he firmly believes.

Two other neighbors join Mehmet to help hold and bind the animal. Deb and I notice that once bound at the lower legs, the goat displays a strange, relaxed resolve. There is no more flinching, resistance or nervous looking about. Its head is pulled back to expose its throat. Mehmet compassionately folds its ears over to cover its eyes. He takes the knife in hand and continues to sing softly his sacrificial hymns. Deb and I stiffen as we prepare for the moment. At the last second before he makes the cut, we hear his wife's name, Reyhan, recited – this is her goat to take away the guilt of her sins...for now. For this past year. But what about tomorrow? Next month? They will kill two more next year. Reyhan says she gets goose bumps during these religious experiences, yet she admits that despite performing this faithfully every year, all she can do is hope that Allah *might* accept her at judgment. She says, "But I can't know."

Both animals slain, our children rejoined us and matter-of-factly investigated the head, hoofs and watched the whole butchering process. A great home school anatomy lesson! For me as well, there was one strange

friend Mehmet sacrificing a goat

detail I had not previously witnessed before. It was the technique used for separating the skin from the meaty parts. A small hole was cut in the skin near an ankle. Gungor, a neighbor and building custodian, knelt, placed his mouth over the hole and began strenuously blowing air into the carcass. Gradually, the air could be seen inching its way up through the leg and eventually around the whole body, in the end forming a misshaped, furry balloon. The skin was then easily stripped away from the muscle and removed. From there on, everything was similar to my hunting experience and butcher shop observations, the carcasses being sectioned into various cuts of meat. Certain portions would be given to the poor. Others distributed to neighbors, including us. For the first time in our lives, Deb and I would need to personally grapple with and apply the Bible's teachings for Christians about handling meat sacrificed to idols.

After the sacrifice holiday, we spent several evenings watching the World Cup soccer matches with Mehmet and Reyhan. Talking religion amidst these relaxed get-togethers was something they often initiated, and did this time regarding what we'd just witnessed that week. In response to their further explanations, I told them what we believe about Jesus being the *last* sacrifice and that a Christian doesn't need to make another one. Their response was a polite nod. They had their beliefs, we had ours. It was no light matter for either family. In both of our respective convictions, our eternities were wrapped up in this bloody conversation. It's why Deb and I had transported our family to this foreign world. With a slight discomfort and awkwardness, we eventually agreed to leave the subject for further discussion in the future.

Ellie may have offered the best temporary relief to this weighty yet touchy topic, as the sacrifices happened to fall on her seventh birthday. "It's kind of a gross birthday present."

After this provocative experience, we decided to escape the city during the sacrifice holidays throughout our following years in Turkey. Not only did we prefer to not deal with the potential issue of avoiding participation if offered meat again, but the city stank for a full week afterwards, and likely harbored germs even longer. We made plans to take an annual camping vacation during that religious event. A side benefit to going at that time was the emptiness of campsites. Everyone was celebrating the holiday with family and we often had entire campgrounds to ourselves. These were not contrived, semi-natural KOA-type camping environments. Most of these were gorgeous spots in the mountains or on the Mediterranean, Aegean, and Black Seas. For all of four bucks a night, if not free.

Prior to coming to Turkey, we had purchased all the basics for camping and were well equipped for most seasons. We had a six-person tent, sleeping bags rated to minus five degrees, a Coleman gas stove, and piecemealed the rest together over the years as experience taught us. Although many people find tent camping more of a chore than a vacation, it was heaven for us. To get out of the concrete jungle for a week and sleep close to the ground didn't feel like suffering to us during those sacrifice holidays.

One of the highlights of these vacation adventures that we developed was a tradition of naming each campout based on a few main events that took place. We can still pull up vivid mental pictures of particular trips by simply recalling the names:

Dung Roll Knoll – We found an unofficial campsite on a mountain clearing just before dusk. We awoke to find ourselves surrounded by grazing sheep and a probably stupefied shepherd. When the wooly residents eventually moved on to other fields, they left behind their droppings so well known to that part of the world – marble sized balls of manure. At some point, movement of these little spheres caught our girls' ever-curious eyes, revealing miniature haulers called dung beetles. These acrobats hike their rear legs on top of the balls of dung and walk backwards on their front legs! Thus, our little mountain top retreat got tagged with "Dung Roll Knoll" and began our tradition of naming campouts.

Sahil Holiday Hoedown – Coordinating plans to incorporate our American Thanksgiving, one year we headed south near the popular vacation city of Antalya on the Mediterranean coast. Teammates David and Cindy joined us. One night around an animated fire, David being a southerner from Yazoo City, Mississippi, entertained us with some blue grass on an improvised branch turned bass violin. Before long, all of us had natural wood instruments and were dancing around the fire in an old-fashioned country jig. *Sahil* means "seaside" and the spontaneous hoedown also got featured in the naming.

Solo Star Splash – For another excursion in the same region, we went as a solo family to a campground sandwiched between the base of steep mountains and the shore. Lined up like beached sardines near the swishing surf, we lay face-up on the sand surveying a splash of stars in the night sky. Another constellation name in the universe of family vacations was being formed. In terms of contact with other people, I talked to a shepherd as I hiked in the mountains, and the wife of the camp manager came by our tent to sell us eggs a couple of times. That was it for a whole week. We soaked up the solitude.

camping hoedown on the Mediterranean

4-H Flop – With another family, we ventured north to check out a new area, the Black Sea. Finding a grassy bald on a seaside cliff seemed almost too ideal a spot to camp, but a local person assured us it would be fine to set up there. After several days of some great exploration and stomach-crunching laughter with our friends, Mark and Sue, we narrowed the contending elements for a camp name to four words beginning with "H." Hill was an obvious choice in view of our fantastic location. Hurricane was a bit of an exaggerated commentary on the winds that nearly flattened our tents one night. Hazelnut reminded the girls of their outing to pick nuts with a village lady. And finally, Herd, for a bovine alarm clock that plodded through our campsite early one morning. The trip was absolutely *not* a flop, but we did just flop ourselves on the first Black Sea spot we saw and had another collection of "accidental life" experiences to take home with us.

It was on the morning of one of these inner-city slaughters that we exited our apartment to jump in our van, which we'd already mostly packed the night before. We wanted to get out of the city before the carnage began. I had parked our vehicle along the curb, but unintentionally at the lowest point of a dip in the street. To our revulsion, we hadn't made our get-away early enough. There, in the middle of a nice residential area of Ankara's four million people, was our van straddling a river of blood! The flow centered on my driver's door such that I had to enter the van's passenger side from the raised sidewalk in order to pull it out and load my cringing family. As we drove away from the nauseating site, we discussed how an apocalyptic scene of the Bible seemed more plausible than ever before. *"And the blood came out of the wine press, up to the horse's bridles, for a distance of two-hundred miles."*

As I remember those juxtaposed sobering sacrifice holidays and our happy family vacations, I am grateful for yet another Scripture in which God says, *"For I desire steadfast love and not sacrifice, the knowledge of God, rather than burnt offerings."*

a skeleton from the closet of my personal journal

The Bible confronts reality, with an insistent unwillingness to accommodate fantasy.
- Howard Hendricks, my much-admired professor at Dallas Theological Seminary

Anytime a person makes himself vulnerable by sharing personal feelings, let alone failings, it's a risky thing. The hearer can run with that information in any number of hurtful or helpful directions. On the optimistic side of that potential, the revelations can open up increased perspective, greater empathy, and a deeper relationship. On the pessimistic side, the exposed elements can invite ridicule, spawn unjust judgments, and dash trust.

Nevertheless, at the risk of shattering or confirming some people's views of Christians and missionaries, I have decided to expose myself by lifting a section straight from my personal journal of twenty-six years ago in Turkey. This particular passage does not present me in a favorable light. And yet, just possibly, the naked sharing of it may have virtue in the act itself. I'm actually happy to hazard it since I owned the blame many years ago. And, if nothing else, it fits the way I choose to approach life on the whole; that is, take risks that, if successful, can bring great benefit. If they fail, it's rarely a matter of life and death...except to the ego...which I'm forever learning is a good thing.

The events in the following *verbatim* journaling account took place in probably less than five minutes. I believe the impact of my own reflection on this experience has been producing some inner changes over the years. If not, the same dirty laundry will likely show up on my lifeline somewhere again.

Jim McCracken

[Journal Entry, August 4, 1990]

Two days ago I was eating lunch by myself at an outdoor table near my office. My table was on the perimeter of the area and right next to the passing people. My meal had not yet come, but I had poured half my Coke in the glass. As I watched the people pass, I saw five or six little girls (about my girls' ages, 4-8), filthy from head to toe and obviously on the prowl for handouts. They had previously been scavenging in dumpsters across the walkway. As they walked next to the table adjacent to mine, one girl with animal-like passion snatched a coke bottle from one man's placemat and began voraciously guzzling. Within a second, another girl had seized the man's glass and poured it down. Before I could even begin to put this scene together in my mind (this was a little more aggressive than the beggars I daily encounter), I saw a hand, as black as any car mechanic's, reaching for my glass!

I immediately put my hand out and instinctively said, "Dur!" ("stop" in Turkish), not loudly but firmly. She quickly let go of the glass, but returned her hand to dip all four fingers of her filthy hand into the Coke as if to say, "There, now you'll have to give it to me." As quickly as the mind thinks in such situations, I thought, "Oh yeah, well watch this!" and lifted the glass slowly and took a drink. She cast a spiteful glare at me and returned to the others who were "sharing" (as lions do a downed gazelle) the previously seized bottle and glass.

As my frustration calmed and I wondered what new wave of germs I had swallowed from the little girl's grimy hand, I observed something that really made my stomach begin to churn....

It was the four men – Turkish men – at the adjacent table, whose Coke had been stolen. Their response dropped me dead in my tracks. They were laughing about it. Not only that, they talked with the children and one volunteered his partially finished bottle, which they eagerly devoured. Then it was over. The men lightly shooed them away as the waiter also firmly told them to go.

My mind – my soul – was suddenly flooded with thoughts and rebukes certainly from the Spirit within:

"If someone asks for your coat, give them your coat and offer them your shirt also." (But they were rude and didn't ask. After all, this is a restaurant. And those men are Turks and are used to this.)

"If someone asks you to go a mile with him, go with him two miles." (Yes, but if I gave them the Coke, then they'd keep badgering me for money, my meal...then again, look at them. They're just little children, poor children without any guidance to teach them better.)

"Whoever welcomes one of these little children in my name welcomes Me." (It really would have been a small thing for me to have given such a small thing. I have so much, especially compared to them.)

"Go and sell all you have and give it to the poor...but he went away sad because he had great wealth."

As the waiter brought my nice plate of food, I continued to more honestly search my heart. Here I am in Turkey for the sake of bringing these people a message of love and light, yet guarding my little glass of Coke to the point of shunning a poor beggar child. And at the next table are those without the light that I have and know, yet they say, "Bosh ver." (Turkish for "Don't give it a thought." or "It's nothing.") and treat them with some degree of care. What would it have cost me to let her take the glass...and to have offered the rest of the bottle? About 45 cents. I'd have been a good testimony to those around me, felt the joy of giving, and pleased the Lord's heart. Instead, my immediate reaction (from the real man) was one of hoarding and greed, and worse yet – a lack of care for these lost children, victims of this fallen world.

I am searching my heart anew for the real love of Christ. I pray for another chance, a second try.

Now, nearly three decades later, the recollection of this encounter still produces a painful regret. But there's also a healing chagrin. If life was a seamless garment of perfection, these kind of rips wouldn't even happen. If there's any real hope in this life, it's not in ignoring the reality of evil or denying our own failures. It's in knowing where to take them both for mending.

my Turkish ID, serious expression required

in camp with the Kurds

The poorest man would not part with health for money,
but the richest would gladly part with all his money for health.
Turkish Proverb

I still have the Newsweek covers and articles about the Kurdish refugee crisis in 1991. Televisions in America and worldwide broadcast the unfolding tragedy from varying distances and perspectives. Without pronouncing guilt or excuse on the Kurdish people and situation at the time, the fact was that hundreds of thousands of them were fleeing the threat of genocide in northern Iraq. Another fact, that they were fleeing into the mountains of southeastern Turkey, is where they and I came together face to face.

An American friend and fellow worker in Ankara, Chris, told me that he was considering dropping his present responsibilities for a few weeks in order to go to the region and see if he could be of help midst the devastation. As we talked, I mentally compared the value of what I might accomplish in a few weeks of work in Ankara versus that time possibly invested on the southern border in relief to these ravaged people. It was an easy decision and one with which Deb readily agreed when I presented it to her. Initially, she and the kids were going to go as well, but we later determined that wasn't prudent. I would go first, assess things, and then we would decide whether she or they join me later.

Chris and I gathered basic work clothes, got a Viet Nam veteran medic friend to give us gamma globulin shots to stave off hepatitis, and caught a thirty-hour bus to the village of *Hakkari*, about 35 miles from the Iraqi border. Arriving, we were introduced to other expatriates who were there for the same reason. The persons coordinating efforts proposed which of the numerous refugee gatherings in the mountains we should go to. Chris, one other guy, and I left the next afternoon to hike six hours up the mountain pass to the village of *Uzumlu*. Along the way we came across supplies dropped by parachute for refugee relief. Most of it had been taken away, but two items were clearly left behind – cans and MREs with meat in them. Muslims don't eat pork...apparently even when literally starving they wouldn't take a chance with meat that looked unfamiliar. We picked up a few and ate along the way. None of it was pork, but it met our need for some sustenance during the hike up. It was after dark when we arrived.

Although the isolated, pastoral village of *Uzumlu* had a tiny population of a few hundred, it had been overrun by tens of thousands of Iraqi Kurdish refugees. By the time of our arrival, these desperate families had already stripped every tree and bush from the land to combine with parachutes, cardboard boxes, and whatever else they could find...to make tent-like shelters for themselves. One small stream flowing through the village was sufficient for the native residents, but now had to service the drinking, cooking, and bathing needs of a massive throng of people. Squalor, sickness, disease, and death were the obvious outcome. We would learn from medical volunteers (especially *Medecins Sans Frontieres,* Doctors Without Borders) that in addition to vast dysentery, we would encounter cholera and typhoid fever in the camp.

Military personnel were also present keeping the area secure while coordinating the crucial transportation of people and goods to the camp. Sargeant Ed, leading the U.S. Army Special Forces in charge there, became my good and respected friend during the next three weeks. Prior to our arrival, the men under his charge had set up a perimeter of safety and stopped some sniper attacks. They had also located and removed *most* of the land mines. Tragically, there would be about a half dozen more mine explosions and victims during our time there. All air transportation in the region was provided by various military branches, which we were privileged to utilize on a "space available" basis.

One of my inherited responsibilities would be to act as a liaison for our group and meet daily with the military, United Nations representative, and the leaders of the formal NGOs (Non-Government Organizations). One specific role requested of me was to communicate to the sergeant when there were critical patients who might be saved by helicoptering them out to the closest hospital in Iraq, a detail that explains my journal reference below to being "displaced" briefly in Iraq.

with Special Forces Sgt Ed

This is the context into which we arrived, and where my personal journal picks up. The following pages are excerpts taken verbatim from a journal in which I wrote by flashlight most nights before bedding down. Typical days began around 6 a.m. and ended around 10 p.m. So most journal entries are first blush, reflective, often weary, and as they say, "close to the bone"...here offered fittingly unscrubbed of raw emotion and coarse writing.

Journal Entry, May 1, 1991

Somehow, the Lord has seen fit to let me be sitting in a Kurdish home in the furthest SE corner of Turkey, housed with 5 women and 14 men.... My comrades are from England, Holland, USA, Australia, Germany, Switzerland and Norway.... Sounds as though my role will be a combination of evangelism, digging latrines, hauling garbage, and helping the medical clinic in whatever way I can.

May 2

Upon my arrival in camp, I was informed that the team leader was heading out the next day and that I was voted the new team leader...for the next two weeks...in a place I'd just seen for the first time in the dark!

The weather is tough. At night, it gets down into the upper 30s F and up to nearly 100 F afternoons.... There are several camps in this area. The largest neighboring one (Cukurcu) has 170,000 people. Ours (Uzumlu) had 40,000 when our group came, but 8-12,000 have left. They are going back to Iraq, which is ill-prepared to accept them. Many will certainly die. Our camp (an 8-man tent with 11 people) is about 25 meters from the clinic we assist.... As the second wave of patients came through in the afternoon, I "became" a full-time aid at the clinic for IV assistance, mixing re-hydration solution for babies, showing the mothers how to give it and basic trouble-shooting (plenty of that!).

May 3

The highlight of the day for me was to find (after much searching) enough cable to wire and light all three clinic tents.... Until we put lanterns in here the night before, the people were in complete darkness all night long. Women would wake up to find their children had died in the night and they'd not been able to know.... I awoke today to see a beautiful sky (the rain finally passed) and was excited to get up and get going. As I stepped out of the tent, I was met by a fellow worker, Kathy, carrying a dead baby that didn't make it through the night. I felt like a balloon suddenly punctured. This little one was 4 days old and just yesterday Kathy had brought her to me to show me how healthy she looked and how she seemed to be doing better.

May 4

As I tried to take a breather in the tent (for the first time in 3 days), someone came asking for a white sheet – we supply these as body wraps (their tradition) for the dead. Upon accompanying the young man, I found a 3 to 4 year old boy dead – eyes staring, mouth open. The neigh-

boring patient's mother (only two feet apart on plastic we spread out over the dirt) was crying as she'd just seen the patient on the opposite side die the day before – not giving her hope for her own child. Not even the doctors knew yet that he had died. The neighboring lady asked me to close his eyes. My hands over-rode my emotions and pried the lids shut (already quite dry and stiff with rigor mortis). I wrapped the boy in his blanket and informed the doctors. Inquiring about where the mother was, I learned through an interpreter that the mother, a brother and a sister had died in the previous 4 days. The father was paralyzed and my young escort was a refugee camp neighbor wanting to take responsibility for the body. I offered to carry the body back to an uncle who would take care of the ritual wrapping, prayer chants and burial. As I left the compound, I was met by the dead boy's remaining sister who was doing all she could to contain her grief. At this sight, I could only keep walking ahead as the tears streamed down my face and onto the dead boy's blanket wrap. I carried him nearly half a mile through the camp as on-lookers' faces sorrowed at the sight of yet another death. Some sighed, some stared, some ignored – either hardened by so much loss before or unable to acknowledge the reality of another.

May 5

I find myself switching languages from moment to moment. Most of the Kurds only speak Kurdish, some a little English or Turkish. I am often taking a message from an American soldier in English, translating it in Turkish to a Turkish Kurd who, in turn, converts it to an Iraqi Kurd in Kurdish. Then the answer comes back in the reverse order. One often wonders if the message got through as intended.

May 8

I haven't written for 1½ days now. The main reason is not just busyness, but rather "displacement." In an attempt to air-vac (by Blackhawk helicopter with guns ready out each side) two emergency patients from our clinic to the hospital in Zakho, I (along with Kathy, our nurse) ended up stranded in Iraq – with only the clothes I had on (tennis shoes, old pants and a white undershirt) and no passport or money!.... The advice given concerning us was to catch a chopper to Silopi, Turkey, and then from there to our base. To make a very long story short, we got to Silopi, but there were no flights to Uzumlu. We were stranded for the night and were sent to "refugee assistance" since we had nothing. Finally, the US army set us up in a tent with cots, casualty bags (no sleeping bags available), nice meals (the first ham I've had in 1½ years), Star Trek on TV, and the first shower in a week.... When we finally arrived "home" in Uzumlu, our team was quite curious to hear what had become of us the last 26 hours!.... No lack of adventure.

May 9

We have been able to reach out with the message of hope in addition to all the physical help. Jarle (a Norwegian partner) and I went up to a family near the minefield (in which several refugees have lost life and limb). Talking to two young men and finding that they read Arabic opened the door to give them New Testaments.... Chris (another worker) and I took a Turkish-Kurdish translator and re-hydration salts and headed for some more remote areas. This process also gets us in tents for discussion. We had an hour-long talk with one Kurdish family (with 4 men while the women sat outside). Canned Islamic and fatalistic answers were given for each probe. These people feel deserted by God....

May 10

Sometimes the flurry with which new events hit me leaves me feeling as though I'm living out some movie script or fiction.... Last night after getting settled in the tent for our nightly time of prayer, singing, talking... the wind began to pick up.... Within 30 seconds, I was leaning with all I had on one of our tent posts to hold it up – unsuccessfully! Kathy and the bulk of our team were hanging on the 2-inch metal pipe braces of the clinic's pediatric tents. It was lifting them several feet off the ground.... With the help of several doctors who arrived on the scene, they were able to keep it from going completely. IVs were ripped out of several babies and we lost our electrical line. The scene was horrific – wind (clocked at 40 mph by the military), swirling dirt, pitch blackness, children and mothers yelling. Thanks to the Lord's protection, we didn't lose any lives that night.

It was at the end of two weeks that Deb joined me in the work. She was able to catch an Army transport plane to the ancient, walled, Mesopotamian city of *Diyarbakir*, where I would meet her. It took some courage on her part to make this leg of the trip alone. She carried with her a bag of Bibles and Christian literature in four different and controversial languages. She had to secure a hotel room for us. In her curiosity, she even ventured out for a stroll in this strange city before I arrived.

My trip from *Uzumlu* to meet Deb turned out to be eleven hours by Jeep through rugged mountains and territory in the midst of civil war. I had no map, but only knew I was heading westward and that there were just a few places I would have to make major directional decisions, but there should be signs or people to ask. As I look back on the trip over mountain passes, countless switchbacks, through riverbeds, and seeing less than a dozen cars, I'm amazed I didn't get lost. Three or four times in the course of the trek, as I rounded a mountain bend, I came upon Kurdish, turban-headed Peshmerga ("one who confronts death") militia with automatic rifles on horseback. Each time, they quickly dismounted and trained their guns in my direction. When they recognized me as Western and not one of their enemy PKK, they lowered their weapons, smiled, and even gave me their palm-out salute. My chest tightened with terror each time it happened, but I managed a shaky salute in return and continued.

Deb and I spent one night in the hotel and were able to jump a memorable helicopter flight along the Turkish border with Syria and through Iraq, which included a birds-eye peep at one of Saddam Hussein's largest palaces. This story and others are told in the following journal entries.

May 14

Deb is now here. Although things have slowed down dramatically due to previous care and fewer refugees (they are returning to Iraq), there are still areas in which to serve. Deb has already been able to help redress bandages on the mine explosion amputees, check and help women through a stillbirth, comfort others, be a "go-for" for the doctors, make meals and organize the tent.... On the Chinook helicopter flight from Diyarbakir to Uzumlu, Deb was hooked into a harness and sat on the rear drop-gate with feet dangling while we flew at low altitude over both Turkey and Iraq. After half an hour, I took her place and she ended up in the cockpit with earphones and microphone to observe the rest of the flight and talk with the pilots. It was royal treatment by the Royal Air Force of the UK!

May 18

Among Deb's most memorable moments in life has been an experience with a little girl she emotionally adopted from her first day here. The girl was 4-5 months old and brought in like most with malnutrition, diarrhea and severe dehydration....

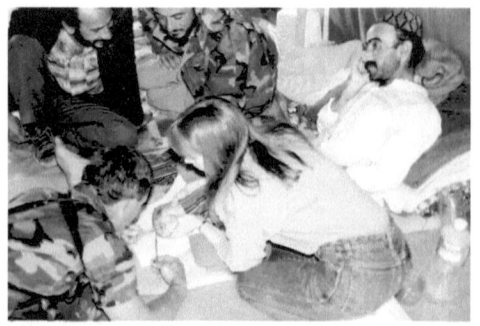

Deb helping mine victim amputees

On Deb's 4th day in camp, she was approached first thing in the morning by the mother. There was a problem. Rushing to the tent, Deb found that the baby was having difficulty breathing.... [2 hours later] I was being interviewed by a reporter in our tent area. I saw Deb busily starting to work on breakfast and tried to introduce her to the reporter. She turned away quietly and began to cry. I knew what had happened. A little later, she told me that some improved vital signs were only a last effort by the baby fighting to survive. Once back in the tent, the baby again vomited, inhaled some and went back to prolonged gaps between breaths. As Deb comforted the mother and looked on, the pause continued and another breath never came. No sooner could each one present realize she was gone, the grandmother picked up the baby, covered it and helped the mother away to prepare for the burial. As the mother exited the tent, she turned and embraced Deb. They both cried for a while. Deb watched them walk toward their tent home until they were out of sight.

We have now returned home and, at least for a while, appreciate in a special way our comfortable house and healthy children. More than anything, I am aware that the hope I have in Christ is the greatest of my possessions – not a hope that I'll always have these things or that the future will be smooth. Rather, that if I should ever face something such as these people are facing, I have an anchor. I have a confidence that He does know and He does care. I can't imagine being able to withstand such disappointments and sorrow, but I know He is faithful in that time.

As an American, moving to a place like Turkey seems like a huge and daunting endeavor to many of our friends. And it was a decision arrived at with much thoughtful consideration and preparation. However, just two years in country, we had already become enough acclimated to be able to consider an even further step into the unknown and risky by going to the refugees. We hadn't planned beyond city life in Ankara, but the "accident" of unscripted life presented an opportunity. And what came of it? Not only did we enter into the work of extending life to needy souls, we encountered a reciprocal experience of life that we never could have anticipated or engineered. I believe that's the way it works. With every step of unbridled faith in the One who is trustworthy, we are purposefully stumbling into meaningful existence.

a man's been shot!

A generous action is its own reward.
Turkish Proverb

I guess you could call it my "parting shot" before leaving Turkey to return to live in the Untied States. But it wasn't I who pulled the trigger.

We had moved from Ankara to live and work in the northern city of Samsun on the Black Sea. My office was downtown, but we lived on the outskirts in what was typically a quiet neighborhood along the beach. What a daily pleasure and relief from the city clamor to wake up each morning to the waves only a hundred yards from our bedroom window and balcony. The only unnatural noise came from the four-lane in front of the apartment building. Even that was muffled a little by our third floor roost.

"Jim, a man's just been shot out front!" Those were Deb's words screamed to me about six months before we left Samsun and flew Stateside. It was high noon, I was just off a plane from Istanbul, had been in the door only fifteen minutes,

my Turkish mining business, far right

and was temporarily "indisposed" in the little room down the hall. Sounds like a sick comedy already. Deb had heard a series of gunshots, looked out the front window, and witnessed several things: Two men were running full-tilt to the left. Another man lay in the middle of the highway directly in front of our house. Several people at the car wash, lumber shop, grocery, and carryout across the street were watching the whole event unfold. It was after seeing this that she yelled to me.

In the midst of hurriedly trying to get my attire together and my shoes on, our three girls were crying and Deb was giving me an on-the-fly, rushed summary of what she'd seen. All I could process was a man possibly dying in the street. We told the kids to stay put (not that they were entertaining going outside) and ran downstairs together from our flat.

I'm no hero. I must admit that I was not enthusiastic about going out in the street where numerous shots had been fired. My one attempt to break up a domestic fight several years before, but instead getting pummeled myself, did cross my mind. Still now, as then, the example and teaching of Jesus to lay down one's life for another superseded my fear...barely. I told Deb to hang back. Somewhat to my surprise, but more to my frustration, *no one* had yet reached this man lying in a puddle of his blood, pitifully trying to crawl from the street while weakly waving to stop traffic or get help. It became obvious to me then that no one intended to come to his aid. As I checked the man's numerous wounds (the police report I signed later revealed *seven* bullets in his abdomen, hips, groin, and thighs), Deb ran to pull our van from the garage. My anger at my neighbors increased with each passing car and second.

Finally the neighbors trickled to the scene to gawk. Deb brought the van. The police who just arrived ordered some bystanders to pick up the wounded man and put him inside my van. The officers didn't dirty their hands to pick him up nor to check the wounds, let alone give medical assistance. They didn't offer their official vehicle to be bloodied. My blood was about to boil over. Then they commanded me, "Go, get him to the hospital!" It was obvious that I was ready to assist by the fact of my active presence and my voluntary use of the van, but I wasn't going to take responsibility for a crime victim who might die while in my care. I replied that I needed one of the several police on the scene to come with me. They resisted and said, "No, you just take him. You know where the hospital is?" By this time, the poor man was loaded and lying on the bench immediately behind my driver's seat, and blood had already smeared the vinyl cover and was dripping on the floorboard. Incredulous, I insisted I would not take him unless I was given a police escort *inside* the van with me. It took several back and forth stalemates before they relinquished an officer who reluctantly climbed into my passenger seat with an Uzi.

As I sped to the hospital with my writhing patient and captive police officer, I wrestled again with feelings of anger over my neighbors' lack of compassion and apparent total concern for themselves. This wasn't the first time I'd struggled with such feelings. My well-worn, self-addressed sermon replayed - *You can't expect regenerate behavior from unregenerate people.* Then a tandem message immediately followed - *But if I am regenerate, that's what I need to deal with. I'm not responsible to judge or make them do what's right.* I relaxed some and listened as the officer questioned the victim who was moaning from the van floor where he'd tumbled in pain. There was no sophisticated alibi or excuse in the man's answers. He had previously gambled with some guys, lost, and had a debt he couldn't pay. His two attackers were the guys he owed, and they had decided to take it out of his flesh. (In Turkish fashion, they went for a part of his body that would shamefully maim him if he did survive. Thus, seven shots to the groin area.) When asked, he gave the names of the two guys without hesitation. At the hospital, my conversion ambulance was emptied as quickly as it had been filled. Returning my uniformed passenger to the police station, I gave a brief statement in writing, and left. Before reaching my driveway, I realized the guys at the carwash could probably do a better job than me at removing the blood. The well-manned crew gathered to see the condition of the inside and concluded they needed a couple of hours. I left it and walked across the street to find out how my family was handling things and to personally debrief as well.

When I could see the van was finished and waiting, I went over to pick it up and pay. Once again, all the usual suspects huddled around to hear what I might say, offer their volumes of good-old-boy speculation on the big event, and make sure they didn't miss any of the drama. As I paid and started to field or avoid their questions, the police showed up in the conspicuous crowd and began their own questioning. An officer asked the whole den of men what they had seen. Comically, the group's former bravado about what happened and what must have been the case vanished into a single, uncreative consensus – "Nothing." There is a general distrust of the police in Turkey, who routinely take bribes and use abusive force to get information or gain control of a situation. Each angle the officer tried in order to elicit some piece of evidence was met with the same blank-faced response followed by glances around the circle to see who might be stupid enough to insert himself into this business. From this culture's perspective, it was best to stay uninvolved and say nothing. But with certainty, once the police officer would leave and the threat gone, the conversation would revert back to the omniscient interpretations they'd been espousing only minutes before.

I *knew* some of these guys had to have seen something because they are always sitting out front doing just that – watching whatever might be going on. It's what the older men do – sit and watch. I lived right across the street and had done my own watching of them. But still, "nothing." One said he'd been out back, another was working with a customer, and the rest laid low hoping to not be singled-out. The policeman, being even more aware of what was going on than I was, saw a possible chink in the armored clan gathered. He asked a young boy who worked at the carwash what *he* might have seen. Another street-smart, learned response: He hadn't been there at the moment the shooting took place…"Oh, but, this American here (indicating me), he took the wounded man to the hospital in his car." The light was dawning on my naive horizon – not only were these people unwilling to risk their lives at the initial scene, but they also feared the repercussions if they should testify of whom and what they saw. This young, targeted boy saw an even softer target to which he could deflect the interrogation - the *yabanci*, the foreigner.

As I rode in the paddy wagon to the police station to "give a simple statement that you took him to the hospital" for the second time, I shook my head with unbelief at the lying, selfish ways of my neighbors. In honesty, I seethed with feelings of frustration, naiveté, self-righteousness, anger at them.... Again the self-directed sermon rolled - *You can't expect regenerate behavior from unregenerate people*. I can't expect them to think and do otherwise. They had no confidence that Allah would faithfully reward right living. He *might*, but that's about as far as most of their faith assures. The Allah of the Koran is largely capricious. At the station, I again made my simple statement of what both Deb and I did and didn't see and hear, and what I did with the shooting casualty. On the way out, I met the detectives as they hustled past me the two alleged criminals the victim had identified by name. It looked like an "open and shut case", as they say. As they *say*....

Once back home, I rehearsed the day over in my mind. *Should I have done what I did?* Answering our girls' questions, I repeated what I'd taught them many times before in various situations – "It's always right to do what's right." I emphasized that even if everybody else does what's wrong or differently, we need to do what we believe is right. As if to test my resolve, only four hours after the shooting, a loud screech and crunch out front of the house signaled a sizable accident. Within thirty seconds, the scene was crawling with forty or so of the same neighbors, this time in a non-threatening situation, pointing accusing fingers and confidently *telling all they saw*!

Play it again, Jim – "You can't expect regenerate behavior from unregenerate people."

Punch the button for "fast forward" about five months, well after the shooting drama and even after the buzz of hushed talk along *Atakum Bulvari* (White Sand Boulevard) had ceased. We were exactly one month away from loading all our possessions on a ship and boarding ourselves on an airplane. I opened the mail to read in Turkish, and re-read to make sure I got it right, that I had been subpoenaed in the shooting case and was to appear in court…three days before our departure.

My gut reaction was, *I won't do it!* My head said, *What if you don't show, and you get arrested in what is supposed to be your last seventy-two hours in Turkey?* My conscience sided with my head, and in turn, reminded me what I had said to my girls – "It's always right to do what's right."

From a positive standpoint, I had an entire month to think about how I would formulate my testimony in the courtroom. From a negative standpoint, I had an entire month to think about how I would formulate my testimony in the courtroom. I dreaded it. *I have no idea how a Turkish courtroom trial proceeds.* My only mental framework was from the movie "Midnight Express", which, to put it glibly, was no help or comfort! *What if the case isn't resolved and they order me to stay in Turkey?* Not likely, but I had been in country long enough to know how much I didn't know. I was sure there were more "unknowns" ahead than "knowns." Was that ever true!

We were to fly out on Monday, and on the Friday before, I entered a large, open waiting area of the courthouse. It was surrounded with doors leading to what I learned were separate courtrooms. The only instruction I was given was to wait in this anteroom with everybody else until our case was summoned. I lingered among tens of folks, all of us dressed in our best, nervously waiting our respective cases. I had no idea who was who. I didn't know how many cases there were and which people might be part of "my" case. Not recognizing anyone, I stood against a wall and tried to relax, shifting weight from foot to foot, and involuntarily rehearsing my brief and refined story.

One grouping of men began to draw my attention because of the obvious intensity of their conversation. They leaned in close to each other, talked in diminished tones, and had that guilty look of scheming that, in my perception, resembled a movie version of dirty dealings. One guy in particular, wearing a putty-colored suit, gave the appearance of a ringleader. Several times, I thought they glanced over at me and might be talking about me. I had just about convinced myself that it was only my overly sensitized imagination, fed by nerves and being the only foreigner, when the putty-suited man waved me over to the group. My stomach muscles snapped to attention. I approached very tentatively and was almost physically pulled into the circle. Rather, they closed in tightly around me.

There were no introductions, but the conversation started with Mr. Putty Pants asking me a question. "Aren't you here with the (victim's name) case?" Although it seemed a bit strange, so did everything else, and I merely answered "yes." His next question, however, had a genuinely creepy feel to it. "What are you going to say you saw?" It felt wildly inappropriate. I answered probably more wisely than I could have thoughtfully intended, and said, "I don't know who you are or what you have to do with the case. I don't think I should answer that."

The ringleader began to reveal a story to me that was so childishly fabricated and embellished, I felt embarrassed to stand there and hear it through to the end. According to him, he was also a victim of a shooting. In fact, several months previous, the victim in *my* case had shot him, Mr. Putty, in the stomach. He even pulled up his shirt to reveal a scar on his abdomen. More importantly, unlike Mr. Putty, my victim was not a good guy but actually a bad guy, and deserved to have been shot. Mr. Putty was present as the victim of that *other* case, and was just curious to know what I was going to say in *my* case. "What are you going to say you saw?"

By this time, I was convinced that my fictional movie thugs were real, and I answered as evasively as I could think to. "I'm just going to tell the truth." He was relentless and pressed me for specifics. I repeated that I was going to simply tell the truth. When he didn't get the information he evidently wanted, his demeanor and body language began speaking an even uglier dialect. He moved in, locked eyes with me, and said very firmly, "You're going to say you didn't see anything." I was almost certain I wasn't missing some nuance in the Turkish, but asked just to make sure, and then almost wished I hadn't. "Are you asking me or *telling* me?" His answer left no doubt, even though he stayed quiet and calm in repeating, "You're going to say you didn't see anything." With much more composure than was going on inside me, I was able to echo my previous answer about telling the truth, and walked away back to my place along the wall.

Some time later, a man (whom I guessed to be a bailiff, and proved later to be exactly that) emerged from a courtroom and called our case name, so I followed him inside along with a number of other people, including the entire group of thugs in the "other" case. The fishy story was really getting stinky, but I still couldn't sort out the players or plot.

The room sloped amphitheater style. I took a seat in the center section right next to the aisle I came down. I began to take in my surroundings. Up front was a high, dark, wooden bench that stretched nearly the whole width of the room. There were five men in black robes with high collars. The one in the middle, whom I took to be the presiding judge, had an even more pronounced collar that I can only describe as very much like that of Dracula. Down in front of him and the long bench was a small round pedestal with a half-circle rail on it facing the judge. I recognized it as "the bar." In the far right corner, I saw my victim, who was in much better shape than when I'd seen him last at the hospital. Toward the left front corner of the room, I saw the two defendants I'd seen brought in the police station the day of the arrest. Then I saw the plot connector that started to pull the rotten story together. Sitting with and obviously advising the two defendants was Mr. Putty. He was no victim. He was the defense attorney and had been imitating a victim...and intimidating a witness – me!

As I sat and waited for the case to begin, I could hardly accept that something so blatantly wrong had taken place. The thought of telling the judge lasted only a few seconds before I reeled back such a crazy inclination. At that point, I just wanted out of the courtroom and out of the country with my family.

Finally something was happening. The bailiff who was talking to the judge dismounted the platform, walked right past me and up to the door we had all entered. Then clearly and loudly I heard

a typical Turkish courtroom, like a gallery of Draculas

him yell outside to the waiting area what I'd heard many times over six years – my name read phonetically in Turkish. "*Zhames Mujjra-jken!*" I turned toward him, raised my hand and piped up in Turkish, "*Benim, buradayim*" ("It's me, I'm here."). He whirled around, came down the aisle fast, extended both hands palm-up at me, which gave the same rebuke as his voice did. "What are you doing in here? We didn't call for witnesses yet. You're supposed to wait outside!" Before *I* could say it, the judge mercifully stepped in saying, "It's alright, he's a foreigner and doesn't know." The bailiff had to let it go, but was still visibly frustrated that I had violated *his* miniature kingdom of authority.

Then I got my last round of shock treatments before being discharged. The judge asked the bailiff about other witnesses, to which the bailiff replied, "There aren't any others. He's the only one." With that information, and before I could fully embrace that fact, the judge called me to the small railed pedestal and asked me to give my name, where I live, what I do for work, and what I saw. Part way through my story he asked, "You're an American, but you live and work here?" I confirmed his understanding and finished my not-too-helpful story, emphasizing what I'd pre-planned to say, that "I didn't see any of the shooting, but only came outside after the shots in order to help. I just took him to the hospital, that's all." He asked a few more questions to establish for sure that that was all, gave me a smile that communicated a warm and genuine appreciation, thanked me, and dismissed me. I went back to my seat and sat down. Before I could get settled in my seat, the judge said, "You can leave, that's all we need from you. Thank you." As I proceeded to leave, I was more relieved than probably anyone might have guessed! I was exiting the left side of the courtroom and couldn't resist one last glance at Mr. Putty. For some reason, which I think I know, he was very intently concentrated on the papers in front of him and didn't seem to be aware or care that I was there or leaving.

As I left the courthouse light-stepping and feeling pardoned, I knew I was going to make my Monday departure. I never did get to hear whether the defendants were found guilty or not. I never got revenge on my neighbors who hung me out to dry as the only witness that could be found. I never got up the nerve to expose that dirty defense attorney for lying to and intimidating me! I never got to....

Play it again, Jim. "You can't expect regenerate behavior from...."

career development

For every complicated problem there is a solution that is simple, direct, understandable...and wrong.
- adapted quote from *Prejudices: Second Series* by H. L. Mencken

My problem was actually quite simple to identify: I needed to figure out what to do with the rest of my life. Now that I was leaving the mission field (the direction my entire adult life had prepared for and worked at the previous seventeen years), I needed not just a new job, but a whole new career.

It might seem obvious on the surface that a logical choice would be pastoring a church, but that was one thing I was fairly certain I would *not* do. Many times during my seminary years, fellow students or new acquaintances would assumingly ask, "So, are you going to be a pastor?" I'm sure my defensive response at the time made them feel like they'd asked some socially inappropriate question. I was evangelistic in proclaiming that I had *not* entered seminary to be one of *those*. "I'm a cross-cultural missions major. I came to Dallas with foreign missions as my goal from the start." And then I'd make the fatal statement with my own mouth: "I don't *ever* see myself being a pastor." Why do we say those kinds of things? Of all people, I, as a staunch purveyor of "Accidental Life", should know that's the very sort of comment that one often has to eat later. I ended up with a three-course meal.

But I had a tasty snack on the way to the pastoral buffet.

Not having concrete plans in mind, we decided to move near good friends in Arkansas and launch our career and inner search from there. This move was no small decision in itself. It entailed shipping a twenty-foot crate with all our belongings from the Black Sea by truck, ship, railroad, and truck again to this small city of 10,000 people in the Ozarks. It was not the recruiting center of the nation. We didn't even have a place to live, but our generous friends offered to set us up in a hotel for a short while in order for us to look around. We didn't want to take advantage of their liberality, so we rented the first and cheapest place we could find available to someone without a job – College Hill Apartments.

The name of the place did forewarn us that it might be housed primarily with collegians, not necessarily notorious for quiet or upscale living. We could handle that for a while. And after all, the college was my main target of possible employment. The much clearer caution that I overlooked was standing right in plain view - the building itself. In retrospect, I think I was so desperate to get my family settled somewhere, I ignored the blatant fact that the apartment had no windows, dark chocolate vintage shag carpet, plaid furniture way too similar to my long-gone orange Hornet's upholstery, and it used to be a gymnasium. A long time ago. I must describe the structure to reveal the extent of my impaired vision.

This had been the college's original and subsequently abandoned gym. Rather than demolish it, some penny-pincher decided to maximize occupancy by cramming as many housing units as possible into the rectangular edifice. The *sane* stage of construction was to frame-in individual flats around the entire perimeter of the building. Next came a suspicious loop-like run of hallway inside the building to access each flat. Then came the sinister genius of the plan. *Inside* that looping hallway, was a series of back-to-back, "center court" cellblocks whose only window was a small one looking from the living room...into the hallway. It more resembled the payment window of a questionable doctor's office. No natural light. No way to see or even hear what the weather was like outside. No ventilation except via the smoke-infused air handler system. But at least there were two bedrooms. Both were so miniscule, the entrance doors to them could *almost* open all the way before hitting the beds. It was horrendous...and all ours!

We hadn't been there but a few days before it was painfully obvious to me that I needed a job and we needed a different place *soon*. As I stated before, the local liberal arts college was my first (and only) idea for employment. It was late September and the academic year had begun, but I learned of a position that they had not filled as of yet. *Can I do this job? Am I qualified? Can I sell myself?* Despite these dissuasive doubts reverberating in my head, I had never been more motivated in my life to go get a job.

The Dean of Students would be conducting the interview, and for good reason. The position directly answered to him. He received me warmly and professionally, but his prefacing comments were deflating to my ginned-up enthusiasm. Although the salary was allocated in the budget, the college was reconsidering filling the position after it became unexpectedly vacant. Nevertheless, we discussed all the ordinary relevant factors about the position and my background. The more we talked, the more I was convinced *"I could do this."* The Dean was hesitant and deferred to giving it some more thought. I left without the job or the hope of getting it.

The phone call came within just a few days. Karen, his administrative assistant, informed me that for the time being they had decided to not re-fill the position...however, if they changed their minds, they'd let me know. The news was more than depressing. It felt like a mistake. So I did something I'd never done before nor have since. Without invitation, I went back to get the job. The Dean had not given me reason to hope, but I decided to try to convince him they needed me anyway. He graciously welcomed me again into his office, let me unjustifiably ask the rationale for the decision, and boldly offer myself once more for consideration.

As I drove back to Deb and the girls incarcerated at College Hill, I knew in my heart that there had been nothing in my formal training or vocational direction that qualified me for the position. I knew it had been a risky long shot to go back to the Dean and potentially be perceived as badgering him in his decision. Once home, I walked into the stale smelling lock-up and performed my best and slightly altered rendition of the 1958 hit by The Silhouettes singing, "Yip yip yip yip yip yip yip yip, Mum mum mum mum mum mum, Got a Job!" All my girls gave a screech of excitement and began crying. Their dad and husband, who was trying to figure out what to do with his life and what kind of job to pursue, was now the "Director of Career Development." Ironically, I would be counseling college students how to figure out what to do with their lives and what kind of job to pursue.

Now, if that's not "Accidental Life", I don't know what is.

It turned out to be a wonderful year of transitioning back into American life. We got a pardon from College Hills and moved into a nice two-story house with a huge yard. I may have actually helped some students that year. I taught them to put together a resume…while I worked on mine. I boned up and passed on skills for interviewing… making sure I retained the knowledge for myself. I made some great friends and learned what a rich environment working for a learning institution can be.

At the end of the school year, my position was revamped to incorporate a new endeavor into the local business community, and the college was entertaining applications. I was encouraged to re-apply. Although I knew the job had evolved far outside my strengths, I tossed my hat in the ring anyway. We truly loved being part of a college atmosphere and especially near our good friends. Even applying all my recently sharpened job acquisition skills, they hired a different candidate. Bruce, the Dean, who had become a friend and sometimes tennis partner, called me in his office and quizzed me in a chummy way, "What happened? You didn't sell yourself at all. You didn't convince us you wanted the job." The truth had surfaced. As much as I *wanted* it the year before, I really *didn't* want it now. And it showed.

The big question was again on the table – what to do with the rest of my vocational life. Partly out of desperation and partly from inner changes in my perspective, I began bouncing off Deb the possibility of me being *some kind* of pastor. Maybe it wasn't an option to dismiss offhand. I still had cold feet, but we would keep the door open.

A phone call from Tom, a former missionary associate and buddy, broke the ice. He presented two separate propositions. First, he knew of a large church that was searching for an associate pastor, if I was interested. And second, he was remodeling his own house in Colorado and could use some help, if I was available. Since I was in limbo, I accepted both invitations. He was glad to make the church introduction. I was enthusiastic as always about making a road trip.

Pulling out the roadmap to plot my trip from Arkansas to Colorado and choosing a route that cut through Kansas, a loosely-related and quirky conversation with our girls popped up from my memory. It took place a year earlier when we had just gotten back to the States and were having one of our free-flowing dinner talks. As we discussed our uncertain future, I put the positive spin on it: "We can go anywhere we want! We're not limited by any constraints. Which state would each of you like to live in?" The girls used their limited geographical knowledge and started tossing out ideas coast to coast. Deb, a heat-seeking missile, picked sunny southern climates. Then a random idea came to me. Since our preferences were all over the map, "What if we just decided to live in the center-most place in the nation? I wonder where that would be." I brought an atlas from the shelves and displayed it in front of us on the table (another brilliant home school trick of slipping in an incognito geography lesson). Opening to the USA map and roughly finding midpoints east to west and north to south, I located the cross-section. It looked to be in the middle of nowhere. "Let's go to the Kansas map and look closer" (obviously before the days of Google Maps and zooming in). Finding the rectangle that was Kansas, I dropped my pointer finger on the relative spot. What was there? All of us gawked and then followed with a flurry of ways to exclaim, "*No way!*" My finger was on top of *McCracken*, Kansas.

Now a year later, planning my current road trip and recalling this past minor miracle, I knew I had to stop in McCracken to see what's there. And I did.

It *was* in the middle of nowhere, and its existence didn't seem to do much to change that fact. The population sign read a little over 300 inhabitants. According to other signage, it was obvious that rodeo was, or had been, a big attraction there. There was a McCracken library, so I knew there must be some literate folks around somewhere, but at five in the evening on a weekday, I hadn't seen a soul yet. I found what was obviously their main street and cruised the length of it, turned around, and came back the same slow fifteen-second distance. It looked as though there were two establishments open. One was a creepy looking bar called "Frog Hollow" with a sidewalk-to-sky mural showing clothed frogs as the patrons. I decided against it, and chose instead an average, seedy-looking bar across the street. Maybe there would be somebody there who could satisfy my curiosity about this little cow stop with my name.

Just opening the door into a bar as a stranger in town is daunting to most guys, I think. For an unaccustomed lightweight barfly like me, I forgot my opening lines as soon as I stepped inside. The bar was directly opposite my squeaking entrance and, like something out of a spaghetti western, every head at the bar turned around to see who came in. All three of them stared at me with expressionless beerface. None of them said anything, but the gruff bartender welcomed me with, "Can I do something for you?" Not only did the accent really throw me, but he apparently thought I was lost and probably wanted directions out of town. By his glower, I wasn't sure he liked the idea of me sidling up alongside the others for a cold one. But then I remembered my opening lines and said, "Hi, my name's McCracken. I'm passing through and wondering if I could find out something about this town."

To my satisfaction and relief, the bartender announced, "Hey guys, we've got us a McCracken in the house!" They all nodded "Hi" and even smiled. I ordered a beer and sat down, feeling pretty hopeful about my amateur traveling journalist reception. I asked a few questions that brought out a few interesting facts. The regulars did all the talking while the bartender did the usual busy stuff of wiping things down, washing glasses, straightening up bottles, and stopping periodically to listen with folded arms.

Even though nobody could remember exactly who the town was named after, it was for sure a McCracken. I could find out at the jail right there on Main Street if it was open, but not at this hour of the day. The jailhouse was built of natural stone right around the turn of the century and was now the town's museum. I might be able to talk with someone there about the town's history tomorrow, if I was staying around. (What was around?) A few scenes of the 1973 movie "Paper Moon" with Ryan and Tatum O'Neal were shot in and around McCracken. (Now that truly was something noteworthy!) Rodeo was the town's biggest draw for outsiders. Their high school team was full of champions. (Rodeo as a high school sport?) The school mascot name was, not surprisingly, the Mustangs.

About the time I was finishing my beer and had seemed to exhaust the historical faculty at the bar, it came to me that in the midst of my interviews, I had forgotten a question I'd meant to ask since our initial introduction half an hour ago. When the bar tender had first greeted me, "Can I do something for you?" it rolled out of his mouth with a totally out-of-place Australian accent. I was sure of it from my exposure to lots of my dad's clientele from Down Under. It seemed like a natural curiosity to ask the obvious, "You're Australian, aren't you?" He didn't answer, but his fans at the bar offered, "Yeah, he's an old sea captain from Australia." Since I was right on that first surmise, and I was starting to feel like a truly insightful reporter, it seemed like a sequitur to ask, "So what's an old sea captain doing here in land-locked Kansas?"

I didn't see it coming, but I sure got its force when he delivered his answer. "What's with all these (bleeping) questions? What are you, the bloody FBI? I think that's about enough questions for now. That'll be three bucks." I'm pretty fair at catching the subtleties of language, so this wasn't a difficult "G-day, Mate" to interpret. I paid with a five to ensure a generous and fast tip, and made my exit. Once I made it across the street and safely to my car, I was able to laugh. Even though the main street looked like an old western, no boots had followed me outside to challenge me to a draw. I saw an old coin payphone and called Deb collect. "Hey, you know where I am?"

It was a fun reminder when I got my phone bill that month. I didn't even mind paying the extra fees to see "collect call - McCracken, Kansas" on it.

My bare bones Nissan pickup truck did make it all the way to Colorado. I wedged a portable tape player between the dashboard and windshield, and blasted my conservative tunes by Loggins and Messina, Seal, and James Taylor as I dustbowled through the desert. Tom and I accomplished a lot on his house, then watched old Cary Grant movies with his family each evening. I read Peter Jenkins' "Walk Across America" before I fell asleep in my comfy basement bed. Tom told me about the large church in Illinois to whom he was referring me. It sounded like a great place to work…if someone wanted to be a pastor, that is.

A week later, I was physically beat as I set out for the long return trip back to Arkansas. My no frills, no comfort truck multiplied the effect of the miles. As I made my way toward home, I saw the most incredible rainbow in New Mexico. It formed a full circle instead of the usual half arc. I survived a lonely night in a dumpy motel in the Texas panhandle. I fought off sleep in numbing Oklahoma, and blinked away at dry eyes my last sleepy leg through the winding back roads of Arkansas. The lights of our small college community and the smell of the Tyson chicken processing plant let me know I had made it home. Just three minutes from the house...*squeal* and *wham!* After two-thousand incident-free miles across strange country, some young punk pulls a hit-and-run on me with my house almost in view. There goes the two-hundred bucks Tom gave me for helping him. And I'm still out of a job.

Two months later, Deb and I were in the beginning process of learning twenty-three hundred faces and names. They all called me Pastor McCracken. As I taught on topics like "faith versus doubt", "your sins will find you out", and "God, our Protector", things like window-less apartments, bartenders on the lam, and hit-and-run drivers were more than just memories. They were sermon illustrations!

preaching, an unplanned privilege

helping people die

My constant in the chaos...
From the song "Christ Remains" by Phil Driscoll

His name was Don. That's almost all I know about him, other than he had a young family at home, drove an eighteen-wheeler, and "should have known better" according to his boss.

Like many sheltered modern Americans, I hadn't been directly exposed to death much as a child. Death is not something we easily forget unless maybe when it's been a constant companion, or when it's so traumatic that remembrance gets shoved out through sheer survival of the soul. My earliest memories were pretty much confined to the sanitized and mannequin-like caricatures in satin-lined caskets at funerals.

First was Grandma 'Guire, our elderly neighbor two doors down. She wasn't my real grandma, but it's what we called Mrs. McGuire. I was preschool, so when most of my playmates were at school, Grandma 'Guire sometimes filled the gap with crafts, cookies, or might be my "unsuspecting" recipient of May Day flowers. This latter surreptitious act of love involved wildflowers stealthily placed on her porch, a ringing of the doorbell, and running for cover. I always got caught. That was part of the game. When Grandma 'Guire died, my mom took me to the funeral home and let me look in the casket. All I felt was confusion. Once home, I went to my room where death's reality somehow sunk in. Mom heard me crying and came up to console me. That's my earliest remembrance of death.

My *real* great-grandma, Bobbin, was next. I was ten when she passed away at age ninety-three, thus I had vivid memories of doing things with her. She lived with my Grandma B in our little village. A fairly common occurrence was spending Saturday evenings watching Lawrence Welk blow bubbles while playing Canasta and drinking Seven-Up with three antiques - Bobbin, Grandma B, and Blanche Williams, a neighbor. In the morning, we would walk together to the Methodist church where, after making something biblical with construction paper, glue, and cotton swabs in Sunday School, I would rejoin them for big church. I was familiar with every crack and smell of the heavy, dark wood sanctuary. I could choose either of two giant stained glass windows as my subject for meditation that Sunday. To the right was Jesus sleeping in his mother's arms. On the left was Jesus retrieving the one lost sheep. I almost always went left. I guess it was prophetic premonition. Anyway, Bobbin was a fixture throughout my first decade. Before entering their little house on Elm Street, I already knew her likely placement and form: Sitting prim and smiling in her chair next to the kitchen archway, her dowager's hump hid beneath a simple mid-shin length dress, and clunky black heels. I could feel her pointed, bristly chin and smell her ancient breath as I kissed her hello. The impact of her funeral on me was less scary, but felt more permanent. I wouldn't see her when I cut Grandma's grass or raked the mountains of fall leaves in their yard.

There was the traumatic emptiness in junior high of losing my hero, Robin – he was no longer playing his guitar and singing for us. But at least I was spared going to his funeral, leaving only his healthy, handsome face and crisp tenor voice for my memory.

And Mr. Troutman was a gregarious yet gentle giant next door who had played lineman for the San Francisco 49ers. I had recently helped him clean out a rental house and gone camping with him and his son, George Jr. His abrupt death at only thirty-seven years of age stunned me some as a high school senior. I guess it was toughest watching his three kids, one nearly my age, working through it. It wasn't the right time in anyone's mind. It was different than the compulsory exit of the elderly.

But Don's death was different. I hadn't been there in person when the others' spirits left their bodies. Deb and I were driving with another couple in a van from Dallas, Texas to San Jose, California. We were to attend an orientation with a prospective mission board there. Approaching Reno, Nevada, I was driving through a series of intermittent, sweeping curves in an otherwise featureless desert. I saw the front of a semi truck approaching fast in my rearview mirror. By the time he was on me, a curve ahead prohibited him from just continuing on around me. I heard him downshifting and by the way he hugged our back bumper, I could tell he wasn't appreciating this hindrance in his streak across the open sands of the Truckee River valley. I was driving the speed limit and felt a bit annoyed at his proximity to us. Deb was hugely pregnant and we had two babies in the van. As soon as we made the turn, the truck barreled past me in a way that struck me as impatient. Although, who could blame a guy having to endure those desolate wastelands for a living?

The s-curve started right, then left. It was as we neared the second half that we saw the truck. It was upside down in the desert, sand and dust still settling, and wheels still spinning. The guys, Miles and I, suggested the ladies stay put with the kids while we ran to see if we could help. Advancing around the front to the other side of the cab, the sight of no visible windshield was ominous. Cautiously, because of the smoke and dripping diesel fuel, we approached the driver's door. Upside down, with one arm and head outside the open window, was the driver who had moments before been riding our tail. He was non-responsive as we spoke to him and it was hard to imagine where his body could be in what little space was left of the crumpled cab.

As I tried to check his pulse, black diesel fuel was dripping on him and me. I was surprised to find a pulse, which prompted Miles and me to give words of encouragement to him even though he showed no signs of consciousness. Our few efforts to extract him proved right away to be out of the question. There was simply no space to do it. I stayed with the man while Miles went to see if another trucker who had stopped could radio by CB for help. He had already contacted someone. As a few other travelers made the scene and stopped, each one instinctively asked, "Is he still alive?" I kept repeating that he was, but his pulse was getting weaker and slower. I was sure he had to be bleeding out somewhere inside the wadded metal.

It was a helpless feeling, squatting in the sand, trying to shield the driver from the warm dripping fluid, and waiting. Miles and I prayed for this nameless man. We kept talking to him, saying things we didn't really believe like, "Help's on the way…hold on…don't give up…they'll get you out." The time between his heartbeats was getting longer and increasingly harder to feel. And then, they were gone altogether. I told Miles I thought he was gone. I didn't let go. My right, white hand was in a sort of handshake with his right, black hand, while my left hand fingers were on his wrist. It felt wrong to let go. It felt like abandoning him.

Right about then, a man came running up and asked what everyone else had. This time I answered, "He had a pulse the whole time, but it just stopped a little bit ago. He's gone." The man stomped and bent over shouting toward the desert surface, "Dammit, Don, you knew better! You knew better." This was the driver's boss. He was not just angry, but already grieving. He told us that Don (the guy now had a name) was married with kids at home, had driven for him a good while, and knew this was a dangerous section of road. They had lost others on these curves. He should have known better.

At that, I did let go. Miles offered to drive, but I wanted to continue. I felt the need to *do* something. It wasn't long down the road that my throat tightened and eyes burned, and I knew what was coming. I just stared straight ahead and let the hot tears drip down my face.

Deb checked on me a few times. I couldn't talk except to repeat, "I'm okay. I'm alright." That had been my only firsthand encounter with the moment of death. I didn't know it would be the first of several. It never even entered my mind that there would be more. Quite a few more.

The Kurdish camps in Turkey presented me with a handful of hands-on encounters, which included last gasps for air, closing eyelids, and fighting rigor mortis. As new as that was to me, the extreme situation and conditions somehow made it seem normal, or at least expected. However, I must say that helping people die was not in the forefront of my mind when a few years later I signed on as a pastor in a church in the Midwest. But I soon became aware that it would be a regular duty in such a large fellowship.

In three busy years, I would bury about 24 people and make literally thousands of hospital visits. Along with the other pastors, my share of calls on the infirmed averaged three days a week with anywhere from five to fifteen patients a day, spread between three hospitals. I knew the hallways, stainless steel paraphernalia, and names of conditions and procedures so well, at times I felt like I was medical personnel. I also learned early on that people in the hospital often want or need to engage in a form of "show and tell" as part of the healing process. I saw more incisions, bloody bandages, vials of bile, and exposed human anatomy than I cared to. Probably one of the most unforgettable moments came from a man, quite under the effects of painkiller, whose answer to my inquiry as to his health was, "If it wasn't for this damn catheter, I'd be fine!", flinging the sheets away to make sure I got the full picture. Thankfully, that candidness wasn't daily fare.

Interacting with the terminally ill was by far the most challenging and emotionally draining. I grew in the ability to talk in straightforward terms about death, and help prepare people for the inevitable demise of themselves or a loved one. It is truly one of the great responsibilities and privileges of a pastor. Only twice was I called on to confront what I consider the most heart-wrenching end-of-life situations – the decision regarding discontinuation of life support, and a suicide. The latter prompted me to take immediate responsibility for the owner's truck that had several inches of blood on the floorboards. To this day, when I encounter the smell of his particular brand of chewing tobacco, it still resurrects the gut feelings of that odd undertaking. Through these demanding duties, I learned that when it all shook out, I couldn't personally be the one to bring folks the deeply needed comfort. *The Lord is near to the broken-hearted and saves those who are crushed in spirit.* Often my best pastoral contribution was being silently present.

A little blue slip of paper on my desk was my first notice from the administrative assistant that a funeral was scheduled and I was expected to perform the services. I was already involved and spiritually prepared for some of these, while others crept up completely unexpectedly. In either case, once I had notice, this important event in the life of a grieving family would take over the better part of *my* week as well. Many of the family gatherings to plan the service would involve laughter and soothing stories among those "survived by" members of the family as they worked through the typically bittersweet process of grief. I usually felt privileged to be invited into this tight circle of vulnerability and intimacy.

Although most funerals transpired in a familiar and predictable manner, a few left marked impressions on my pastoral recollect. One lady had preplanned to have a fork placed in her folded hands in the casket. She wanted people to be prompted and consoled by this reminder that she was enjoying the *feast* of heaven.

My sister's husband was a retired Light Colonel in the Marines and had served in Vietnam. When Tim finally surrendered his battle with cancer, he won the war of life as a courageous and humble man of God. It was a wonderful thing to be interrupted a few times during my part in his memorial service by the loud, unison shout "Oorah!" from his fellow Marine buddies.

On television or in movies I had seen a "fly over" with jets during a high-ranking military figure's memorial service. But when I was asked to participate in a "drive by" salute, I was admittedly skeptical. The man for whom I was performing the ceremony had owned a trucking company. Just before closing the graveyard interment service, I asked those present to observe a moment of silence. Perfectly timed, after a few seconds of peaceful meditation, the rumble of huge equipment could be heard approaching. As everyone naturally turned toward the sound, they witnessed a long line of Mr. Alkire's dump trucks driven by his men slowly passing the cemetery. The effect was quite touching and profoundly honoring.

Being a church of about twenty-three hundred people, there were a number of times that I was called upon to perform a memorial service for someone I didn't know at all. In those cases, I did a sort of friendly interview of family members in order to receive some general background or to glean a few second-hand anecdotes to eulogize the deceased. If a family member desired to handle the eulogy portion, I was happy to incorporate them into the service, allowing me to focus on presenting God's word of truth and hope.

In one such case, I had never met the elderly woman who had passed away. I met with her son, a mid-fifties gentleman who had flown in from Las Vegas, in order to gather some personal facts and plan the service together. This very animated and aggressive personality offered to do the eulogy about his mother. In view of the circumstances, I agreed and asked the son what he could tell me about his mother's spiritual life. His initial answer wasn't a complete surprise, but did seem a tad unorthodox. "Oh, my Mom loved your church almost as much as she loved the Vegas strip." I assumed the comment was a light-hearted joke, and probed a little more. It became apparent with each question that, regardless of what his mother's spiritual knowledge was, *his* was about as vacant as a casino confessional booth (I don't think they have them). I resolved to simply leave the personal stories of the loved one to the family while I preached the Gospel.

After welcoming those present, reading some Scriptures, and before giving my message, I introduced the son "who has offered to share some things about his mother." For the next twenty minutes, I sat fighting the urge to run, cry, laugh hysterically or yell out "Enough already!" There was one theme to Junior's eulogy. "Mom loved to gamble." He told how much she missed living in Vegas since moving to Illinois. He listed her favorite games and dramatically described in detail some of her biggest wins and losses at the tables. He talked about her love for the splendid buffet foods offered at such great prices in the casinos. He pictured for us this little lady running back and forth from the teller windows to the one-armed bandits. And finally...finally...he wanted to conclude by sharing with us "how fortunate I feel for the last time I had with my mother." (*Maybe there's a redeeming moment coming...*was my grasping, vain hope.) Junior, almost mesmerized, expounded about her visit with him just a few months before her passing. He drove her down the strip and let her glory in the lights she so loved. She got a bag of coins and, despite her weakened state, was able to play the slots since they have push buttons now. (*Well, praise Elvis!*) She had made it *home* one last time.

And now it was my turn. At least I didn't have any second-guessing about what to say. "Let me read and share some things with you from the Bible...."

The newspaper article blandly began: *PONCA, Ark. (AP) – The National Park Service says a Louisiana man floating on the Buffalo River in North Arkansas has collapsed and died in his canoe.* The opening sentence was accurate in the matter-of-fact journalistic style characteristic of papers, but it sure communicated little of my intense memories from that weekend.

A friend, church member where I pastored, and leader of the group, Arden, had organized a family-oriented canoe trip on the Buffalo River for twenty years. This was Deb's and my second year to join them. Arden didn't start the Memorial Day trip tradition. Another man, James, had done so twenty-five years ago, and Arden took it over. James was now a 68-year old art and music teacher with many talents and in great shape physically. He still broke horses at this age. James had decided to return for the trip after not participating for twenty years. In a sense, it was partly a reunion of this man and his brainchild that had developed into quite an event under Arden's enthusiasm. Some of the excursion's embellishments included comfortable cabins, evening board games, ice cream churned from your favorite soft drink, southern barbeque on the grill, and a share-your-photos-and-videos night. Straight-up fun.

I was attracted to James from the start, in part due to his kindly manner. But I also wanted to hear about his art. I had recently told Deb that I'd like to learn to sculpt in stone or to tool leather. I found out from James that he had experience in both.

Day one, Arden's was the first of thirteen canoes since he knew this section of the river from Steele's Creek to Kyle's Landing quite well. He asked me to take the anchor position to make sure no one got left too far behind or to help from that end should anyone get in trouble. The group enjoyed a great day of floating with stops for lunch on a beach, swimming, and jumping from the rocks. With only about one hour left in this initial day's float, James and a teen-age girl tumped in a little rapid. She was momentarily under the canoe, and despite hitting his head, James quickly wrestled the canoe off her and both appeared fine. We were nearby and sidled-up next to their canoe to check on how they were doing. His head injury looked minor and he acted fine. We proceeded down river, but half an hour later, Deb and I came upon the last four canoes on a shoal and could tell there was trouble.

The girl in the front of James' boat had heard a strange noise behind her and turned to see James slumped backwards in the rear of the canoe, gasping for air. By the time we reached the group, James had lost consciousness and turned blue. The assorted assembly from our group responded with great composure and surprising coordination.

Interestingly, a pharmacist and nurse were among those present. Three people in our ad hoc triage team took turns doing heart compressions. Having been a lifeguard with resuscitation training, I joined another two in shared rotations giving mouth-to-mouth. The pharmacist was even able to provide two shots of epinephrine. Deb helped in various ways - checking James' pulse and ministering to the young teens and others dealing with the scene…including James' recently adopted 13-year-old son. Spontaneous prayer undergirded the activity. The intensity of the situation was dramatic, but the cooperative calm was impressive.

We sent for help via some other vacationers who came floating by the scene. We were able to keep his body pink and at least looking alive for a whole hour through our pooled first aid knowledge. EMTs arrived by trail from Kyle's Landing. After our hour of resuscitation attempt and then about twenty minutes with the EMTs, they decided it was time to give up the efforts to revive. James was gone. His body was put in one of our canoes with the EMTs and floated to the landing where he was pronounced dead by a coroner.

That evening at camp was spent helping one another deal with the experience. All but four couples understandably decided to abbreviate their holiday and left for home the next morning. James' son had gone home from the river with other family members. Arden, being responsible for the trip and as a long-time friend of James, was hit hard by the crisis. He had only arrived on the accident scene with the EMTs because he was at the head of the group. Melanie, Arden's wife, insightfully suggested that Deb and I accompany Arden and her the next day, canoeing the same section of the river in order to show them the place of the initial tump and revisit the shoals where James had died. They needed to see where it had happened and work through the whole tragedy.

It was a sobering journey, especially for Arden. It also proved a little tense for Deb when we went through some of the rapids, including the one where James' canoe had flipped. However, the quiet, reflective day on the river proved to be a good decision. Arden wanted to "know"... and we all sensed the need to get back on the horse, so to speak.

We never did learn the exact cause of James' death. Maybe the hit to the head - although it appeared minor. Heart attack or stroke – strong as a horse, no history, and on no meds. He did canoe all day, hiked to a waterfall, swam a good bit, and maybe

James' death spot marked by stick cross, Arden & Melanie reflecting

most significantly, strained hard to get the canoe off the young girl who slipped underneath. An autopsy followed, but no revelations resulted.

One of the couples who stayed behind the next two days at camp with us had videotaped that first day. We sat together in the lodge that second night watching the real life retrospective drama unfold. There were many segments with James laughing and enjoying the day...some actually less than two hours before he died. As we relived the day on the wall of the lodge, one in our little clump said, "Just think...James could say 'This is how I spent my last day on earth'... what a way to go!" Good perspective for us all.

James was known as a sincere man of faith and action. I only had a couple of days with him, and a single extended conversation, at that. He offered to teach me some leatherwork and sculpting...sometime. I owe him fifty cents that he loaned me that morning in the convenience store.

These days I wear my hair in a gray ponytail, and have for the past seven years. It's for my Dad, kind of. He'd actually think it was silly. I may cut it off someday, but not just yet.

Dad was eighty, but still very sharp mentally and fairly active. His

Dad, that thought-filled smile

engineering design and consulting business was still operating under his mainspring role. I discovered, in settling his affairs after his death, that his briefcase contained an active blueprint on which he had been doing trigonometry and calculus in old school longhand with a pencil. And it was accurate. And it was dated exactly two weeks prior to his death.

Dad had taken a few falls recently. One was triggered by a dog that ran up behind him while he was walking the neighborhood. Another, strangely, happened in the hospital when he tried to enter an elevator at the last second by sticking his foot between the closing doors. It caught and he fell backward on the marble floor. Blood had built up in his skull and needed to be drained surgically. Although I lived twelve hours away, I wanted and needed to be there. I arrived just in time to accompany him, along with my mother and sister, to the surgical prep room. We laughed with him as he comically sported his standard-issue blue bonnet. We prayed with him, engaged in family small talk, and they wheeled him off. Our "see you in a while", now in retrospect, seems incongruously casual. Then again, much of life in hindsight feels inopportune. How often do we think or say *If I could go back and do it over, I would...*? I don't know exactly what I *would* have done or said differently, but it wouldn't have looked just as it did.

The surgeon's comments after the procedure expressed an expectation of full recovery, but cautioned of some possible strange and erratic behavior or speech as Dad would be coming out from under the anesthesia. "This is the brain we've been working with, after all" was his approximate wording. The three of us family members were eventually invited to come to the recovery room to see Dad once he was awake. We were encouraged to find him sitting up and somewhat coherent. It seemed like the typical slow and partial lucidity we'd all seen before in other post-op situations. After a short semi-linear conversation, we left to let him rest per the nurse's instruction. It wasn't but a short time later that I was asked to come back to see if I could help out with my dad. He was at times being "unmanageable." That immediately struck me as alarming, being a description foreign to Dad's character.

Out of respect, and honestly, some heart-sheltering preference, I will simply describe the next fifteen hours as possibly my most painful ever. Dad was in a confused state ranging from sentimentally tender and needy, to caustically berating and perverse. What he seemingly thought and expressed rarely resembled the dad I had known for fifty-two years. Sometimes he knew me, sometimes he didn't. This quickly vacillating, inconsistent behavior continued for a few hours, after which Dad transitioned into a fitful, semi-conscious unrest. I physically wrestled with him for fifteen hours through the afternoon, evening, and night just to keep him in bed and from tearing out the tubes and wires attached to him. It was exhausting, but worse yet, breaking my heart.

The doctors explained that they were unable to sedate him because it was essential that he fully come out of the anesthesia. Despite his constantly disturbed state, nothing could be done. Early the next morning, Dad went into heart failure. I was forced outside the door as a large team of attending medical personnel applied the heroics associated with a code blue.

The following forty-eight hours brought our nuclear family of five together at his silent bedside. My mother, married fifty-six years, displayed great clarity and peace in the decision to remove life support. We held each other and shared the intimate conversations only family can share. We spoke to Dad in his unresponsive sleep. We even listened to his familiar snore at times. We knowingly soaked up every final look and touch we possibly could during those last ten hours after the support was removed. Quietly, peacefully, we were present...and we knew when he left us.

To our closest of friends and family at an intimate lunch after Dad's memorial service, I said rightly, "There's no one in this world, possibly apart from Deb, that I enjoy being with and doing *anything* with, more than my dad. Not everyone has the privilege of saying that with confident sincerity, but I'm happy to say that I can."

These days, I wear my hair in a gray ponytail, and have for the past seven years. It's for my Dad, kind of. He'd actually think it was silly. After his death, I just found myself letting it grow. It was an expression of sadness. I may cut it off someday, but not just yet.

shadows of a ponytail

helping people get hitched

"People Are Crazy"
Bobby Braddock and Troy Jones' country song
recorded by Billy Currington

Although I've raised three girls and have an admitted big bias toward enjoying that gender's idiosyncrasies, I am not by any stretch what I'd call a *froufrou* guy. I'd have been happy to do the simple backyard wedding or let the kids take the money (it wasn't a lot anyway) and run! But in both the family sphere and ministerial, I've been part of officiating tens and tens of weddings. My conclusion: Like the country song infers...God's idea of marriage is great. Some of the celebration of weddings is good, like beer. And weddings can bring out the nutty part of people.

My personal stories probably can't compete with the plethora of YouTube wedding fiascos, from marching bands surrounding a proposal, to brides breaking out in dance with a ninety year old codger, to grooms galore throwing up and fainting. Gladly, I have none so extreme to my resume. But I have had my share of Bridezillas, grooms being real "guys", and distracted pint-sized ring bearers tangled in aisle runners. Some flat-out entertaining memories.

As a precursor to specific wedding oddities and being one who has a high view of marriage, I have not been in the habit of performing services willy-nilly. Although I have made some exceptions for folks in unique situations, I typically meet with couples for five two-hour premarital sessions before marrying them. I want to offer them the best chance I know to not just survive as a couple, but to thrive and to love the whole wild procession of years. A few couples have impatiently endured the discussions, fidgeting on a couch until they can *finally* get to the altar and Hawaii. But I've found most of them have been grateful for some new insights or perspective they might actually use. And sadly, I have had the uncomfortable occasion of declining to marry a few of them because of serious hitches surrounding their plans to get hitched. Don't get me wrong. I'm not expecting complete maturity or perfect compatibility before I marry a couple. I *did*, however, have a problem with one guy on Sunday morning right before our church service started....

I was at my office desk gathering notes and Bible in order to walk to the sanctuary to start the service. Hearing a vehicle skid to a stop in the parking lot right outside my window, I turned to see who was arriving late and might need help getting inside. A young man in T-shirt and jeans hurriedly jumped out of his pickup, slammed his door, and ran to the church entrance. It being Sunday morning, everything was unlocked and my office door was open as well. He had no problem finding me as I got up to meet him halfway across the carpet of my office. With his hurry, I thought he possibly had an emergency, so I asked the obvious question, "Can I help you?" His story was to the point and simple, but pathetic. "I'm getting married at two-o'clock this afternoon and I'm twenty bucks short. I was wondering if you could help me out?" I didn't mean to be insensitive, but I started laughing before I could answer with words. He looked certainly surprised, and possibly shocked, by my knee-jerk response of incredulity. The young man didn't know how many times each week people came to the door with stories of "need", but the final chapter was always titled "Show Me the Money." He *wanted* twenty dollars. He *needed* something a lot more substantial. Since it was time for me to be getting to more spiritually serious folks, I let him have my help without frills. "Son, if you're twenty bucks short for your wedding, I *can* help you...with some advice. You've got no business getting married!" He wasn't interested in joining us for the worship service and let me know what he thought about Christians who wouldn't help somebody in need. I can't say he persuaded me that he had a better understanding of Christian priorities than I did. I think I prayed for him as I walked to the sanctuary and he huffed off to his truck.

If it weren't for women, I doubt we'd have weddings. I know that sounds terribly obvious, but I didn't say "marriages." I'm talking about the ceremonies that usually necessitate a lot of things guys run from, not toward. Things like showing affection in public, talking *ad nauseam* about details using words that all sound French or like they demand to be said with a squeal of delight. And then there is the whole issue of making a bunch of decisions, let alone a lifetime commitment. I joke, but it's been a rarity to find the guy who's "had the whole thing planned in my mind since I was age seven", or the gal who says "Can't we just sign a piece of paper somewhere?" Let me put it this way: The *affects* of wedding ceremonies are generally for the genteel gender. And that presents some challenges not just for the groom, but every male involved, and the pastor in particular.

For instance, I was running the rehearsal for the largest wedding I have ever performed. There were nine bridesmaids and nine groomsmen. One Maid of Honor wasn't enough, there had to be two. (And here's where I'll support my thesis about feminine impetus.) When I asked how many Best Men there were, the bride's answer was, "Two, of course...since there's going to be two Maids of Honor." *Of course*. The groom just dimpled one cheek and shrugged his acquiescence.

Those present for this warm-up to the big day were not just those fitted for tuxedos and matching formals. It also included several family members, spouses or friends of those in the party, musicians, and two sound tech staff. It was already a larger gathering than some weddings. I had succeeded in getting the twenty wedding party members carefully arranged in ascending order up the breadth of the stairs to the platform. I always placed the participants in their respective "landing positions" before walking through the entire service pace by pace. With this large of a group, that alone had been a major task. As I verbally informed them about the order of family members that would be ushered down the center aisle (which no one on the platform cared about or was listening to), I saw the mother of the bride get up from her seat. Standing front and center and staring at me with grave intensity, she pointed a finger at me, turned her hand over, and gave the well-known signal for me to "come here now." Up to this point, everyone there had been politely semi-attentive, but now it got keenly quiet as I received my summons. Despite a hesitation to give in, I excused myself, encouraged everyone to relax for a moment, "but *please* don't move from your spots", and walked down to her. Fortunately, I had presence of mind to silence my lapel microphone.

There in the center aisle, I began to learn in hushed tones that there had been some divorces and remarriages that necessitated highly elaborate and confusing arrangements and seating order on their particular side of the aisle. Once I got the gist of the "crisis" and could see this developing into either a lengthy explanation of the family tree or even a feud, I leaned in a little closer to the mother and whispered with a forced smile: "I understand. You can work that out later, but right now I need to keep this rehearsal on schedule." Brides can be scary, but mothers of brides can be downright menacing!

And there was the time I forgot one tiny element in the service and you'd think the validity of the covenant enacted was now in question. It was just one little kiss! Yes, I forgot to say, "You may now kiss your bride," and so they didn't. Once the congregation was dismissed to join the couple in the reception hall, they stood and began to filter out as usual. But then, one by one, the women and girls of all ages came up to me saying, "Where was the kiss?...What happened to the kiss?...Did they decide *not* to include the kiss in the ceremony?... Do you know what you forgot?" All the men, on the other hand, waxed eloquent with elaborate commentary like, "Good job...Nice service...C'mon, lets go get something to eat...What are they serving?" Actually, there was one guy who mentioned the missing kiss. "You forgot the kiss. You're in big trouble with my wife!"

The people it should've matter to most, Chuck and Becky, were a little older than many newlyweds and had become friends with Deb and me. They were fine with the oversight and laughingly said, "It's okay, we took care of business when we got outside the doors of the chapel." I'm sure they've made up for my omission many times over.

What do you get when you marry an amateur magician to an overly emotional bride? It sounds the beginning of a groaner joke and a lot worse than it was. But it could have been better. The groom was a locksmith by trade, but did magic for small events on the side. I'd never thought about the similarity of those skills, and it wasn't very reassuring when I did. Nevertheless, the bride-to-be was the granddaughter of a dear, elderly couple in our church, and I agreed to do their wedding even though neither went to our church, and the ceremony would be held at another church building in town.

During our premarital counseling sessions, I found myself the willing audience for some pretty good sleight of hand. In the last of the five sessions, we talked about the wedding itself. That's when little Copperfield made the request to float the ring through the air onto his bride's finger during the wedding ceremony. It was then that I got a foreshadowing of their marital communication through the premarital interaction that ensued right there in my office. He was childishly grinning and trying to convince me he could pull it off. She looked mortified and pleaded with him, "Don't you dare! This is *not* one of your performances." And then to me, "Please, don't let him do it!" Since I'm a guy at times also, I was giving it some curious consideration. But I decided instead to use this "moment" as a mini marriage practice run, and let them work it out while I observed. She was dead serious and panicky at the possibility of such a display at the wedding. He had no such parameters or inhibitions, but showed the sense to pretty quickly let it go...but not without one last "It would be really cool..." before stuffing the rabbit back in his hat for good.

The momentous day finally came and we met at the other church facility. It didn't bode well to be greeted with the news that the air conditioning had gone out, but they would move a few fans into the sanctuary. It was going to be a hot day and an afternoon wedding at that. The bride was already crying.

By the time the bridal march began, the small sanctuary was filled with guests and I was soaked. To begin with, I sweat easily and profusely. Additionally, I was wearing a suit and tie *underneath* a heavy black robe (the tradition of our churches). The cool and calm groom even had beads of perspiration on his forehead. And then came the radiant bride. (My mother had passed an old adage on to me that "horses sweat, men perspire, but ladies glow.") Well, this poor little lady was lit up! Not only was her foundation makeup melting, but her tears were challenging any waterproof mascara she might have had on. It wasn't Alice Cooper, but it wasn't pretty. She cried as she came down the aisle. She sniveled during the prayers. She wept during the songs. She whimpered during my message. She sobbed during the vows. She was a mess.

Desperate times call for magical measures, but that had been vetoed. So, as her groom and I attempted to comfort her by whispering, "It'll be alright. Relax. It's all fine," I handed her my only slightly used handkerchief I had tucked under my Bible after a few dabs to my forehead. It helped her a little. The only redemptive thing I can say about the ceremony is that it's a good thing we nixed the floating ring.

Certainly one of my favorite debacles came from a Best Man. He was the brother of the groom. It was a family with several boys who all acted like boys. Once again, a factor not necessarily conducive to prim and proper expectations in a formal wedding. The rehearsal and wedding preparations were uneventful. But at one point in the service, I noticed the groom looking meaningfully at someone other than his bride. As I talked, he was obviously trying to give a subtle high

fun officiating a favorite couple

sign to his brother standing a couple of steps away. He bared his teeth and made a chewing motion. His brother got the message, and I caught a glimpse of him removing a large wad of chewing gum from his mouth, hesitating for a moment unsure what to do with it. He finally stowed it in the front right pocket of his tuxedo. Some of the party and the congregation also saw it, letting out a few constrained snickers.

At the appropriate time in the sequence of wedding etiquette, I asked the groom, "What do you have as a token of pledge to your bride?" He responded with the compulsory "a ring", and turned to his Best Man brother for the article. Brother reached in his pocket and, of course, pulled...and pulled...and pulled out a long strand of pink gum attached to the ring. No one tried to suppress laughter this time. We all knew it was a classic moment in the history of misplacement of mannishness in proper weddings.

One of the greatest privileges with which I have been honored is being asked to officiate all three of my daughters' weddings. The double duty and blessing of giving away the bride and pronouncing them "man and wife" goes beyond easy description. In order to avoid any likeness to turning page by page through one's thick wedding album, I will refrain from what to Deb and me alone are a trio of rich, meaning-filled weekends with our girls. And yet, to abstain from giving at least one anecdote from each wedding would be, if not remiss, a lost opportunity.

By the time Ellie was to be married, I had enough weddings under my belt to not worry about logistics or form, and was free to totally enjoy the unique occasion. In preparation, I did something that evolved into a personal tradition that I hold close to my "father's heart." A few weeks before the wedding, I watched for a beautiful, cool day. I went to the back part of our four acres behind the pond, built a fire in the ring, and sat down to think about my daughter. With each of the three upcoming occasions, I sat for hours in a lawn chair, poked at the fire, and jotted thoughts on a legal pad as they came to me. I reflected on her as a child, her emerging personality, her developing maturity, her strengths, her brand of humor, her contribution to the family mix...and her step into the world of romance and love. Each time was far from sad or melancholy, but was a rich pause of joy and gratefulness. When the fire finally got tamped out, I had a yellow pad full of notes that became a father's comments in the wedding service. For this experience alone, I should be the envy of all men.

Despite what I've joked about men being unfit for wedding ceremonies, I was jazzed about tying the knot for Ellie. I was not only well-prepared, but genuinely enthusiastic about the whole wedding event. However, the very first words out of my mouth went awry. In order for me to walk Ellie down the aisle, she arranged for her boss, Dr. Kevin, to handle the opening prayer and remarks. When he asked, "Who gives this woman to this man to be his wife," without a blink I said, "His mother and I do." *No...wait...that's not right.* "I mean, *her* mother and I do." *Nice start.* Thereafter, everything flowed smoothly and full of happy celebration, as such a day should.

One highlight before the kiss (which I *didn't* forget) was the opportunity to praise Ellie for a rarity in our modern era. I commented that the kiss in the ceremony was not only their first kiss as a couple (rare enough), but her first ever from a guy. It wasn't a naive father's blind wish. It was fact. Drew, a healthy man of conviction had led the way in this decision, and Ellie followed his lead. In my mind, a pretty good start on a marriage. Fourteen years and six kids later, if a happy home is any indication, they did great!

Middle kid, Sarah, is probably what I would have been like if I'd been a girl. Adventurous, spontaneous, and creative, she welcomes new challenges. She went to Guatemala for seven months as an English teacher, fell in love, and a couple years later we had a wedding in the chapel of a missionary compound. My Spanish wasn't up to speed for a whole wedding service, so we had a wonderful national friend, Vicky, translate for me. It was a "Guatemerican" ceremony, incorporating elements of both worlds, reflective of what their marriage would be. During our two weeks there, to watch my daughter navigate so fluidly between two cultures and languages was a deeply satisfying experience.

Sarah's cross-cultural marriage accomplished something we never thought we'd see. My father used to light-heartedly lament that the McCracken name was going to end with my generation because my brother and I have six girls and no boys to our literal name. My sister would take her husband's name, and our surname would perish as far as our immediate lineage was concerned. But Sarah stumbled into an accidental solution by marrying a Guatemalan and having three kids. In that culture, the children take *both* parents' last names, so our first grandson from them became *Samuel Jacob Castillo McCracken*. Leave it to this sweet, inventive gal to discover a way to make something happen.

Kate being expressive and dramatic, I knew the ceremony had better be fun. But she's also a deep thinker, so it had to have content. No fear – Kate had it all planned out. She was one of those little girls who'd thought about that day since she was wearing...well, she said it best herself at about age four while dressing up in her favorite white, frilly, lacy, poofy dress (you learn those kinds of words as a Dad of girls) to go out for some fancy event. She announced (holding her dress out for all of us to see), "I'm ready to go. I've got my wedding dress..." (then lifting her dress over her head) "and my Micky Mouse underwear!" Of course, that *needed* to be shared in my comments at the wedding.

One other anecdote I thought would be a fun jab to share during "a father's comments" harkened back to a dinner table conversation when all three girls were in their teens. The girls were postulating about marriage (which happened often). This was before there were any *real* men on the horizon. It was all theoretical at this point. This was what we called a "rotic" evening - "romantic" without the "man." This particular evening the discussion topic concerned what were good names for a husband, and the consensus *then* was an adamant, "No J names! Everybody has J names these days." So, for Kate's wedding congregation's consideration, I introduced the male side of the wedding party: "Starting with the groom on the left and moving right, this is Joel, JJ, Jeff, Justin, Jake, Josh, John, and, the newly dubbed, J-Drew."

Helping people get hitched was another one of those serendipities I never saw coming as an element of my life. I sort of fell into it as part of the job description - both the church and the family "jobs." But I'm convinced having all girls was no mere accident. I suspect an intelligent and smiling Cause had something to do with it. It was no mistake for Deb and me to give ourselves to those three beauties as our highest priority over the formative years. And it was no misstep in letting them fly away to do the same for themselves.

our grownup gals, as I love to see them!

big bending

It wakes you up to take a journey for a while, wherever it may be.
Kenko in his *Tsurezuragusa*

Sometimes you just got to get away. You just know it. The prompting can be due to a specific conscious issue, decision or troubling problem. At other times, it's not so much a particular cognizant matter, but you're generally burnt out and need a break from the stress, noise, and constant badgering of mental "to do" lists. Or it's the doldrums – no big issues, but lethargy, brain fog, flatness, and overall lack of energy let you know it's time to get out of Dodge.

We express in lots of different ways that intuitive inner poke and the corresponding felt-need fix of places foreign to our daily norm: *I feel stuck. I need to clear out the cobwebs. I've got to have some alone time. A change of venue is in order. If I don't get out of here for a while, I'm gonna blow! I just need quiet, to be able to hear my own thoughts, to simply think. I want a road trip...some windshield time. I think I'll become a hermit.*

Many of us find our getaways in little snippets. Going for a walk or run. Loading the earphones with escape music in a quiet nook with eyes shut. A glass of wine to either soften the clamor, or on the flip side, to cheer up the mundane. But lots of us eventually get to an intensity of ache that won't be massaged out by a quick rubdown or realigned by a chiropractic *crack*. We really have to get *away*.

I've learned increasingly over the years to hear that inner voice saying, *Get out of here.* Early on, however, it sometimes took nudging by external prods...called friends. I remember one such time in seminary settling myself in for a long weekend of writing in the library. As I greedily staked-out my own section of wooden tabletop, glancing left and right to make sure no intruders tried to come within my mandatory bubble of study, I was intermittently sighing in dejected resolve to another energy-draining mental marathon. I was already burnt to a crisp. Enter Miles.

"Hey, McCracken, lets go climbing!" For just a second my numb soul saw a flash of light projecting a vision of us hanging by finger jams and toeholds on the side of a lichen-specked rock face, but quickly lapsed back into a responsible anesthetized state. "I can't. I've got an exegetical paper due next week and I need to make some significant headway this weekend." Saying it, my inner rock climber just peeled off a layback move and was dangling lifelessly at the end of my 11-millimeter, dynamic Edilrid rope...barely library chair height from the ground. It was excruciatingly depressing. My best bud, Miles, was no slacker. In fact, he was about as disciplined a guy as I knew. Much more so than me. But he also knew how to break away and have a blast, and saved my tail from the study blues many times. This was his current inventive tactic: "Look it, Mac. Ten years from now, what are you going to remember? That you wrote this stinkin' paper...or that you went climbing with Miles?"

We had a blast that weekend, hands covered in powdered chalk and bleeding, muscles screaming for relief, and "sewing machine legs" bobbing up and down before finally giving out. And there I was dangling uncomfortably in my seat harness seventy-five feet off the ground...empty of strength and full of life. I did turn in a paper that next week, but like Miles prophesied, I have no recollection what it was about. Miles has been one of those faithful guys in my life that taught me how to break away for a season so I could stay alive for a lifetime.

A few calendar flips later, our family was on a scheduled four-month furlough after three successive years on the mission field.

Furlough (definition according to *Webster's*) – *a leave of absence from duty*

Furlough (definition according to many foreign Christian missionaries) – *a leave of absence from duty, which leaves one longing for duty again!*

We had heard that this ironic experience was not unusual. Spiritually battle-worn soldiers often spend their home leave running about, speaking, meeting, and reporting to the extent of wishing only to be back on the field of fire. We *knew* we needed a respite, so in addition to fulfilling necessary commitments, we landed for a few days in Arkansas at the house of close friends Karl and Terry for some R and R.

You know you have true friends when they tell you to "Get out of here" and it feels right. These good friends are a few years ahead of us and have many times levied good advice, but never in an intrusive way. Insights usually came about as a by-product of natural dialogues. Whenever we got together as couples, we scraped the Milky Way of topics and frequently came away mutually inspired and refreshed. It's what Deb and I looked forward to most in our interactions with them – long, lively, heresy-airing, no echo chamber conversations. Nightly walks around town, daytime lawn chairs in the creek, and exactingly crafted nachos were common catalysts for our in-depth discussions.

One particular evening's wobbly walk along the rocky bank of the White River raised a troublesome issue in which Deb and I were gridlocked. The evolving conversation revealed a flaw in my character. I needed to "bend" significantly, but being fearful of breaking, I wasn't giving ground. As Deb and I passionately bounced differing perspectives off our soundboard allies, what was a stubborn blind spot for me was apparently clear to Karl and Terry. After a long, fruitless, and tense *tete-a-tete* between Deb and me with our friends officiating, we returned to their house. Right before bed, Karl came to me holding out his car keys. "Here. Tomorrow morning I want you to take my car and tent, go upriver, get a canoe, and float for two days in order to think about what's going on and what you need to do about it."

Karl is often matter-of-fact and holds strong opinions, but he is rarely directive, so this got my attention and didn't elicit any resistance from me. I needed to "get out" for a couple days.

Day one was hot, beautiful, invigorating, and challenging as the river's level was high and its current swift. As the sun began to lower, I wanted to get off the main river to camp in cool and seclusion. Finding an inviting tributary required me to paddle hard upstream for a ways, but yielded a perfect spot. A few hundred yards inland, I found a deep, clear pool in which to swim and an island sandbar about twice the size of my tent on which to pitch it. I have to admit that my reflections and prayer throughout the day and evening were mostly circular and felt unproductive. I was still thinking and arguing the same old thoughts and arguments. Awaking the next morning, I began to panic with the anticipated possibility of *not* returning with anything new and helpful.

Back on the river, the sun was intense and my Celtic skin was getting red, so I scanned the map for every parallel, looping rivulet into the woods, and took as many as I could. These excurses were like a watery service road alongside an interstate, with on and off ramps connecting.

Midafternoon that second day, I finally had a breakthrough of insight. I could very clearly see my erred approach to our dilemma and standoff. My handling of things was exacerbating an already critical challenge we were facing. I could see what I needed to *stop* doing. (This is one of the values of getting away, taking a trip, leaving one's familiar cycles, etc. New environs at least provide potential for interrupting stuck cycles of thought.) The next part was harder to see and harder to embrace. In place of what I needed to *stop* doing, what would I *start* doing differently? I couldn't see it easily, and even if I could, would I be willing to follow through? (This is another of the values of this kind of trip and getting outside in creation. Sometimes the *metaphors* of nature communicate the message needing to be heard.) Let me attempt to describe this particular metaphor as it played out.

Deb and I were logjammed despite wanting to work together

to address a problem. We were being moved quickly along a river with heat oppressing our heads to the point of frustration and irritation. We were being carried along in a flow, but getting nowhere. We needed a different course. And right at the moment, Deb wasn't capable of navigating this swift current. I needed to find a new stream and lead the way. This much of the analogy was coming into focus for me, and I knew it. Then, in what I can only attribute to the sovereign "accident" of Divine planning, my map showed one final rivulet before I was to be at my landing. This time I wasn't just needing to get *off* the main river. I was conscious of needing to enter *onto* a new path of unknown water.

At first, this side stream was much like the previous ones I'd taken. The canopies of trees on each side were almost, but not quite, touching each other and providing patches of shade. Blue herons were being spooked off perches to lead me for a while before careening off into the branches ahead. Turtles were flopping off logs in fear of my shiny flotilla. The current was strengthening as it became narrower and shallower. Nothing new to catch my attention or spark new thoughts. But then came more of the analogy…the revelation, gradually.

What's that sound? Are my ears stuffy? No, they're clear. Is it industrial machines nearby? No, it's natural. I know that sound, but can't place it. Is it locusts? No. It's definitely getting louder and closer. It's running water. I know…it's white water. No, not exactly, it's too steady and loud now. Oh, I know…oh no…it's waterfall!

As soon as I realized it, I began straining my eyes trying to see ahead while also quickly diverting the canoe toward the right bank of tangled tree limbs hanging over the water. Soon I was able to barely distinguish the change of crest on the water tens of yards downstream. I reached the trees, and fortunately was able to trap my canoe in them without turning sideways, filling, and rolling over. The current was just strong enough to make it a constant struggle, but I could hold it long enough to assess and plan. The obstacle ahead was a cement bridge or cattle crossing that the high water had overflowed, and was now forming a small but rapid spillway. Some of the metal rails were bent and others gone. The sound was really loud now, creating a battle between simultaneously distracting my thinking and heightening my concentration.

Then came the silent, lightening-round metaphorical lesson in my mind: *Can I handle it with my canoeing abilities? (Do you have what it takes to do what you need to do for Deb?) I don't know because I can't see how high the drop-off is. How rocky is it on the lower level? I can't tell that either. (No, you can't see in advance all the unknowns and rocky details of what it will require of you.) I could portage past it through the woods. No, I'd definitely turn over in this current. (No, if you try to escape the test, you will go under.) Okay, I know I can't just float, I've got to at least get up some speed in order to steer through it with some control. (Yep, no half-hearted effort will work.) So, are you going all in, or not? (Are you talking about this stream or the issue with Deb? Same same…I get it, I get it…!)* At that moment, I let go of the branches and started paddling as hard as I could toward the white noise. My heart was pounding, but my concentration was acute. When I reached the crest I could see it was only about a 3-foot drop with a few large rocks below. My canoe nose shot downward and glanced off a rock, throwing me one way, then hit another, fortuitously knocking me the other way, allowing me to stay straight through the remaining white water. It was over in seconds, and apart from a little splash, my canoe and I were dry and upright.

The decision was made. I would bend, and break if necessary. I had committed to the daunting and uncertain spiritual course I'd visualized while I was acting it out in this physical, man-versus-nature conflict on the White River. I would do what I knew to do, and I had a tangible memorial on which to draw in the future when my resolve would certainly be tested. I had something new and helpful to tell Deb. I also had personal commitments to keep without telling Deb, in order to not burden her. I knew which were which. Clarity. Commitment. Hope. All, from "getting away."

Some five years later, another set of circumstances urged me into the wilds. This time, it turned out my faithful friend, Karl, was ready for a road trip himself. In fact, he had actually adopted the habit of getting away alone on nearly an annual basis. As Ben Franklin proposed, "An ounce of prevention is worth a pound of cure." By taking this hiatus, I was hoping to prevent future heartache instead of needing a more painful cure down the road. I was once again at a juncture of deciding how to proceed in my career. An unexpected bend in the road made me question whether vocational ministry was still the path to pursue. Fittingly, Big Bend National Park in Texas, along the Mexican border, was Karl's chosen destination. Sounded good to me.

To make travel all the more intriguing, but not more comfortable, we would be driving the two-thousand mile circuit in Karl's recently partially refurbished, rusting, copper finished, 1966 International Scout 800 - a beast with noisy-knobby tires, 3-speed on the floor, no power steering or brakes, a top cruising speed of 55, a 10-gallon tank offering only 15 mpg (so we stopped every two hours to refuel), and two-window AC for the Texas desert. It was perfect! The great C. H. Spurgeon poetically understood, "There are joys of pilgrimage which make men forget the discomforts of the road."

I progressively acquired an appreciation for the southwest desert terrain. If you've ever made the highway trek westward across Texas, you know there's not much to report unless something goes wrong. Thankfully, nothing did. At first exposure, "monotony" pretty much covers it. Expanses of sandy, inert soil. Snaggley scrub and sage brush, dotted with spindly trees – mesquite, acacia, and more varieties of oak than I cared to know...mainly because none of them were big enough to get the attention of a Midwesterner used to huge, hearty hardwoods. Everything my eyes saw could fit in the "scrub" category. On the other hand, I did at first find something intriguing about the oilfield pumpjacks. To an Ohioan, they smacked of romantic cowboy movies. After a few thousand of those slow-motion rocking horses, even they blended in to the scrub. The misery that is Midland-Odessa just makes you want to cry.

It wasn't until we hit the far reaches of Fort Davis, Alpine, and Marfa that I began to wake up to a bit of the subtlety and beauty of the desert hues. What at first looked brownish took on rust, umber, camel, burnt sienna...the scattered greens grew into sage, olive, avocado, hunter...purples separated into fuchsia, concord, amethyst, lavender...and all those other wonderful names of colors you find on the cards in the paint section at Lowe's. Once I saw it, I was hooked. I would describe myself as a lover of beauty, and many subsequent trips through various deserts have continued to capture me in awe.

A bonus to our excursion was the anticipated exposure to the night skies in the Davis and Chisos Mountains. I had heard before of their magnificence, and was really geared up for a good show by Karl's testimony and itinerary. He had lived in this area years before and was friends with Rex, who headed up maintenance of the property at the famed McDonald Observatory. We would be staying with Rex just a few hundred yards from the main telescope. As if that personal touch wasn't enough, we were arriving in the peak of a meteor shower. After an evening of stimulating conversation, we stretched out in our mummy bags on chaise lounges on the back patio, all set for the celestial fireworks. As we settled in, about one shooting star a minute had me primed. *This is going to be good.* And then it happened...a hazy cloud cover rolled in. Somewhere above that wispy cirrus blanket were hundreds or thousands of meteors streaking the sky. No matter how much my imagination strained to see them, my eyes eventually accepted the insistent facts, and I was asleep...several layers under the stars.

All was not lost. A few nights later, camping a few feet from the Rio Grande, I witnessed more stars in one sky than I'd ever been able to see. In the black spaces I was used to seeing between stars and other luminaries, were multiple times more stars. These newcomer costars to my experience almost camouflaged familiar superstars like Cassiopeia and Ursa Major and Minor (the few layman's constellations in my galactic repertoire). I learned firsthand that with skies so far removed from light pollution, it was possible to see two of Jupiter's moons with the naked eye. Simple field glasses revealed more than I'd seen before through cheap telescopes. It was truly awe-inspiring and no disappointment.

Scout, Karl, camping 30 feet from Mexico

Staying in government campgrounds has its pros and cons. One misses the spontaneity and isolation of just stumbling upon a stunning, natural setting, but you gain access to the great national sites and things like running water and bathrooms. Not always a bad trade-off. Karl and I planted our tent in the Big Bend designated campground, and it being November, happily found ourselves quite alone. Except for "Bill", a cowboy who pulled up in his muscle car just after we committed to our spot. The good thing was that he didn't talk. The weird thing was that he didn't talk! Bill wore the ubiquitous boots and hat, but strangely kept his dark sunglasses on well after dark. He kept to himself, never made a noise, and other than an initial nod of acknowledging our existence when he arrived, avoided us completely. We were fine with that. We had come for solitude.

Karl led our hike the following morning to The Window, an impressive opening between two stone walls, naturally framing a gorgeous watercolor-worthy panorama southwestward toward Mexico. Scrambling a little on the red rocks rewarded us with silent vistas, just the ticket for two wannabe mystical hermits. Without verbalizing parameters and schedules for our time, we instinctively fell into a balance of shared expeditions, personal moments, campsite jobs, and general wandering of minds and bodies. But eventually, we both needed some total aloneness. Karl was once again my forerunner in this and recommended we take two days apart. He let me keep base camp in the high desert, while he mounted the Scout to the low desert. As much as I enjoyed his company, I knew my greater need was a fast from socialization. If I was going to seriously *listen up*, I not only needed to temporarily forfeit his companionship, I needed to lose my human audience in order to *shut up*.

Since I didn't know the area well and wasn't there to simply explore new ones, I decided to go with what I knew – the section of the basin and cliffs within a few miles of camp. On the previous days with Karl, I had scoped out some ridges and perches that looked like promising vantage spots for enjoying the scenery and getting above any foot traffic and noise. I easily found my way to a promontory that allowed me to see both into the far distance of Mexico, but also back into the canyon I'd traversed from camp. On the crest was what I called my pulpit. A waist-deep crack along the ridge opened into a roundish, waterless well in which I could turn and face any direction. It even had a small ledge surrounding it for my notepad, Bible, music headset, lunch, and thermos of water. I had found my place to listen and reflect.

But how long can a fairly social creature like me stay in such a place? Two days. Though I would normally get bored, distracted, long for company or just need a change, I stayed put the better part of this pair of designated days. I knew what I was there for and felt a sense that I needed to stay until I got whatever it was I was supposed to get. For sure, I changed positions by standing, sitting, lying down, pacing, and minimal bouldering just to keep from getting stiff. But I remained there. A number of well-worn Scriptures came to mind that kept me in that pocket: *Be still, and know that I am God... You will seek Me and find Me, when you seek Me with all your heart... Behold, there is a place by Me where you shall stand on the rock, and while my glory passes by I will put you in a cleft of the rock, and I will cover you with my hand until I have passed by. Then I will take away my hand, and you shall see my back, but my face shall not be seen... You have said, "Seek my face." My heart says to You, "Your face, Lord, do I seek."*

I watched various birds of prey ride hot drafts, lizards zip and tarantulas creep over sandstone, admired antelope wandering in the valley below. I read passages as they came to mind, sometimes out loud, yet subdued. Several times throughout the day I put on my headphones and listened to music. One song in particular was speaking to my soul, and I was bellowing it *acapella* such that I could hear it echoing off the rising walls on each side of the canyon. Soon afterwards, I had my only interaction with another person. A guy a little younger than I was hiking past me, and stopped for about a half hour to visit. He said, "I heard you singing, but I couldn't make it out." I didn't offer the name or words of the song. It felt too personal. I decided to not broadcast my music anymore. Mostly, I was uncharacteristically quiet.

When the sun began to lower, I could tell by the early hues that it would likely be a fantastic sunset. As I said before, and as a fortune cookie one time rightly pegged me, I am "a lover of beauty in all its forms." Colorful sunsets are way up there on my scale of soul-filling wonders. I wanted to stay, but didn't think I knew the way back well enough to venture it in the dark. As the colors intensified, I felt torn and bit-by-bit packed up my stuff and began a stop-and-go hike along the trail toward camp, stopping to glance back every once in a while. I got to enjoy a few glimpses of the Western twilight, but not as much as I wanted.

Supper on the Coleman stove was simple, but tasty. When camping, men tend to choose a combination of easy and spicy, and my canned chili, mozzarella sticks, and fruit cocktail wasn't exceptional. The cement picnic table and bench wasn't any more friendly to my backside than the rock all day, especially as the temperatures dropped. While I sat scraping my metal spoon on the metal pan and lifting it to my mouth (men don't mess with plates if they don't have to), I could see the red glow of Bill's cigarette periodically appear and then disappear. I couldn't see him...just the blinking, bloody Cyclops in the dark of his haunted tent site. Creepy. *Why is he here alone? Why doesn't he talk? Does he live on the road? Why? Did his wife kick him out? Why? Is he watching me?* I turned my gas lantern down low so he couldn't see me as well, just in case.

After a while, I thought I heard something move near me, but quickly recognized my own creep factor and dropped the thought. Then, something unmistakably brushed against my leg! How I kept from startling, I don't know, but it was fortunate I did, as my dinner guest was the largest skunk I've seen anywhere in the wild or in captivity. His vertical tail came up to my knee. This was one bold intruder. I'm not talking about the skunk; I'm talking about *me*. It was clear that this big boy was right at home around people, and I was the new interloper on the block. My presence didn't concern him in the least. Nevertheless, I certainly wasn't going to shoo him away, so I let him wander all around me for a couple of minutes sniffing for food until he was convinced I wasn't messy or generous enough to drop stuff. He headed toward Bill's. I doubt Bill said a single word to him. That red eye kept winking at me until I finally crawled in my tent...and made sure the zipper was *completely* shut. Karl had told me of a time a skunk was able to poke his nose in the junction of three zippers, enter, wander around inside the tiny tent with him and his son, find nothing, and exit. Other than warn his son to *not move*, that was the whole of it. I'm not that cool a customer. Ever since hearing that story, I've lashed my tent zippers together.

Day two I went back to the pulpit. I wasn't trying to be creative or adventurous. I needed answers. Keeping the same kind of regimen, I passed the entire daylight up on the mountaintop. One of the authors I've read and respect, a Greek Orthodox priest named Kallistos Ware, in describing the monastery on Mount Athos in Greece, expressed a "silence, not so much the absence of noise, but the presence of active listening." That's what I was going for, and think I found a modicum of that second day. I had no detailed roadmap or ten-year goals, but a few personal insights and some perspective to guide my next steps with confidence. It was enough.

The sinking sun was forecasting yet another gorgeous sunset. To stay and watch the whole progression of it seemed to me like an apt finish and reward for my perseverance in the desert. But, there had been a sign. Not of the mystical kind during my meditations, but of the paper kind posted at the head of the trail that morning. I can't remember the exact wording, but in effect it alerted: *Warning. A mountain lion has been recently seen in this vicinity. These are potentially dangerous animals and should be given due respect. For your own safety, do not hike alone if possible. Do not stay on the trail after dark.*

But I *really* wanted to see the sunset.

Now, here's another little peephole into the personal wiring inside my "accidental life" head and heart. I don't even claim to fully understand it, but it's there, nonetheless. I really wanted to see the sunset. I wasn't naive to the carnivorous nature of a puma. Two desires were clearly at odds with each other. Prudence was patently on the side of leaving now, before dark. A love of aesthetics didn't trump prudence. And yet...the very *fact* that there was a conflicting dynamic for me actually heightened the inner debate, instead of resolving it. How much of this kind of attractive fear is a guy thing of testing my own limits, I'm not sure. (In a previous conversation as couples, Karl and I realized we had the shared experience of driving our vehicles as far as we could by using *only* the rearview mirrors, just for the challenge of it, to which revelation both our wives looked stupefied and said such a thing would never even cross their minds, let alone be something to actually try! The ladies also weren't thrilled about Karl's and my mutual enchantment at seeing how long we could dare ourselves to turn off the headlights going down a country road in the pitch dark. Karl and I had tried it together once on a motorcycle at about 90 miles per hour.) Maybe that's part of it. But I know that's not the bigger part. I'm truly not inordinately brave or a daredevil. Case in point, I get shaky on heights despite being a climber. I consciously took up climbing partially in order to *overcome* the fear, not because I didn't have it. In this current sundown versus takedown scenario, there was also an element of faith involved. The sunset was God's creation, and something of His that had repeatedly inspired me to worship and trust Him all the more. The lion was also His. Logic and faith told me that He could control both. So I asked Him to let me enjoy the one, and to avoid the other. And I stayed to watch.

I won't try to describe the sunset and be boorish with what Twain complains is too much "weather" in books. Simply said, it was worth it – both the actual display *and* the decision to wait it out. Once again, there are, for me, metaphors to be acted out sometimes in order to drive home a deeper point. I was being called on to persevere in a challenging arena of work, so waiting out the sun and facing the potential beast was serving as a practice round and memorial in one.

In the canyon, there was very little transition time between day and night. It seemed almost immediately black. Trekking in that morning, I noticed that the trail was fairly obvious, so getting lost wasn't a major concern. My flashlight was sufficient to make out the path a few paces in front of me. I wasn't a rattling Tinman or molting Scarecrow repeating, "Lions and tigers and bears, oh my!" but I was on edge. At one point, it dawned on me that I was being very quiet. The futility of it was laughable. A mountain lion would smell and see me, as easily as hear me. In fact, my childhood barbershop reading of *Field and Stream* had taught me that it would actually be better to *make* noise. There was a much greater chance of drawing an attack from a startled creature than from a hungry one. So, I decided to make some noise that would give a lion a heads-up, if not scare it away. I picked up two baseball size rocks and tried to figure out how to "clack" them together while holding my flashlight. I tried wedging the light in my armpit for a while, but it proved too cumbersome and the light was flashing off branches making everything look like an attacking lion. I finally concluded it was better to be heard than see ahead, and put the light away in my daypack.

Per my habit, any steady rhythm brings a song into my head. Thus, the *clack clack clacking* of the rocks ended up being a drumbeat and I was singing tunes in my head much of the walk. Despite a degree of forced calm, I was still periodically mentally re-reading, *For your own safety, do not hike alone if possible. Do not stay on the trail after dark.* My next thoughts personified a curious cat wondering what that rhythmic beat might be, so I made myself stop the songs in my head that were creating it. I consciously kept the cadence irregular from then on.

Finally, having covered the two or three mile march, I could see some lights from the campground ahead. Ascending the last small hill into camp, I tossed aside my pair of makeshift percussion, and sighed relief. I'd made it without any confrontation...until I took my last step out of the brush. Both of us jumped as we came eye to eye. "Oh my goodness...we wondered what it was!" said the wife of an older couple leaning and straining to see down the trail. "We were walking back from the bathrooms when we heard this strange popping noise out in the canyon. We were trying to figure out what kind of animal could be making that kind of sound. *Pop pop pop*. We could tell it was getting closer, so we walked to the trailhead to see if we could see anything. And then it stopped...we waited...and *you* popped out! We didn't expect a person." We had a second good laugh together as I explained my side of the story.

getting away above the Rio Grande

Getting away isn't magical, but almost. I believe it's necessary at times and the payoff can be surprisingly rewarding. I find myself wanting and doing more of it as the years roll by. I'm not sure how much the need for it is a growing work of wisdom, simply a retreating inclination tied to aging, or...I'm also wondering how much is the result of a world going increasingly mad and driving us away from society! I tend to think it's a smattering of each. Regardless, it's definitely one of the key ingredients in "accidental life." A significant part of getting away is *counting on* something popping up unexpectedly that does exactly what you need. An unlocking insight, a backside boot, a calming hush, a driven stake, an inspirational vision. I've had them all at various times.

Have I always gotten what I thought I needed? No. I believe it's possible to respond to the itch to go, scratch your ticket for the open road, and come back home with what seems like only burnt up fossil fuel and used-up days off. But I've found disappointment to be the exception, especially when the craving for an answer is intense. It's possible to wander and simply stay lost. A working inner absolute compass that recognizes a spiritual true north is essential. I suppose it really comes back to an even deeper belief in the words of the One who holds all the answers: *Ask, and it will be given to you; seek, and you will find; knock, and it will be opened to you. For everyone who asks, receives; and he who seeks, finds; and to him who knocks, it will be opened.*

Right now...I need to get outside for a while...take a walk or run...get away...before revisiting the uneasy events of the next chapter.

flying with Karl, a favorite thing

success in reverse

*If I spit upwards, there's my mustache.
If I spit downwards, there's my beard.*
Turkish Proverb

That's the Turkish equivalent of our English *damned if you do, damned if you don't, stuck between a rock and a hard place, between the devil and the deep blue sea*. Spanish speakers word it *between the sword and the wall*. The Jews, *between the hammer and the anvil*. Other English adages describe similar nuances – being in a *vicious cycle* or *Catch-22*, *on the horns of a dilemma*, hearing *heads I win, tails you lose* or *pick your poison*, and the graphic, intensifying *out of the frying pan and into the fire*. Since various cultures have a lot of ways to say the same thing (but the Turks win the prize for the most colorful expression), it must be a pretty universal experience. And that makes me feel a little better about "getting resigned" twice. That's *my* personal idiom. Uncomfortably squeezed between those last little quotation marks is the self-protecting euphemism I adopted for vaguely admitting that I've been fired two times.

Technically, it's not just verbal spin on a pair of painful experiences. In both circumstances, I never was actually told, "You're fired!" I didn't get a pink slip and wasn't escorted by security out of the office to my car. The wording in both situations was, I believe, intended to soften the impact and consequences. The first went something like this: "Jim, I want you to be looking for another job. I want you to keep doing *this* job, but report to me your search results. I want to know you're actively looking and I don't want it to take too long. No one else needs to know about it." When it finally came down to action, it was abruptly and unexpectedly announced that "Jim has resigned," despite the fact that I hadn't, and that I didn't have other employment in hand yet. In the second job situation, I was presented with a letter in the morning board meeting which I was leading. I remember it seeming odd that two easily decided agenda items I raised got immediately tabled for "later." That hardly ever happened. Then, in the letter that was handed to me, the leaders briefly expressed that they felt we were heading different directions and asked me to resign...in two days. And so I did.

Bottom line: Both sure felt like being fired, but technically, I resigned. Thus, I feel justified (and rather *precise*) in saying, "I got resigned."

Retrospect usually sheds light, and my case is no different. There are things I would definitely change on my part. I can also say with conviction and the evidence of time that I hold no grudges and withhold no forgiveness, and assume the same on the part of the decision-makers who issued my notices. I consider the ultimate outcome of those experiences to be "good" – like the good wine that comes from crushing grapes, the good jewelry that eventuates from the refiner's fire, and other such pertinent and useful analogies. They were two very wonderfully tough ordeals. So now, with the objective of accentuating the *good* involved (sprinkled with a dash of ironic humor), I'll elaborate on a few details of those two purgatorial times.

At the first site of ill-fated employment, my beginning title was Assistant Pastor. My responsibilities included the usual gamut involved in a large congregation – teaching, preaching, counseling, hospital visitation, management, oversight, and ceremonies (*a la* my previous references to marrying and burying a host of folks). Early on, I had a bellwether of who was who when I questioned a decision being made, mind you, in the privacy of the Senior Pastor's office. Shortly after the conversation, he came into my office and clarified matters. "Your

baptizing Simon, a real Scot

title is Assistant Pastor, not Associate Pastor. I don't have Associates. I have Assistants. You need to trust my decisions and just implement them without question when I direct." *Wow!* We were the same age, of the same training and years of experience in ministry, but my assumption of us being peers in ministry was inaccurate, and unmistakably corrected. I was his employee. A hireling.

About midstream in my three-year tenure, due to theologically technical difficulties (and a few more death knell attempts at saying to the Senior Pastor, "I have a concern about..."), I was re-directed to a lower tier position over college students and adult singles. These were two sizable sub-congregations in themselves. Despite the formal demotion, I found myself increasingly energized and fulfilled to be molding more generally malleable hearts and minds, as I perceived it. From my perspective, this was another upside-down positive resultant in an apparent fail. I ended up in a specialized niche that fit my skills and passions. I spent less time in the office and hospitals, and more time in coffee shops and "The Shack" – a natural wood lodge a family in the church generously volunteered for use by the college students. I gladly embraced my stumble from the ladder of success. Decades and thousands of miles later, I still have interaction and input with several of those "kids", now in their forties and with kids of their own.

When that three-year stint did rudely end, I had to quickly find something to do that brought in some financial remuneration. I was sitting on a mortgage and was living with eight women. Yes, eight... ranging in age from two to forty-three. Of course, I had my harem of four, which included three teenage daughters. But I had also invited a

Accidental Life

family member going through a divorce, along with her three daughters who were elementary and preschool age, to live with us. For one year, I enjoyed the fluctuating and unpredictable world of female qualities and hormones...eightfold. Indescribable, so I won't. But in all sincerity, it was more often than not, a giggle-filled privilege.

It was during that lady-laced season that I needed a job, and fast. I took the first offer that came along as a stopgap. A stopgap that lasted about a year. I began using my two degrees to transport me to the lofty heights of local rooftops. I accepted a gracious offer from a congregant and friend, Bruce, to tear off shingles for his roofing crew. The pay wasn't nearly what I'd been previously bringing in, but the hours, social interaction, and physical exercise were...killer also!

Being forty-two, I was at the age where most guys in the construction business had gained enough experience to transition into more planning and less pounding, more managing and less manhandling. Mine was a backwards success track, dressing down from white-collar headwork to no-collar hard work. I was starting at the bottom, grunt level with a bunch of scraggly, young punks. I don't mean to use such derogatory words to degrade, but rather to accurately depict. One example was a young high school dropout, whose successful, professional dad had given up on him, tossing him to the roof-riders. This fidgety, blond mophead would take his breaks by walking the ridge to the chimney, light a joint, and when finished, toss the remaining evidence in the opening. One day, his already wired personality exaggerated by the weed led him to flee a single honeybee by jumping off the second story roof we were repairing. We had to call Bruce to report his broken leg. Another drug-addled, emaciated regular on the crew considered himself a philosopher and music critic. His ability to indistinguishably represent Aerosmith and Aristotle, the Scorpions and Socrates, offered a truly dizzying experience for rooftop conversation. His lunches were no less remarkable. Every day he erected the same sandwich: two slices of Wonder Bread, three slices of baloney, two more slices of Wonder Bread, three more slices of baloney, and finally, two more slices of Wonder Bread. No condiments or garnishes. That was his cheap and efficient bachelor's all-in-one cuisine. If by now you are picturing a monstrously tall, impossible-to-bite, let alone swallow, unappetizing stack of filler, you'd be accurate. But his brilliant solution to that physical impasse was his crowning achievement. Leaning his full weight on both of his overlapped hands, he would smash the four-inch townhouse into an efficiency flat, and choke it down with a Doctor Pepper chaser. Most days, he could demolish two of those hideous, pasty piles.

Such were my daily co-workers. But they had at least one thing going for them that I didn't – youth. I managed to keep up with them, but the wear on my body was motivation to move on. In the winter, I was able to switch from tearing off roofs to framing houses with another good buddy from the church, Jimmy D. His coaching in carpentry, self-deprecating humor, and gratifyingly greasy lunches at the Dirty Squirrel (our affectionate name for Grandma's Diner because of the ancient, dust-layered taxidermy decorations) kept me working and sane for the remaining duration of my hard labor sentence.

From there I went to my next limited duration pastoring gig in the bayous of Louisiana. Pursuing and accepting this outpost was the outcome of my Big Bend reflections. The first and founding pastor of this church lasted seven years before moving on elsewhere. As number two, I had the same exact longevity there. Maybe it was due to an odd combination of the biblical number of perfection and the seven-year itch that governed our respective terms of service. As in the previous church, my retrospect of this second pastorate is a mixture of gratefulness and regret. Some really good people involved there definitely leave a sweet savor to the memories. Some grave misunderstandings and disconnects leave an altogether different taste in the mouth. All in all, from my perspective, it was a decent seven-course meal. But the after dinner drink had a real kick to it!

As I said before, I was asked to officially resign as pastor of this church two days after that Friday meeting notification. That would mean addressing the congregation on Palm Sunday morning. That would also be on April 1st. That would also be on my 50th birthday. Now, am I making something out of nothing, or does that not just seem to be an apropos closing curtain for an act in an "accidental life?" First off, having a birthday on April Fools' Day sets the stage. Second, this Palm Sunday the ass was heading *out* instead of *into* town. And then third, getting booted on your 50th? It seemed to me like a fitting bow-out into a mid-life crisis.

Similar to watching a re-run of a failed TV series, once again I immediately needed a new job to cover the usual commitments of house, cars, insurances, food, etc. Our unique home was located on a beautiful four acres with a half-acre pond, all of which demanded hours of weekly hands-on interaction with the Genesis 3 curse on Eden. Louisiana seemed to get an extra dose of the curse in the form of heat, humidity, burrowing armadillos (armor-plated opossums), relentless mosquitos, Devil's Walkingsticks (human-height broomsticks with shark's teeth), sawbriars (grabbing vines with saw-like barbs), invasive mold, the popular poison ivy, sumac, oak, and the periodic promise of a copperhead or ground rattler mincing your steps. Our homestead was truly a paradise, serpents included.

We were also exactly in the middle of a short, five-month breather between two daughters' weddings. I was playing the dual roles of father of the bride (the one who pays) and officiating pastor (which I was no longer). It was a strange and stressful time.

New work came easy. It just wasn't easy work. Once again, a church friend came through. Generous entrepreneur, Scott, hired Deb and me to clean his office complex twice a week. Deb became queen of cleaning bathrooms – something on the nasty order of twenty-three of them. I was king of vacuuming miles of carpeting and emptying hundreds of trashcans. In addition, I started my own handyman business. That business's non-stop jobs ranged from a myriad of honey-do's at an ad agency to painting a convenience store/gas station. As the sad joke format goes - The good news is that I never lacked work. The bad news is...that I never lacked work. Physically demanding work, especially for a guy now in his fifties. Rub it in.

How do you respond when you "get resigned" from a church of 2,300 people? Strike one. How about from a church of 100? Strike two. Given the baseball analogy, it's not yet time to give up. No one wants to strike out, but then again, I've never seen a batter sulk to the dugout with only two strikes. But that's exactly what I did for a season. After the second swipe, Deb and I took a timeout from most people for a few months in order to evaluate our game strategy. And honestly, to lick a few wounds. I realize it's beginning to sound a bit monotonous, but the next painful seven months of hibernation from humanity turned out to be restorative. New insights and refreshed spirits prepared us for the last step of reverse success – a house church of less than twenty adults. Seven months into our seclusion, I was asked to preach at a church plant that had lost its pastor. With great hesitation, I agreed, "I'll preach once." One need led to another, and I was back in the business of teaching souls, this time moving twenty delightful adults into our house.

Over the course of pastoring three churches, the congregation size had plummeted to less than 1 percent. Salary took a nosedive to 60 percent. Satisfaction and peace...rose in direct contrast. Solomon knew what He was talking about when He said, "Better is a little with a reverence of the Lord than great treasure and turmoil with it." That small, intimate fellowship encouraged one another over a rich four and a half years in the comfort of our cozy great room.

What are my takeaways? Too many to list, but a few worth highlighting.

A friend and singer-songwriter, Michael Kelly Blanchard, insightfully writes of "the Other God...the broken One...Who patches years as they come undone...."

A full four years after my brusque exit from the large Midwest church, I received an unanticipated letter. The body of twenty-four elders was formally apologizing and asking forgiveness for their past lack of insight in the situation that led to my departure. They hoped our path since that time had nevertheless been a blessed one, and that this letter brought some added closure and encouragement. My response to them sincerely communicated that their letter was no less meaningful with the elapsed time...in fact, maybe meant even more.

My wise friend and office manager at church two, Lorenzo, was right in prodding me to question my frame of reference. It was in the midst of my Louisiana resignation, when I was bemoaning my frustrations to him, that he asked, "Did you think life was going to be easy?" I almost immediately recognized the bulls-eye his question pierced. As most reading this account of my life so far can easily conclude, I've had a pretty privileged, varied, and favored existence when put up against the whole of humanity and history. At least *I* know it's so. Life's been pretty rosy. My kindly interrogator hadn't had such a start. In pretty severe contrast, Lorenzo had grown up in the hood with circumstances that would make most men angry and unfruitful, as well as convinced that "life stinks." However, he had become a godly and successful man who learned through the years that life can be pretty wonderful. Conversely, I had been gradually learning from the opposite direction, through some inescapable trials of adult life, that it could be pretty rough.

Bottom line – life's a mixed bag, and it *is* partly what you make of it. Personal responsibility is an immense factor. But another reality is also a significant component in the composite of life – the element of surprise. That surprise, in whatever form it takes, is either accepted and welcomed as a potential agent for good, or it's resisted, denied, and missed for all its would-be positive effects. So, I'll reach way back to my parents' quizzical quip: "Jim, you seem to be able to fall in a pile of horse manure and always come out smelling like a rose." Well, I'll just borrow the cock-eyed optimism of an old joke - maybe the piles of manure indicate there's a gift horse somewhere nearby!

And faith must turn loss about, so that life can be explained.
- Michael Kelly Blanchard in "The Other God"

Lorenzo, my brother from another mother

part three: season of serendipity

Men on frontiers, whether of time or space, abandon their previous identities.
Neighbourhood gives identity. Frontiers snatch it away.
— Marshall McLuhan quoted in *Marshall McLuhan and Northrop Frye: Apocalypse and Alchemy*, by B.W. Powe

breaking good

Men rush toward complexity, but yearn for simplicity.
- from *Robert Louis Stevenson* by G. K. Chesterton

In my opinion, "cutting edge" is bleeding out. That popular phrase adopted by everybody wanting to convince others that they are truly going somewhere new is, I believe, definitely going somewhere itself – it's on the gurney heading for the morgue. In our current culture's lust to always come up with something innovative and edgy, we're jettisoning everything previously done or sold, as if they were useless artifacts and ancient history. The shelf life of a product, program or pop song almost expires before the Walmart stock boy's hands front it on racks for the first time. The plethora of supposedly creative things touted as breaking away from the pack *are* the pack. It's things like the truly handy school backpack that's now rejected because one kid's back started hurting. The greatly sought-after Super PAC tramples over the regular old PAC, undermining any semblance of honest elections. Pack my old shredded jeans in an Abercrombie and Fitch store, and targeted trendies will pay eighty bucks for them. *Wish I could actually tap into that naive market!* We've gone bleeding mad about "cutting edge" *anything*.

So, here's my Dennis Milleresque gratuitous rant chapter. I've decided to personally reject the cliché, and everything associated with it. Fear the cliché! Not just "cutting edge", but *all* the modern clichés that are making us a society crazed with being the first one on some fast track to no-one-knows-where. The cliché life of chasing uniqueness...right alongside everybody else. Almost any sane person you can make slow down long enough to have a conversation with and ask, "Aren't you tired of believing in and chasing the latest trend?" answers unhesitatingly, "Yes." If you're then bold enough to ask, "Then what are you doing about it?", you'll likely receive such a blank stare, it'll make you wither as if you've seen the walking dead. You may have! And there you have it. That's a very simplistic version of why and how Deb and I decided on "Breaking Good."

I realize "Breaking Good" sounds a lot like a recently popularized formula from a blockbuster television series, but that's probably mere coincidence, since I've rejected clichés *en masse*. Breaking Good is completely different from Breaking Bad. Let me venture to explain the difference: Good and bad are different things. One is good and one is bad. Yes, it's a complicated concept for progressives (programmed to adopt non-stop, cutting edge, feel good, avoid long-term responsibility, thinking-free notions) to get their heads around, but I'll attempt to flesh it out through the use of an example – us.

Since cutting edge wasn't cutting it, Deb and I were ready for a different edge. I guess we could have tried an absurd knee-jerk counter-reaction, and pursued a *dull* edge...a path actually resistant to progress. But we'd seen enough of that attempt by others retro-wearing prairie dresses, rejecting things like electricity, and rejoicing in a colorless lifestyle, to readily conclude that that may not be a completely level-headed path. There had to be a way consistent with our faith while not going off the deep end. This wasn't just reactionary...although we were decidedly reacting to palpable social lunacy. This wasn't just boredom...although we were bored. This wasn't just youthful "let's go live on love" and join a commune...although there was lots of love between us and some aspects of communal life do have veracity. This wasn't a disappointment in or rejection of our faith...although much of the contemporary religious scene was repugnant to us. No, this was a conscious and confident awareness that we weren't in our niche, and needed a personal redirection if we were going to _____. *What is it? What's at risk? What's to be gained? Yes, that's it.* If we were to stay *alive*.

One might suspect that Deb's and my reverse success track of getting resigned twice had something to do with us searching for a change. A little. But I think it was much more than just sour grapes left over from strained career disappointments. Even while we were in those semi-traditional roles of missionary and pastor, we had an ache for a non-traditional lifestyle. The best way I knew how to word it was for us to become "servants at large." The wording came from Jesus' naked words, "If anyone wants to be first, he shall be last of all and servant of all." Simply go anywhere to do anything for anyone. Part of the appeal in the vision was certainly variety – the potential of confronting a refreshing array of work projects. I like to think on my feet. Deb likes to serve in a pinch. But maybe an even bigger draw was the idea that those opportunities might serendipitously surface in a lifelong series of meaningful work. *What are the chances we could do this for the rest of our lives?* It seemed pragmatically unlikely. *How could we fund it? Where would we start? How could we communicate it?* The question "What would people think?" wasn't a significant concern. In fact, we were realizing that that particular wasted effort was the very kind of worrying that gets the masses stampeding over cutting edges.

Deb was ready to make a jump a lot earlier than I was. She pictured something a little more "out there"…like becoming gypsies. I felt like I needed something a little more stable, like a ministry to gypsies. As always, time, talking, and tyranny of the urgent tempered and coalesced our thoughts as a couple. Thirty years together hadn't been wasted. Something was coming. It was around the bend. A launch pad was being erected.

Among lots of other great literature and widely absorbed input, we had both read the phantasmagorical *Manalive* by G. K. Chesterton, in which the principal character said, "*I don't deny…that there should be priests to remind men that they will one day die. I only say that at certain strange epochs it is necessary to have another kind of priests, called poets, actually to remind men that they are not dead yet."* Deb adopted that conviction and started repeating to me over the months that followed, "I refuse to die while I'm still alive." It was a succinct way to put it. But no matter how hard I tried to find a responsible and practical way for us to do it, I couldn't. Finally, after about five or six years of brainstorming and entertaining "what ifs" together, we realized and accepted the obvious. There was no such thing as a reasonable and practical path. So, an *obvious* conclusion was, *Then don't do it*. But that wasn't the only conceivable conclusion. There was a Manalive conclusion that said, *Do it anyway.* It didn't make rational sense, but it sure woke up our sensibilities. We were at our own edge... an alluring precipice begging us to leap. We just needed a little push to get started. And it came. It came as a gentle shove through the back door of a most unexpected arena, the National Football League. But that fun story will have to wait until the next chapter.

Nevertheless, the NFL nudge gave us the confidence to make Servants at Large not just a concept, but *our* name. We talked with our house church, most of whom already knew of our radical bent and intent to hit the road someday. Although we'd miss each other's regular company, I think each person offered us his or her encouragement and blessing, which added confirmation to our direction to resign as pastor. This time, voluntarily! We put our house up for sale in a stale market. In only two days, prospective buyer, Leo, told us he'd been driving our area for years watching for just our kind of place. He'd even admired our property and wondered if it might ever come available. We accepted a full price offer and stowed it away in investments to fund ourselves in future projects. As they say in those Louisiana bayous, we were ready to "cut and run."

Servants at Large has clocked some significant miles in its first five years. One year in the NFL. A year in Turkey. A few months in Guatemala. Over a year on blue highways serving various folks scattered between California and New Jersey. An entire winter on a Greek isle. And...the travelogue is still being written.

What's it like living on the road, unemployed, and following an agenda that arrives on the wind? Wonderfully unnerving. Tenuously free. Invigoratingly frustrating. Humiliatingly rewarding. Like most things, it's a mixed bag depending on a lot of changing factors. One frequent occurrence keeps us in a regular state of re-evaluation. Peoples' questions. Being itinerant, we're always meeting new people. As expected, the first questions posed to us by others are the conventional conversation starters that used to have simple two-word answers. But not any more. "So, where do you live?" The answer is no longer a simple one like, "Cincinnati, Ohio", since we don't live anywhere in particular, but we do live anywhere in potential. "What do you do for a living?" That's even harder to describe – both the "what do you do" part, and the "for a living" part, since the first always changes and secondly, we don't make any money. I don't think our answers or explanations have been the same in two different encounters. It's actually kind of entertaining to try out new answers on various folks, depending on the mood, time available, and circumstances.

my try at a Guatemalan monastery

"So, where do you live?" One common response we've tendered is, "We're homeless on purpose." That usually stops the dialogue for at least a few cross-eyed seconds. People hurriedly check out our appearance again to make sure we have shoes on our feet. They aren't certain whether they should offer us a handout...until the "on purpose" part of our answer sinks in. A little softer approach we've used has been, "We don't live anywhere. We just travel full-time." That seems to regularly prompt an almost envious "Oh, how wonderful", which assumes we're probably retired, well-off, carefree, and have an RV. It doesn't take long for us to dispel that set of myths and send our inquirers into waves of deep confusion. *So, they don't have a home, job, income or retirement...and just travel...in a small pickup...doing good? But they look clean and sound educated and sane enough.* You see, it's working! Those folks' cliché compartments about "life" are already crumbling and their categories of possibilities are being upset. We don't fit. Candidly, in these chance meetings I get some satisfaction and amusement watching people's brains begin to wake up in new corners of thought.

I must admit that one fairly frequent reaction we receive, especially from snotty-nosed Millennials, does irritate me at times. I've been tempted to pop off, but the sarcasm hasn't escaped my lips...not yet. It all comes back to the cliché thing again. As a case in point, let me verbally paint a beach encounter we had last spring.

Deb and I decided to take a break from an extended service project to clear our heads. We took off in our little Nissan on the spur of the moment and started driving eastward with no idea where we were stopping. The Atlantic Ocean seemed like a logical halt. It was well after dark and Deb, from her copilot seat, called the first online beachside place that didn't look like a hotel chain or dazzle with too many stars over our budget. At The Pelican Motel, owner Tracy answered the phone himself. He had a room, but was just locking up for the night. The price was right, so we begged him to hang on for just ten minutes (we were twenty minutes away, but...). Turned out Tracy and his prehistoric father had been running this place since long before pink plastic flamingos went out of fashion and then came back in. We liked each other immediately. He was in the midst of off-season renovations and we were going to help lessen part of his general vacancy, so we got an even better rate for a whole week...which in the end we extended to two weeks. For a song and a fortnight, we had a kitchenette, balcony with chairs, an unobscured second floor view of the beach, and no neighbors to disturb or be disturbed by. From our vantage point, it was another fortuitous accident into which we were becoming accustomed to stumble.

Our days revolved around all the usual beachside stuff, thankfully minus the crowds. We took naps on the beach and read books in our bed. I ran miles and miles with waves as my companion. Deb did tai chi and stretching routines to make pretzels jealous. Morning coffee with sea salt sunrises. Evening balcony beer or wine. And to make it possible to never need our vehicle, a huge, choice-crazy market and deli lived right across the street. We, the homeless drifters, were enjoying what felt like a timely, if not deserved, getaway. Enter – the snotty noses.

After a blustery night, Deb and I checked out the beach in the early daylight to see what the nocturnal turbulent tide might have left to explore. As we zigzagged the shoreline, a younger beachcombing couple's zig crossed our zag. We exchanged "good mornings" and, to our pleasure, we began visiting. Deb and I like meeting new people, especially people from a different walk than ours. And this couple was different...that is, in a twenty-something uber-chill kind of sameness. Wrinkled, mismatched printed drapery could define their basic garb. The guy's prominent feature was a brown, crocheted, floppy, mushroom-shaped beret that interlaced with his dreadlocks. (I would subsequently learn it has a name - slouch hat. It fits.) The young lady had a sadly sweet smile on a roundish short-maned face. Both were either still hungover or, more likely, had an early buzz going. As we exchanged brief "we're staying over there at the Pelican" and "we're down the beach a little ways hanging with some friends", it was clear that this young couple was killing some time like us. And of course, he asked the typical question, "So, where you from?" I don't even remember the exact version of "homeless on purpose" we shared, but our explanation revealed our wanderings and patchwork work. And then...he said it: "Man, you guys are living the dream." That's not the first time we've heard that envious summation of our current existence. It always makes me feel a number of jumbled reactions. On the upside, I feel a tremor of renewed excitement to realize again that it's true. *We're really doing this crazy thing.* Then there's also a little embarrassment, as if I don't deserve it, because I don't. And usually there's a tinge of obligatory caveat growing inside, as if I'm required to qualify our status since it could all go up in smoke any moment. But that's my problem, which I'm gradually working out. So we just smiled and acknowledged, "Yeah, pretty much so."

I probably would have walked away from this brief dyadic encounter with the usual "that was nice" response, but Mushroom Hat had to finish his thought. Through that slow Cheech and Chong, breathy rasp of stoned visualization, he continued, "Man, that is so-o-o cool. You guys are living the dream. Dude, that's what we want to do." And *that* was when all my insecurities about what we're doing tipped to the downside and slid off into irrelevance. The instantaneous sardonic soliloquy that played out in my mind went something like this: *Great...then go get two degrees, work some hard manual labor and demanding professional jobs without entertaining any excuse to not work for a while and collect unemployment compensation, pay your taxes, stay debt-free, don't get any police records, get married and stay in it for thirty-plus years, learn a couple of foreign languages, give yourself sacrificially to raising a few children into responsible adulthood, own some property and develop a little equity...and sure, Dude, go for it!* But I didn't say it. I just smiled again, nodded, and looked for the first, lame segue to excuse myself and walk away.

That was my silent variation of Pavarotti's spoken zinger (according to urban legend). As it goes, after one of his concerts, an adoring mature fan gushed, "Oh, I'd give anything to do what you do!" His nimble retort: "No, you didn't." That's the difference between the cliché life and real life. Anyone can be wannabe edgy, but you can't be truly "cutting edge" without having some years of honing on the wheel of real life. We're homeless not because we can't manage a home, but because we already have, but choose not to now. We're unemployed not because we're unemployable, but because we've worked hard, but choose to do it now without reimbursement. You can't just decide on a whim to hit the road but *not* take along whatever you packed into the previous years. That is the *reality* behind the proverbial "baggage" often thrown around in conversation these days. To borrow a popular aphorism, Deb and I travel not to escape life, but for life not to escape us.

Deb breaking good

Now that I've beat my spoon on my highchair sufficiently long and shamelessly used ourselves as poster children, somebody could rightfully ask, "Is an itinerant lifestyle the culmination of the 'accidental life' you've been propounding?" To that, I'd quickly reply, "No, not for most people. But it is for us...for this season of our life." What we're doing is definitely not for everyone. If everyone did it, *most* jobs would never get done. Good luck finding your car mechanic, teacher, surgeon, barber, landscaper or pastor...if they all hit the road! Accidental Life can happen in any context. It can happen in the most traditional, mundane, routine lifestyles. It's an expectancy and trust, not a job or non-job description. Not everybody needs to *break* from the norms of society. But some do. Of those who do...some are Breaking Bad. That's just shameful. My guess is that a lot are Breaking Meaningless. That's just sad. As Servants at Large, we're *trying* something we hope proves to be neither of those. Come cliché or cutting edge, we're determined to keep Breaking Good.

loving the roadside stops

a season in the NFL

It never hurts to stub your toe on the moon.
- travel writer, Michelle Witton, quoting her father

If only out of curiosity, at some time most of us watch on TV or read in magazines about the lifestyles of the rich and famous. Hardly any of us ever become one of them. Deb and I managed to get sandwiched somewhere between those two realities for a year. We weren't "them", but we lived and worked among "them." We tripped into the world of professional football through the backdoor.

We had billed ourselves as Servants at Large, and that's what we became. At large in the normal sense of being at liberty and free to go anywhere and do anything. But also at large in that we found ourselves surrounded by people exceptionally large in athletic skill, unusually large in money, impressively large in fame, often large in personality, and typically large in outright size. Our particular colossus measured 6 feet 8 inches, and mobilized a surprisingly trim and agile 335 pounds. Deb, at her impressive 5 feet and 102 pounds, referred to him as "my personal giant." He's popularly known as Big Whit.

It all got started when our oldest daughter mentioned to Deb that this family needed a part-time nanny and she thought Deb might be a good fit. Even though Deb wasn't accustomed to working outside the home, loving on little ones and serving a family intrigued her. We decided to meet together with the couple to explore the possibility. Arriving at their well-appointed house for the interview, we were warmly greeted by what turned out to be a fairly accurate first impression – Whit's bigger than life frame yet subdued, steady demeanor... wonderfully complemented by Melissa's bigger than life personality in an energetic, compact physique (except for the "bump" that was soon to be the number three charge for the nanny). Deb was love-struck from the get-go by the one-year-old twins, Drew and Sarah. It only took about an hour for the two ladies to come to an agreement and schedule. Meanwhile, walking the outdoors with Whit, I got one of my first inside lessons about the NFL. When I joked with him that I was a life-long Green Bay Packers fan, but believed I could manage to also find it in my heart to root for the Bengals, I expected a bit of friendly smack talk to begin. Instead, Mr. Unflappable clued me in on the fraternal nature of the league. "We like all the teams." It's much more the fans than the players who get frothy-mouthed and indignant about their rivals. Many of these players will be shuffled around the NFL deck before their career hand plays out. When the two opposing jerseys mingle on the field after the game with back-slaps and smiles, it's because they've just engaged in something akin to a high-stakes family poker game.

After working four months in their Louisiana house, Deb's energetic, loving, and experienced mothering skills had endeared her to the family. It was also time for the Whitworths to move back to their Cincinnati house for the preseason, and in several semi-serious explorations, Melissa ventured "No chance you'd like to live in Ohio again, is there?" and "It sure is nice in Cincy in the Fall." Although it didn't initially seem feasible, the gypsy germ in us began to ferment and bubble. A couple of weeks later on our vacation, sitting in a Yale University beer garden, Deb and I concocted an email proposal that seemed far-fetched, and yet possible. The Whitworths' response was a generous acceptance – to hire us together full-time as Nanny and Personal Assistant. In another couple of months, Deb and I had moved from our four acres of southern clay to a 550-square-foot studio apartment in downtown Cincinnati. Years of dreaming and brainstorming a way to get on the road had finally materialized.

Strangely enough, it took us back to our home state of Ohio, some thirty-one years after we'd left.

Deb's personal giant, Big Whit

First rookie confession: When Deb and I went to the first preseason game, we both only personally knew one player – Whit. Second rookie confession: Not much better, we only knew two Bengal names and numbers - Whit (77), and Andy Dalton (14) the quarterback, of course. Although we were comfortable with Whit and Melissa, having gotten settled into roles in the work of the home, we still hadn't been introduced to the orange and black universe of The Jungle. As it came time to accompany them to our first official football event, Deb helped Melissa herd the three little ones and their paraphernalia from the house to the game. The day was a sweltering 92 degrees in the stadium. Loaded with stroller, diaper bag, and sippy cups, they jostled their way to grandstand seats in the full sun. Deb ended up sitting beside a young, attractive, blond woman whom Melissa introduced, "This is Miss Deb...this is JJ." Per usual, Deb jumped right into conversation and getting acquainted. "Hi...I don't know much about the Bengals team yet. Is your husband a player?" JJ humbly responded, "Yes, he's number 14." Bengals newbie, Deb, didn't know the significance of numbers to positions, but quickly put two and two together to get the correct significance of number 14. A little apologetically and chagrined, Deb admitted, "Okay, that exhausts my entire knowledge of players on the team beyond Whit." To Deb's relief, JJ turned out to be very unpretentious and congenial.

I walked separately at a leisurely pace to the stadium a whole twelve minutes from our apartment to meet them, help corral kids, and try to actually watch some of the plays. When I showed up, Deb, wanting to spare me the same humbling display of ignorance, introduced us with as much emphasis on the second part of the name as subtly possible, "Jim, this is JJ *D-a-l-t-o-n.*" *Got it!* Not a bad start...meeting the quarterback's wife.

I don't even remember what team we played against that day. The kids were so miserable in the heat, and us with them on our sweaty laps, the few plays I did watch were a blur. We did, however, get to meet the players in the bowels of the stadium after the game. Faces, names, numbers, and familiarity with their unique playing characteristics would come in time.

Each season, Melissa had to work out a schedule of the various family and friends she could invite to join her and the kids in their stadium suite for home games. Not every player's family has one of these extravagant boxes. The climate-controlled, carpeted suite has a back area with private bathroom, kitchenette, hot and cold food bar, and TV monitors. There is even enough space for the kids to run or crawl around when they come along. The forward portion looks like a tiny movie theater with tiered rows of cushioned seats overlooking the field at the perfect height just above serf-head level. In inclement weather, huge glass panels are slid into place, but fair weather days allowed them to be retracted for fresh air. Whit and Melissa shared the suite with the family of another player, Leon Hall. If I remember correctly, Melissa was limited to eight guests per game.

For the third preseason game, knowing that I was a Packers fan, Melissa thoughtfully invited me to accompany her to the suite. Deb would stay home with the tikes this time. I was jazzed that I would be watching in person my two favorite players in the league...after Whit, of course. On offense, the record-gobbling Aaron Rogers. On defense, the wild man, Clay Matthews. And as an additional, unexpected treat, Green Bay would move Matthews from his more typical left side position to the right side, meaning he would go head-to-head with Whit on many of the plays. Both were in good form that day, but I have to brag that my man, Whit, capably contained Clay's hyper-animated gyrations throughout. It was great entertainment, even apart from the comfy seats, complementary white-coat catered barbeque, casseroles, veggie trays, desserts, beer and wine.

After the game, Melissa asked if I would get the car to pick up Whit and her near the gate in order to head home. That little request segues my narrative into another whole set of memories from our brief tenure with the Whits – a series of experiences involving one of the family's sweet rides, a new granite-colored Bentley Continental. This is an amazing vehicle worth about the same price for which we sold our house. Looking back on my virgin voyage in it makes me shake my head and grin at the outward absurdity of the mental picture.

I had not driven the Bentley before (I had previously been slumming in their new Ford F-250 Pickup, Jaguar Land Rover, and the enormous white Hummer). Once I found it in the underground stadium parking and acclimated myself to the cockpit (no, that's not a mistake or exaggeration; the official manual for the car calls it that), I began to drive up the ramp toward the gate. I was already feeling a bit out-of-place in this otherworld environment and now driving this luxury automobile, but the next moment *really* threw me into surrealism. Some double doors a little ahead of me opened and from them emerged the entire ambush of Bengal cheerleaders, the Ben Gals, scattering in front of me. I had to stop to keep from running them over. So there I was, sitting in a quarter-million-dollar spaceship surrounded by thirty minimally clad felines waving to me as if I was someone who had business being there. All I could mentally formulate was *What in the world am I doing here?*

I'm not a big car junkie or grease monkey, but the Bentley is one remarkable piece of machinery. I found out just how impressive it is on one longer trip. It was the post season and we were accompanying the family from Ohio to Louisiana, a two-day, eight-hundred-mile trek. The plan the night before was for Deb and me to drive the Ford pickup and follow the family who were in the SUV. When we arrived the next morning, Melissa almost apologetically informed us that Whit had changed his mind and wanted us to follow in the Bentley. I tried to act nonchalant about the new arrangements, but inside I was doing NASCAR laps. Deb just raised her eyebrows and grinned at me.

Whit was cruising about 80 mph most of the way and I kept right with him for the sake of convenient travel and communication. However, twice in congested traffic of Memphis, I got temporarily cut off and was losing sight of him. I simply gave it some gas in order to weave around a few cars until I was back on his tail. It worked, but when I glanced down to check my speedometer at one point, I was surprised to discover I was going 105 mph! Okay, I was *surprised* the first time, but the second time a better description of my sentiment might be "satisfied."

Stopping for gas, restaurants, and hotels revealed just how much of an attraction our means of transport was. At one fueling stop, another customer started circling the car while I was pumping gas. When he saw me observing, he asked, "You mind if I look at it?" I laughed and told him to feel free. He kept smiling and whistling approval. Minutes later, he happened to be walking right in front of the hood when I started it up to leave. Hearing the powerful but smooth, low bass note growl of the engine, he just shook his head longingly and loped off to his all-American sedan. Best reaction of all might have been one local cop's comment in Nowhere, Mississippi. After filling up and waiting for Whit to load up the gang in his vehicle, a squad car pulled up and stopped alongside me. We rolled down respective windows. With a wry grin, the officer displayed his sense of appreciation, and humor. "That's the best looking Bentley I've seen today. In fact, that's the only Bentley I've seen in my entire life." Great line.

Living in our downtown studio apartment was a wonderful change of pace and intriguing experience for us. We couldn't have picked a more ideal place for our tastes. Our flat was front and center on the second floor. We had a French balcony just above the building's classic canopied main entrance, which looked out on beautiful Piatt Park, the city's oldest. Just the perfect height above everything for people-watchers like Deb and me. Our previous Louisiana outdoor view and entertainment of blue herons dipping and kingfishers diving into the pond gave way in Cincinnati to Segway tours, wedding photograph sessions, street people passing out, and lovers nuzzling. After dark we could wave at folks riding in the elaborately lit Cinderella-worthy horse carts that passed by regularly. Our church was a mere 200 feet from our front door. With an 1875 Gothic style cut stone sanctuary, this congregation had been established in 1790. Its previous pastors included some of my heroes of the faith – Lyman Beecher (father of Harriet Beecher Stowe of *Uncle Tom's Cabin* fame) and British theologian, G. Campbell Morgan. The 1,700-pound bell we could easily hear as it rang on the hour was cast by none other than Paul Revere, and bears his inscription. For us, it was a magical place to live.

And we had a charming menagerie of people living on our floor as well. Charles Rudolf Carter, an 89-year-old black man full of stories, weighing 105 pounds, hooked on the blues, and still prone to dance, became a loved acquaintance. He told us to be like the old-timey neighbors who borrow eggs and the like. When Deb made an especially good meal, I'd take him a sampling. In return, he'd give me a scarlet-hued story from his colorful past. And there was Mr. Koon, probably also in his 80s, who wore his pajamas in the halls, was bent-over about double, still walked to work, liked art and Italian women, and told us to watch out for the lady in 203 who hogs the laundry machines. Newly graduated Chad gave me updates on his budding career as an accountant. Flamboyant, single, middle-aged John who lived with his mother, Mary, sometimes wore a multi-colored, sequin-bedazzled vest and had a gregarious opinion on every topic. We'd go back there in a heartbeat.

Accidental Life

Deb & neighbor, Charles Rudolf Carter

Our domicile was downtown, but we worked from the family home just five minutes over the river in Fort Thomas, Kentucky. The Whitworth's seven thousand square feet of comfortably beautiful decor became our office. Although we were employed by them both, we mainly took our marching orders from Melissa. The tasks they desired from us were decisive and clear, and yet we were welcomed and treated like family. They shared their home and things openly and generously. Rich and famous they are. Stingy and snooty they aren't. And still, this is *not* your average couple. One couldn't find a much more enchanting, real-life Beauty and the Beast or Prince and Princess Charming.

Whit is not only huge physically, but has qualities that make him able to utilize that physique to big accomplishments. In the football arena, he has made his mark with "All This" and "All That" accolades in high school and college, and continues in the pros. For instance, as left tackle who protects the quarterback (think the movie *Blindside*), he currently leads the NFL and is blowing the top off the record of allowing no sacks of his quarterback. Almost 900 plays *in a row* without it happening. To talk in nerdy football stats, he has a PBE (Pass Block Efficiency) of 98.7%. What that means to us laymen is, he's almost perfect all the time in doing what he's paid the big bucks to do. One day in their kitchen, two-year-old Sarah was trying to get around Whit and into the other room. As she fought and ran left and right to get around the giant who merely had to slightly shift his feet to stop her, he lightly said, "Sweetheart, I can do this all day. I do this for a living."

In much of America's armchair sporting opinion, big guys like him who play football are supposed to be mentally dull, have volatile tempers, and not care about anything but that little pigskin projectile. To whatever degree that stereotype might bear some truth, I can testify it's about the opposite of this number 77. As a team captain, Whit's often the go-to guy for the media, partly because he's an effective locker room leader, but also because he can express himself well. It isn't the old "Yeah, dude, we just gotta get out dar an' give it our best, and you know...." He actually says something, despite the fact he has a limited range of topics he gets asked about. Part of the reason he has the playing stats he does is due to using his head against his opponents. He plays smart. In terms of temperament, he's about as steady and controlled as he is large. He's a real life Hoss Cartwright (for those of us old enough to know the gentle giant of black and white TV's *Bonanza*).

Deb's and his juxtaposed sizes when up close are quite amusing to witness. Their friendly banter as well. On one occasion, some good-natured jab Whit said to her prompted a wonderful scene. Deb had just purchased a stepstool for her kitchen use, so she picked it up and placed it in front of Whit. Mounting its topmost platform, she was finally eye-to-eye with him and simply said, "Yeah, this'll do." Whit responded with his warm, tickled grin. I think they both liked it all.

And regarding priorities, family and benevolence ranked way up there. Whit and I were getting barbeque sandwiches at a local restaurant when a young lady approached him. "You don't know me, Mr. Whitworth, but I was part of the prom group last year. That was such a great thing! Thanks so much." When she walked away, he humbly wouldn't have explained a thing to me if I hadn't asked, but I did. A bunch of high schoolers had been enjoying their prom dinner at the same restaurant in which Whit was eating. Behind the scenes, he paid for all their dinners just for the joy of it. On another very different occasion, he learned of the on-field death of a high school football player near his hometown. In sympathy, he quietly covered the funeral expenses for the family. His pleasant demeanor also flows over into his family. His four kids are as happy and delightful as...as my own twelve grandchildren are. And that's saying something!

Melissa is an altogether different batch of talent and good things. When Whit met her, she already had her own leg-long list of accomplishments. Little things like being Miss Louisiana, competing in the Miss America pageant, and holding a job as news anchor for the local NBC affiliate are among them. Obviously, her physical stature isn't up to Whit's, but she makes up for it in her turbo-charged, high-octane personality! Melissa is a "hot mess" in the best sense of that Southernism.

When the team traveled for away games, Melissa, then the mother of three children, realized it wasn't worth the disruption to go as well. She ended up staying home, watching on the big screen TV with us. I'm not sure which was more entertaining – watching Whit play or witnessing Melissa react and give high-spirited running commentary. Long hair and arms flying, she covered almost as much ground in the living room as Whit did on the field.

We watched the kids one evening so Whit & Melissa could go to the Reds Baseball game. They'd been invited by the team's owners to sit in their suite. They arrived to find other celebs there – Rob Lowe's brother and dad, the guy who invented Crocs, and Charlie Sheen. Melissa texted Deb: "I'm sitting with Charlie Sheen", to which Deb replied, "I'm not sure if that's good or bad." Given Melissa's gregarious and exuberant story-telling ability, debriefings after their evenings out were for us often almost as much fun as having been there. As it turned out, this night's group watched the game together and then went to some reserved hotspot for food and drinks. At some point, Melissa ended up talking about her faith with Charlie. As he was so vocally against it, she simply said things like "Let's be fair here..." and "not all Christians are like that...." Classic Melissa – she is who she is, regardless of the audience.

There's another Melissa moment I enjoy recalling. I had been commissioned to cull through and hire painters for the downstairs walls and ceilings. The one detail Melissa would understandably reserve for herself was to choose the colors and pick up the cans. The morning the crew painted the kitchen, Melissa happened to be out with her mother who was visiting. Just as the painters were finishing, mother and daughter drove in. Melissa wasn't in the kitchen a millisecond before she announced, "Oh, no...this won't do. *Way* too dark. I'll be right back." And with that, she and Mom were gone. Immediately, the painters looked at me with dread. I assured them they would be fairly remunerated for their extra effort and encouraged them to take a little break until she got back. In typical short order, Melissa came flying back from the paint store and into the kitchen with a lighter shade of the previous hue. As the workers began reaching for the cans to restart their task, Melissa headed again for the door saying, "I gotta go back to the paint store." I asked what she needed and if I could make the run this time. Rolling her eyes with exasperation and a little sheepishly, she said, "No, I gotta do it...I forgot and left my mom there!" A hot mess. I love her.

As I expressed before, our jobs were defined but flexed with the ebb and flow of a busy family. Deb's day was filled with filled diapers, gallons of Boudreaux's Butt Paste, and an adorably alive trio needing her help and enjoying her love. She also made meals, picked up clutter, did laundry, and ironed Whit's massive shirts. Nearly everything in the realm of nannying came instinctively to Deb. She speed-shifted gears, from the organizing of stuff to meeting the emotional needs of little ones, without touching the clutch. Nurturing and running the home just rolled along naturally. She did, however, have to make a few adjustments now that she was doing these things where resources were plenteous. One experience near the beginning of her employment was particularly comical. Deb was doing what she'd done for years in our conservative home and given our restrictive budget – she was washing out the Ziploc bags and drying them on the counter.

Dismissing the mental hint of wondering what Melissa might think about it, she continued the practice regularly. One day when Melissa came home and saw the bags, she finally let her feelings about them come out. "Miss Deb, do we need to have these laying around...like we can't afford another box?" The housecleaner, who had more time in the home than Deb and was observing the interchange, said, "I knew you were going to get in trouble for doing that!" Deb felt a bit embarrassed, but the three were soon laughing together over the difference of worldviews expressed in a little thing like quart size bags.

My role encompassed a wide variety of things. Anything pertaining to the house and property was mine. Landscaping, hanging drapes, putting in a golf driving practice area, purchasing and stacking firewood. In addition, hiring and overseeing an assortment of tradesmen was a regular responsibility - painters, landscape lighting crew, playground and fence installers, pest control inspectors, air-handler servicemen, car detailer, and auto storage specialists. Although not my forte, I was also able to create a filing system for all their paperwork. Periodically I got to be Jeeves or Mr. Carson, especially when Whit had knee surgery. I enjoyed carrying him trays of food or setting up the ice therapy system. There was also the periodic necessity for me to find and recover misplaced personal items like Whit's Breitling watch, diamond encrusted wedding ring, or a single game paycheck that happened to slip unnoticed between the car seat and console. Some might consider much of this to be menial work, especially for someone with a Masters degree and with years of leadership experience. But I typically found it interesting in its variety and rewarding to meet practical needs for good people.

Deb and I shared a few responsibilities like the majority of the family grocery shopping. I got to become familiar with and could quickly locate Pampers Cruisers #4, Aquaphor Healing Ointment (by the tub), and Gerber Graduates Lil' Crunchies (styrofoam-like vegetables for littering the backseat of the Land Rover). I also helped with some of the direct dealings in the children's care. Deb fulfilled the strategic stuff of teaching numbers, kissing boo-boos, and making sure they ate their vegetables. I performed the less purposeful, but necessary tasks of demonstrating how to slurp spaghetti noodles as noisily as possible, letting toddlers chase and catch me with dramatic overacting, and singing the goodnight song to them before turning on the white noise machine. Deb and I sure got attached to the happy and loveable triad in our charge. Delightful.

A winning season and playoff showing for the Bengals finally came to an end. In the meantime, among other great experiences, Deb had also gotten her turn enjoying the stadium suite for one game. But the perks hadn't been exhausted yet. We were informed that reservations were made for us all to spend ten days in Vegas, and maybe go from there to Hawaii if Whit made the Pro Bowl selection. *Well, if we must.* In flight to Vegas, Whit got the message that he was in fact selected for the Pro Bowl. A big *whoop* went up from our two first-class rows as we all learned about it! We had been optimistic enough to bring along our summer shorts and bathing suits.

Deb and I had never put Vegas on our list of places we hoped to visit. It never appealed. But that quickly changed. I guess it makes a difference when you stay someplace like the Wynn Encore Resort. Our 2,000-plus square foot palatial suite with high altitude view, room service, and a few outings on the strip gave us a privileged exposure that changed our opinion...at least for ten days. Even though we were there to work and spent much of our time with the kids, the Whitworths generously made sure it was a special time for us as well. Off hours were punctuated with treats arranged by them: massages in the hotel spa; dinner at Sinatra's (the *best* Tiramisu we'd ever had); front row seats to Cirque du Soleil's Beatles LOVE show.

One of the most noticeable characteristics we observed about Vegas was the standard use of hyperbolic schmoozing by employees everywhere, and especially in the casinos. When we ordered food from room service, each item we selected received a response of "excellent... wonderful...perfect", as if we'd made the best decision a human being could...in ordering a BLT! Every time I walked through the lobby, every staff person behind a counter (not just the *concierge*, and often as many as 3 or 4) would stop their work momentarily to look up and say, "Good morning...How's your day going?...Have a wonderful evening." *I feel like Bond...James Bond.* And I'm sure that's their exact hope and expectation. Those over-the-top pleasantries, every door being opened for us, and the upbeat music...all subliminally say, "Go ahead and give it a go...roll those dice...you're a winner waiting to be discovered." The casino has no windows or clocks, so no one's reminded what time it is. "You're timeless." The oxygen level is slightly higher than normal to increase the sense of elation and good fortune. It was all so seductively quixotic.

Even having been there ten tempting days (and several more times since then, as our youngest daughter currently lives there), I have still never *officially* gambled. And yet I've won! Let me explain. Whit enjoys playing poker. He does it mainly for the sporting challenge, not the winnings. He shared with me his system of play, which simply disciplines him to determine how much he's willing to "invest" in a given outing, and stick to only continued play based on winnings, not increasing the shelled-out principal amount. It sounded pretty good to me. About three days into our stay in Vegas, I handed Whit a single $100 bill and asked if he'd go to work for me. "Add it to whatever you're betting, and whatever percentage of winnings or losses it is, I'll accept. If you lose, I don't think $100 will ruin me." He smiled, agreed and headed for the casino. About five days later, I asked how he was doing at the poker tables. He laughed and said, "I'm getting my butt kicked." My hopes of making a few bucks sank pretty quickly and I resolved to not give it any more thought. In the elevator as we were leaving for the airport, Whit reached out his hand to me and placed a roll of bills in mine. At first, I thought it was for giving tips since Melissa had earlier in the trip handed me a bunch of 20s and asked me to "please, take care of the various porters and doormen as we travel." But when I saw it was all hundreds, I asked, "What's this?" Whit smiled his ornery kid smile and answered, "I won big last night and this is your share." So, *officially* I've still never gambled, but I walked away with $1,100 from my "investment" in Whit's talents.

Whit & Jim en route to Vegas & Hawaii

Vegas is impressive - man-made glitz on uppers. Hawaii is gorgeous - God-crafted beauty on hallucinogens and muscle relaxants. Now we see why people visit both. Each offers a different taste of unreality compared to most people's everyday existence. If Deb and I had to choose one of these, Hawaii won hands down. In fact, by far the highlight of our trip was the last full day, a relaxed exploration around the perimeter of Oahu. To begin our day, the economy rental Toyota was voluntarily upgraded and discounted to provide us a new Volvo convertible that looked and acted more like one of the Transformers. We cruised top-down at 25-35 mph the entire north coast along famous beaches like Pipeline and Sunset, getting out at several to wade, climb rocks, eat, and watch surfers do their thing in 12-15 foot waves.

However, the bulk of our island time was spent in the Ihilani Resort, which had been itself transformed into NFL'ville. The entire place was filled only with players and their families. By dictate, there were to be no photo-ops and no autographs. *Brilliant.* It created a common, casual feel to a very uncommon gathering of intense guys. It took all the pressure off my mind as to how to relate with everyone else. We found ourselves in the elevator, hallway, restaurants, poolside, and on the beach conversing with a T-shirt and sunglasses, not knowing they were really a Saint, Seahawk, Viking or Giant. But a few times, celebrity revealed itself in ways impossible to not have a few internal flutters of excitement.

For instance, it was hard for Deb and me to not notice we were sitting in the hot tub talking with Eli Manning and his little boy. His brother Payton's handshake at breakfast was as firm and friendly as I would have expected. Jerod Mayo really is an intense workout maniac. Drew Brees does appear to be prone to a bit of a chat.

As the Pro Bowl week neared the end, there was the obligatory Polynesian luau. When the dinner and stage show was over, it was time for Deb and me to put the kids down to bed. Standing and turning around with one of the twins in my arms, I realized the lead entertainer for the concert later that night, Pat Monahan of the group Train, was standing behind me with his wife and child. I decided to say hello. Both very friendly and surprisingly willing to visit for a while, his wife offered, "Let me take a photo of you all together." Deb was a few yards off, busied with the youngest, Michael, so I said in my habitual manner, "Deb, come here a minute, Baby." She didn't hear me. But a second later, to her surprise, the star singer yelled, "Yeah, get over here, Deb Baby!" She heard *that*. And we have the photo as a fun reminder of the delightful moment she enjoys claiming – "Pat Monahan calls me 'Deb Baby.'" Later that night, with the kids in bed, Whit and Melissa spotted Deb and me dancing in the moonlight on our balcony as Train sang below from their pool-top stage. I called her "Deb Baby" lo-o-o-ong before Pat did.

What? No accidents tied to this story of our fantasy island hiatus of indulgence? Oh, no...I didn't get off that easy. But it could have been a *lot* worse than it was. The day of the actual Pro Bowl game arrived, and we were on full-day duty. We had a few hours of daylight left before the game and wanted to enjoy the beautiful outdoors with the kids. We went to an area that had already become a favorite for the family. It was a grassy expanse under palm trees, surrounded on the surfside by a hedgerow. In other words, it was pleasant and largely contained, which is a good thing with two toddlers and a baby. After a while of running in the lush grass, we realized that through an opening in the hedgerow was another potential play area, a natural sandbox walled-in by volcanic rock on every side. *Perfect!* (See? I'm getting the Vegas motivational lingo down.) As Deb oversaw the twins' play in the sand, I held Michael. Although only nine months old, he was taking after his dad and weighed about twenty-five pounds already. He was an armload. The twins were loving the sand.

It came time to get back for dinner and then kids' bed, so I announced such and simply turned toward the opening in the hedge. What I hadn't realized was that in watching the twins play in the sand, I had backed myself up against a foot-high little peninsula of volcanic rock jutting into the sandy area. As I turned, my pivot foot caught in the rock and I was going down face-first fast. More accurately, I was going down *Michael-first* fast! In front of us was a layer of jagged, pocked, black rock. All that came to my mind was my 180 pounds potentially landing on Michael, and him on those evil-looking razors. Who knows why instinct sometimes wins and other times doesn't, but I have never been so retrospectively thankful for fast-firing neurons and the mercy of God. Thrusting my knees outward and extending my arms full length, I was able to come down taking the full brunt on both shins and forearms. Just as I saw it slow-motion in my mind's eye, Michael rolled out of my hands onto the soft sand like a dumpling into noodles. He even came up laughing. I didn't fare so well.

The bony front of all four limbs was shredded and bleeding. It was immediately obvious that some of the gashes were deep enough to reveal the white sinew under the meaty part. The pain was incredible, and yet I was almost exuberant inside at how the tumble had rolled out, literally. Michael was totally fine, so all was well. Deb took all three children in order for me to hobble back to the hotel and find medical help. My first plan popped into mind. *Thank goodness, there's a full-time physician here in the hotel for the team.* Then the quick correction came. *Oh nuts. It's game day, and he'll be with the team on the field.*

At the desk I was informed that one of the resort staff had previously been a paramedic and would come with some supplies to my room. When he showed up with a more than adequate first-aid kit, we sat on opposite sides of the bathtub while he scrubbed my wounds with water and alcohol. He felt certain that at least three of the gashes would need stitched, and suggested I either wait for the team doctor to return later, or go to the emergency room. I opted for Dr. Football.

Dinner, kids' bedtime, and the game on TV distracted me over the next 4 hours. I got news from the desk that the doctor had returned and would meet me in his makeshift clinic off the main lobby. Humorous and easy mannered, he checked me out. He debated for a while about stitches as we talked. He praised the excellent job of scrubbing by the paramed-turned-porter-turned-paramed, but still decided to give it his own professional and thorough scouring. In the end, Doc had used about 15 Steri-Strips instead of stitches, plus a healthy batch of antibiotic cream and gauze.

When Whit and Melissa returned from the game, I met them like an underdressed mummy - fully bandaged with gauze wrappings from ankles to knees and elbows to wrists. I explained as best I could what happened and that Michael was unscathed and his normal happy self. Whit seemed non-plussed. I wasn't sure, but Melissa appeared concerned or possibly irritated. The next morning at breakfast, Melissa first asked how I was. I assured her I was fine. She then revealed what it was I thought I'd detected the night before. "I'm glad everything's okay, but...it probably wasn't the best idea to take the baby out for a walk on the rocks." *Oh, that's what I was afraid of.* I tried to explain more clearly the setting and what actually took place, but I was pretty sure she couldn't hear it. I understood. It's her cub and she's a protecting Bengal momma. It was time to swallow my pride, hope there wouldn't be any lingering lack of trust, and lick my own wounds. We moved on. After all, "it never hurts to stub your toe on the moon"...and maybe even on Hawaiian rocks.

seconds of Turkey

A blind man asks for one eye only, but he will be delighted indeed if he gets two.
— Turkish Proverb

"How cool would it be to show up on Mehmet and Reyhan's doorstep someday and surprise them?" This was a fantasy Deb and I repeatedly envisioned throughout nearly twenty years of reflection, but not one we really expected to see fulfilled. As much as the thought of going back to Turkey someday appealed to a nostalgic ache, our lust for seeing new places and entering new adventures seemed a greater potential reality should we have the time and money to travel internationally again. But as providence played out, even though the green and crusted crags of the Scottish Highlands or the spiny backbone of the Italian Apennines were first course contenders for our appetites, we were invited back for a repeat course of Turkey, on the summit of *Sakintepe*, or Peaceful Peak. And we *would* pay that dream-like visit to our old neighbors.

Whether circumstances and timing are reliable indicators of one's destiny is a valid question to ponder, and it's one that Deb and I certainly have entertained many times over the years. But the transition from America's Midwest to the world's Middle East sure seemed to us to fall into place without any engineering on our part. As much as we loved the Whitworths and our studio apartment, we were convinced that our contribution to their family had reached its saturation point. And Deb was worn out. We had a tearful powwow as couples when we tried to express our reasons for not continuing into another football season. Don't tell anyone, but even though Whit makes a practically impermeable left-side wall against blitzing linebackers, he can still leak a little around the eyelids under the right circumstances. We parted on friendly terms without us knowing the next gig.

I shot out an email to our family and friends around the world simply communicating "We're done here...we're available to go do something somewhere...got any ideas?" The response was almost immediate from long-time friends and former co-workers in Turkey. The situation was this. Our friends, Brad and Ruth, after living twenty-six years in country, purchasing land, and laboring to develop a multi-faceted facility and venture, had their residency revoked. Apparently, the local government felt threatened by their presence. Despite two overturns by the Supreme Court in their favor, this couple was sitting on a million-dollar property, busy business, and having to exit the country for fifty-percent of the year! And our message of availability reached them in the thick of this dilemma.

There are lots of roles we're not suited to fill, but this wasn't one of them. The job called for a ridiculous combination of experience and abilities. "WANTED: Onsite managers for six mountain top villas on ten acres. Must be able to: host individuals and groups ranging from giddy teenagers to chilled-out diplomats; maintain and repair physical plant issues the likes of installing pumps in the middle of the night and lifting cows with a backhoe (that ditty for a subsequent chapter); counsel downcast missionaries while satisfying paranoid and inquisitive *gendarme* police. And the crowning requirement – the ability to do all those things in both English and Turkish. It wasn't hard for us to feel "called" when we could answer, "Yeah, strangely enough, we can do that."

One doesn't just "arrive" from the United States at a place like Sakintepe. There are any number of travel quagmires and cultural hazings to go through en-route. This particular re-entry to our former Ottoman homeland included a suitcase spilling its guts on the baggage conveyor, hiring an ancient hardware truck to tote our multiple Lowe's plastic bins, and realizing we had unwittingly chosen to travel on *the* busiest holiday of the Turkish Islamic calendar. *Seker Bayrami, or* "Sugar Holiday", is like a combination of family reunion and trick-or-treat. It celebrates the end of the month-long fast of *Ramadan.* Families go to their town of origin and everyone is obliged to serve troves of sweets. The bus station was crawling with scarfed women, smoking men, and glucose-empowered children. We sat as two of six people on the rear bench seat of the bus designed for a snug five. For four hours. In the dark. Using Turkish for the first time in eighteen years. All that *after* an overseas flight, a long taxi ride, and four hours sitting in the bus terminal. Deb and I melted down the bus steps for the final midnight leg of the trek, which incorporated a four-wheel drive pickup that wound and bounced through mountain villages reeking of cow manure until we truly did arrive at…one of the more gorgeous spots on the planet, and our home for the better part of the next eighteen months.

As the unofficial job description suggested, every week presented a unique and challenging set of tasks and many accompanying curious adventures. But in the first weeks of being back on Turkish soil and before getting completely entrenched on the mountain, we were anxious to get to the capital city of Ankara, our old stomping grounds. We had no idea how many latently familiar places, customs, smells, and people would welcome us back.

Seeing Ankara after those particular two decades of massive growth and change was like seeing a favorite nephew who's wearing a suave tux repeating his wedding vows in a husky baritone, when the last time you saw him he was a squeaky-voiced adolescent in a mildewed sweatshirt he'd rescued from the laundry basket. We didn't know the place. Two and a half million Turks had grown-up into a strapping five

Accidental Life

million with big-boy up-to-date clothes and toys, batteries included. The old world charm was giving way to Western post-modern sameness. It was simultaneously astounding and a little depressing. I felt like I was living a classic National Geographic article in which the author is astonished at the juxtaposed iPhone user on an oxcart, micro-surgeon meeting the witch doctor, or toothless aboriginal admiring Anne Hathaway's pearly whites on HBO. Turkey is still an awkward contradiction.

I knew we were walking the right way to my downtown office (the eighth-floor one I'd humiliatingly flooded), but I accidentally passed the intersection because it was now an overpass highway instead of just the four-lane street I had known. When I did spy the door and began to enter, the female attorney who managed the building when I first rented twenty-five years before was coming out. "*OoOh...merhaba* Şebnem hanım, nasılsınız? Çok yıldanberi görüşmedik!" ("Oh...hello, Ms. Şebnem, how are you? It's been a lot of years since we've met!"). I wanted to hug her out of that weird feeling of brotherhood that surfaces in such unexpected "long-time-no-see" encounters. Then again, immediately I was cognizant of just how repulsed I had always been by her semi-masculine appearance and icy, yet seductive manner all those years ago, so I held the appropriate distance just as before. She remembered me (and probably could have told me the exact amount of *excessive* lira she charged me for the soggy elevator part) and informed me that no one from my years on the eighth floor was there anymore. We parted ways, but I still had to go inside just to see. The gray, dimly-lit, musty hallway was one thing that *hadn't* changed.

Before we got away from the area of my office, I thought of a stop to make that I hoped might prove rewarding. Out the front door, turn left, walk the tipsy sidewalk pavers about forty paces, another left onto the carless shopping avenue, *Sakarya Caddesi*, stroll among the fishmongers, stationery shops, beer gardens...and eventually arrive at my destination - a glass shack that could have passed for a greenhouse, but actually housed three or four men squatting on foot-high stools. *Could he possibly still be here?* And there he was, with his back to me in his traditional spot, wrapping up with a customer. I would wait for him to finish. As I'd seen him do a hundred times before, he received his pay dropping it in his black, smudged box, tilted his head back to smile up at his patron, and leaned backwards to stretch his lower back muscles. I stepped around him, turned to sit in front of him, stuck my foot on the brass pedestal, and in Turkish asked, "Can I still get a shine here?" Better than I even imagined it in my mind's eye, his warm eyes awoke wide, his open mouth gave an enthusiastic "*OoOh!*", he stood and kissed me, still pumping my hand with both of his hands. Those hands rougher and more leathery than the shoes he worked on. Unlike me, he still had his full head of now gray hair.

Although mostly a man's world among the shiners, Hasan Bey saw Deb who had hung back outside the door and invited her in to sit as well. For the next fifteen minutes, as he massaged the brown paste into my Sketchers, we caught up on families and life. He remembered our three girls and asked about them. When I told him they had produced eleven grandchildren for us already, we received the never-failing response of praise, "*Maşallah!*" ("What Allah wanted has happened!"). I remembered and inquired about his son and likewise heard the fast-forward generational summary. Hasan, himself, was now seventy-five and in his thirty-second year of semi-retirement shining. He might completely retire soon...maybe. He told another customer that we were friends a long time ago, that I and my business partner, Steve, were stand-up guys with good character and nice families. I was so glad I stopped by. This quick pit stop was a much greater reward for me than the double pay I pressed him to accept. Affectionate memories was well-worth the extra three bucks.

As we rambled along, I in my burnished shoes, familiar wafts of seared meats insisted we go for a past favorite, the decadent lunch called *iskender*. This cardiac cuisine is a full plate of fire-roasted beef basted in lamb's fat over *pide* bread, smothered in tomato sauce and melted butter, topped with a dollop of *yoğurt*. A small salad of tomatoes and cucumbers on the side provides guilt relief. The taste was timeless. The price had climbed with the skyscrapers. No complaints.

Primed to reminisce, we were compelled to climb to Ankara's medieval castle, despite having visited it tens of times. As in the years before, the stone steps leading up to the entrance of the citadel that surrounds were lined with women in traditional garb making and selling souvenirs. Our brains' bicultural RAMs were able to call up the delicate social dance of being friendly while evading the ever-escalating pressure to buy something. *Smile...keep walking...compliment their work...keep walking...don't touch or point at anything...keep walking...smile....* It felt good to remember how to pull that off.

20-year reunion with my shoeshine friend

Once inside the open-air ancient walls, we *did* begin to point at things. "Look, the brass and copper workers are still in the same place." "I can't believe we've still got some of those woven bags from that guy's shop." "Wow, I forgot what real antiques are!" Deb and I had gotten used to hitting Stateside antique malls, accepting Scooby Doo thermoses and muted primary-colored Fiestaware as "antiques." Now we were once again rummaging through decor and artifacts much older than our native nation's history. Beachboys vinyl was bowing to Byzantine vintage. The grizzled merchant engaged Deb on some item and I joined them to make sure she didn't need rescued from annoying Turglish - "You like dees? I make you good deal." As I inserted myself into what I realized was a fully Turkish and unpressured conversation, he said to me, "I remember you. Other things change, but the eyes...the eyes stay the same." I was humbled, and relaxed to enjoy the gracious hospitality so pervasive among Turks. He still didn't sell us anything. Ottoman era doors with bronze knockers are a bit pricey and exceeded our baggage limits.

Hüseyin has held a special place in my heart. As a single college student, he was my language helper, hired to painstakingly slog through every tortured syntactical element of Turkish. The Turkish language offers a wide variety of humbling challenges to the English speaker. As a beginner, new sounds make one's jaws ache after an hour of trying to form them. Word order is totally different, so one can't just mentally translate phrase by phrase, like one might in Spanish. A drastically different worldview twists the language into passives and innuendos that frustrate one's instincts. One wants one's *English*! Hüseyin not only patiently explained, repeated, pushed, and appropriately laughed at me throughout the process, he became a household regular at the table and big brother to our girls.

We had kept in touch sporadically over the two decades apart, but now came the happy moment to meet *his* little ones who were now the same ages as ours had been when we'd last been face-to-face. One girl, one boy – just what a progressive high school biology teacher could afford. It was hearteningly clear that his wife, Berna, who'd never met us, had unconditionally adopted Hüseyin's affection and honor for our family. And what does one do to show affection and honor in Turkish culture? Try to out-do one another in gift-giving. Turks are elaborately generous. Despite knowing the cultural odds were in his favor, the "Battle of Deference" commenced.

Deb and I established an early stronghold on the mountain by inviting them for a cookout, selecting choice meats, vegetables, and pastries as our ammo. Afterwards, as we were parting, Hüseyin made a foray to an ATM, withdrew money, and presented it to me. I blushed and refused. He insisted he'd be hurt if I didn't accept it. *Touché.* On another visit, we assaulted them with a small, native American wall hanging from the Grand Canyon, leaded-glass sun-catchers, and action figures for the kids. Hüseyin was not to be overpowered and having preemptively asked in an email for the birthdates of our eleven grandchildren, two large shopping bags emerged with a gender and age-appropriate outfit for each one of them! It was time to retreat and do some mental reconnoiter. So just before returning Stateside, Deb and I counter-attacked by maneuvering them to a fancy restaurant, pummeling them with rounds of delicacies from the menu. But instead of waving his white linen napkin in surrender, Huseyin had a Trojan horse in reserve before we said goodbye. He opened two briefcases that attractively displayed a wide variety of wristwatches, which he sells on the side, and said, "Please, pick one." My Kevlar deflections were useless to his armor-piercing, loving insistence. With a handsome knock-off Patek Philippe Calatrava on my arm, I left in defeat. You can't out-give a Turk.

Now it was time to get to the hopeful task of trying to find Mehmet and Reyhan. Of the many past friendships, with nationals and expats like ourselves, why did this relationship stir in us such a longing to reconnect? I think it was the irony, the unlikelihood, the oil and water nature of us as couples. This was the same couple who, so many years before, had invited us into their intimate circle as they killed two sheep during the sacrifice holiday. They knew we were followers of Jesus. We knew they were adherents to the teachings of Mohammed. We both knew our two faiths would and should never mix. Truth be spoken plainly – we both knew our respective beliefs viewed the other as heretics, idolaters, even enemies among some zealots. And yet, our love for each other superseded the blatantly obvious conflict. In fact, the Gulf War back in 1990 prompted a touching scenario between us that Deb will never forget.

As the fighting at that time intensified in the Middle East, the US State Department warned us as Americans living in the region to consider leaving until the warring was resolved or downgraded. There was clearly an emotional and increasingly volatile divide growing between Americans and most of the Islamic world. Nevertheless, we had decided to stay. During one afternoon conversation with Reyhan, Deb shared the fact of our government's warning and our decision. Reyhan was touched that we wanted to remain, and she wanted to respond in kind. In clandestine fashion, she told Deb to follow her to the bedroom. "When we had this apartment built, we added a special feature...behind this wardrobe." (Turkish homes don't have closets for hanging clothing, but use large wardrobes that, like this one, often span the whole wall of a room.) Reyhan moved clothing aside on the rod, pulled away a removable back panel, and revealed to Deb a hidden chamber behind the entire length of the wardrobe. "If anything should happen...we want you all to come to us and we'll hide you here." Deb was moved by such a gesture, especially knowing the reason anyone would be after us would be our unwanted variant religious belief. *This* is the kind of relationship we had built together that prodded us to find them this eighteen years later.

We knew they had moved away at least sixteen years before. It seemed our best bet was to begin by checking out our old neighborhood in case any of our common friends might still live there and know of their whereabouts. We jumped one of the blue and white public mini-buses that included our former borough in its circuitous route. As we approached the bottom of our old street, without conscious planning, from the vault of dormant cues in the recesses of my mind, the appropriate phrase popped out of my mouth, *"Müsait bir yerde inecek var!"* ("At a convenient place, there's someone who will deboard.") It felt so natural. And yet so weird. *How is it I can pull out that long-unused expression, and I can't remember the name of the movie I saw just last week?* Regardless, the driver did stop, we did exit, and we were walking up a street that was in earlier times home stretch.

What used to be bare, newly-erected construction on a dirt hill, was now a tree-shrouded, developed mass of high-rise apartments. We had to look hard to be certain of our building. Around the corner, we found our grocer sitting right where we would have expected to see him. All I got out was his name, "Faruk...", and he was on his feet... more hugs and cheek kisses and smiles. Of course, we had to sit for *çay* (the ubiquitous tea of the Middle East), reminiscing, catching up, and eventually another farewell that we knew would likely be forever.

Faruk knew nothing of our best friends. Numerous folks came in the store and even more passed us on the street once outside again. No one looked familiar. Before giving up, we reversed course and swung back around for another glimpse, trying to soak up the scene one last time. Walking across the street, right in front of us, was Güngör, our building superintendent (the sheep carcass blower from the *Inner City Slaughter* chapter). I knew his face right away, and he mine. He led us across the street and called his wife & son on our old apartment building intercom, saying, "Come up here... I have something to show you." We had a little parking lot reunion with his wife, Suna, and his son, Ayhan, who had grown from a ragged, dirt-smudged, round-faced boy to a very pleasant, chiseled young man of twenty-six. As we talked, Güngör learned that Deb and I wanted to find our closest friends, but didn't know where to start. He pulled out his cell phone and started dialing. Within a minute, Deb was hearing Reyhan's voice for the first time in over two decades! I was able to capture the look on Deb's face in a candid photo as they spoke. The elated image was identical to the girl of twenty years before.

Two evenings later, as we traveled to their new house, Deb and I looked at each other with "pinch me" expressions, saying, "It's really happening!" We were literally knocking on the door of our dreamed reunion. I stepped back, knowing Deb and Reyhan's embrace would be the center of attention. And it was. The Kasaps' entire extended family and I stood at arm's length around them, watching without embarrassment, letting them soak in the eons between two friends... worlds, civilizations, races, histories. When the moment finally allowed, Mehmet and I would press whiskered jawbones in traditional kiss, and hug with genuine warmth.

We sat for hours with their entire family of wives, husbands, and grandchildren. Their religious convictions had resisted the secularizing direction of the country. All the women were covered to reveal only their faces and hands. Deb and Reyhan giggled and touched like schoolgirls. After dinner, as we had in old days, Mehmet and I sat on the couch closer than any American friends would dare, held hands at times, and championed the same values and beliefs we held years before, only this time running them through the latest world conditions and events. Little had changed beyond our wrinkling skin and wintering hair.

At the end of the evening, as Mehmet drove Deb and me home, Deb expressed to him how much they had been in our hearts over the years, and how truly rich it was to be together. His reply spoke for both couples. "If we should tell people how much we care for each other, most wouldn't believe it...*couldn't* believe it."

Strangely true.

Deb & Reyhan, young years & 20-year reunion

good dog bad dog

Dogs act exactly the way we would act if we had no shame.
– from Get Your Tongue Out of My Mouth, I'm Kissing You Good-bye! *by Cynthia Heimel*

I hate being roused from bed by large noises. Not only does my chest clinch tight with anxiety, but my brain insists on jumping up and running toward the sound without knowing even where my body is. This time, it was in the upstairs bedroom of *Sakintepe*, the mountain top retreat we were overseeing. It was 1:30 a.m. and someone was pounding wildly on the front door downstairs. Once I got my bearings and land-legs under me, I navigated the no-railed wooden staircase and opened the door. Standing there with full-moon eyes, a silly smile, and in his underwear was our work associate, Seth, and his friend, Josh. They were supposed to be camping in the mountains, but were instead beating our door down to share with us their latest adventure. "We just got run out of our tent by a bear!"

The brown bear of western Turkey is kin to the Grizzly. Seth and Josh were awakened by snorting and traipsing behind the tent. After some silence on their part, Seth decided to yell to scare it away. As I remember the story, his attempt at a manly "Hey" came out more like a little girl's falsetto squeak. Fittingly, the bear's response was to begin uprooting saplings, pawing at the ground, and more ferocious snorting. Seth also admitted that his fear made for clumsy, failed efforts to unzip the tent door flap. They eventually escaped their nylon lair and ran as they were, partially dressed, to the truck without looking back. When they went back to check out the campsite the following morning, although the tent and their stuff was still intact, the ground behind it looked like a small tornado had gone through, uprooting and breaking off two-inch diameter trees and shredding the ground with deep claw ruts.

Such is life in those mountain wilds, and one of the reasons we had dogs.

Deb and I are not big "animal people." We've tried dogs of our own. When the girls were young, I buckled to sympathetic and romantic feelings by dickering for the last two chocolate poodles in a cardboard box at the Russian bazaar on the Black Sea. About the only real positive thing about that effort was the first few hours, watching the girls' excitement when I brought them home as a surprise gift for them. From there, it was a downhill plummet of wet and sloppy blankets, stinky apartment, and barks echoing off marble floors and plaster walls. They lasted about one month before we raised the white flag and took them to a pet shop to have them sold for us. According to the pet storeowner, somebody stole them from the shop and we never saw the money. But we did see one of the dogs in a neighbor's yard. Good on them!

A couple years later, we did acquire a sweet Airedale Terrier named Mindy for ten years. Unlike the failed indoor poodle chapter, she lived outdoors on our four acres and had a wonderful dog's life chasing all sorts of critters. We thought we lost her once to a copperhead bite on the snout, and when she plowed headfirst into an SUV fender. But she recovered until old age and some kind of fungus took over. I unexpectedly cried when the vet put her to sleep in the back payload of my pickup. She was too gross looking and smelling to take her in his office, so he compassionately offered to give her the injection in his parking lot. Deb also cried when we buried her. I say that in order to vindicate my claim that we aren't hard-hearted toward dogs. I already told my emotional story of saying good-bye to my childhood companion, Candy. We just don't prefer all that comes with dog ownership. In addition to the incurred expenses of food, shots, vet visits, and complicated arrangements when traveling, we also don't have any inclination to snuggle up to the furry beasts. In all candidness, Deb and I are baffled as to how people who live in clean homes and obviously follow high standards of personal hygiene are able to rationalize allowing a dog to lick or kiss them after it has just moments before been lying on the floor, leg in the air, licking its...well, you get the idea. But somehow, their owners don't seem to.

Nonetheless, a year on the mountain did serve as a repeated tutorial to Deb and me of just how ridiculously maddening *and* impressively wonderful dogs can be simultaneously. Several canine adventures in the context of wilderness life force us to concede that their assets outweigh their...well, less savory habits.

On the positive side of the ledger, everyone who comes to *Sakintepe* soon comes to know, and usually love, the three German & Belgian Shepherds running the place. Montana is the ever-reliable, steady, distinguished elder statesman and patriarch. His mate, Georgia, is the territorial, sleek beauty that can run as if with wings. Their son, Bear, plays the role of a Samson, enslaved to his power and passions, yet with a winsomeness to which one can't help be attracted. (Now, do those sound like the descriptions of a dog-hater?) Children, especially girls, often doted over and planned their vacation days around these hairy friends. I've seen macho Montana patiently endure being dressed in frilly hats and invited to tea parties. When guests at the resort wanted to venture into the mountains for a hike,

with Montana & Georgia, faithful partners

the dogs protectively accompanied them, often leading the way to the most favored spots and vistas, as well as steer them home to camp at the end of the outing. In short, they're part of the family and integral partners in the work of the retreat. That's some of the good news about the dogs.

Another thing about dogs that is bewildering to me is the joy they find playing with, rolling in, and eating disgusting things. One of the few instructions we gave guests at *Sakintepe* was to not leave their trash outside in garbage bags, but to either let us remove it or they could throw it in the back of our pickup truck as they went by the parking area. But inevitably, someone wouldn't get the message or would forget. The next morning, I would walk from our apartment down the long hill toward the villas, and notice the beautiful green, grassy area around the housing and playground...now strewn with garbage. And the dogs wouldn't be satisfied to simply tear open the bag and neatly eat in one place. It was apparently essential to rip every object to shreds and to scatter it far and wide. My worst experience by far was when a house full of young ladies left out several trash bags...from their bathrooms.... As I haltingly picked "things" up, I alternated my angry thoughts between the dogs, the girls, and myself – myself for not checking the porches just one more time before bed the night before.

It wasn't always trash. Sometimes it was animal carcasses and parts, especially bones. One morning, a neighboring farmer walked over to request that we bring our backhoe to bury a cow of his that had died. He wasn't sure why, it just died in the night. By the time Seth and I reached the scene, the bovine had bloated to about twice its normal girth. I was genuinely concerned that it might actually burst as I guided Seth's backhoe gyrations to lift her from where she lay. Once loaded up and driven to the farmer's chosen edge of a wood, we rolled her into the enormous hole we'd already dug in advance. We knew our dogs, the farmers' dogs, the shepherd's dogs, the wild dogs

- that they loved rotting flesh. They would dig it up if at all possible. Thinking we were being extra conscientious, we not only covered her with a foot or two of dirt, but covered the entire surface with rocks ranging in size from baseballs to basketballs.

As I approached Georgia a few mornings later to greet her and see what she obviously enjoyed chewing, I recognized the femur of a cow. She was working her way down the shaft crunch by crunch to get at the marrow with her tongue. It was then that my nose also put together the other evidence. Her matted coat and stench of death sent images of the carnage that must have taken place getting to the cow and removing the femur. I couldn't help jumping on the motorcycle out of curiosity to go examine the burial site. Sure enough, miniature boulders had been dislodged and dirt sprayed aside to reveal the upper side of the unfortunate cow. Certainly, Georgia was not alone in this excavation. I'm sure every dog within whiffing distance had been part of the party that night before. "Determination" is a nice way to spin their gross obsession with meat and bones.

I'm not sure why it struck me as a surprise to be inundated with bones for a whole week following the Muslim sacrifice holiday. Every family in the area had butchered a lamb or goat or cow, and they don't bother to dispose of the remains in those rural areas. All manner of bones and joints and skulls and jaws were showing up on the property. Not out in the fields or woods. Oh no. But in mown grass area around the villas, playground, volleyball court, and outdoor pizza oven. One day I drove the ATV and filled most of a black, forty-gallon garbage bag with bones. Where were our dogs? Playing with kids and guiding hikes? No, lying about, looking satiated and without a hint of guilt.

Humans *can* learn from dogs. I was seriously jolted to sobriety by a lesson Bear had to learn the hard way. In his defense, Bear is young and has received less training than his parents. Despite his truly good nature, Bear cut off a goat from the nearby herd and attacked it before Brad, Sakintepe's owner, could intervene. This nursing mother goat had serious wounds to the abdomen and leg. As the shepherd (a neighbor in the village just below us on the hill) looked on, Brad laid the goat across his lap on the ATV and rushed her back to our place. Cleaning and inspecting the wounds, we realized she was likely beyond our care. I jumped in the truck payload with the goat while Brad sped to the village to find help. These folks have lived around animals their whole lives and would know what was the best course.

We arrived and eventually found a relative of the goat's owner, whose immediate matter-of-fact response was, *"Onu keselim"* – "Let's cut her." While his boys (about six and eight years old) watched, he walked in the house, emerged with a very sharp knife, pulled the goat's head back, and made a series of deep cuts. For the next twenty minutes we talked with him and the boys about school, Americans (they were always curious), and various other topics while their father butchered the goat by hanging it from the teeth of his tractor bucket. Unwanted pieces were tossed off into the dirt for...the local street dog, of course, who crawled nervously on his belly toward the pieces before grabbing them and darting off to the grass to eat.

First, I learned from Brad. He not only took immediate action to try to save the goat, but he subsequently took full responsibility to repay the farmer for the goat. It was the right thing to do. It was also the prudent thing to do. Brad knew he'd just incurred a "debt" to them in their thinking. This religion and culture keep mental tallies of "who owes whom" all the time. When the farmer refused to accept money, Brad had to figure out another means of making amends and repaying his debt in order to maintain his reputation, which he did.

And what did I, this human, learn from Bear? Bottom line, a warning. As a show of good faith and in light of *Sakintepe* guests with children that someday might resemble a playful goat as they run... Bear needed to be either put down or continuously restrained. The merciful resolve for Bear was that his new "job" was front gate security, locked to a 100-foot zip-line. Never again could he be trusted when lives around him could potentially be endangered. No more wandering. No more guiding families to the high meadows. No more midnight cow exhuming parties. No more freedom. My lesson? The reminder that one moment of unchecked passion can sometimes result in a lifetime of imprisonment. That goes for dogs and humans. Bear was a sad and sobering illustration to me every time I entered or exited the property gate. At the writing of this chapter, two years have passed since the goat incident. I went to the website on which the dogs are featured in current photos. Bear's photo, unlike the others', still reveals his ever-present chain.

ill-fated rescue of a goat

If you've never seen a Kangal, it's at least worthy of a few Google Images. A few excerpts from all-knowing Wikipedia are "a breed of large livestock guardian dog originating from the Sivas province of Turkey...to actively fend off predators of all sizes...wolves, bears, and jackals...exported to African countries like Namibia and Kenya... where it protects local herds from lions, cheetahs, and similar indigenous big cats." To see a full-grown one in real life can leave a visceral impression. To have one advance upon you can leave you shuddering, if not much worse. Brad was out for a relaxing ride on the motorcycle in a nearby *yayla*, or high meadow. Out of the corner of his eye, he saw a Kangal on the hillside descending at a vector to intercept him. He decided to hit the gas in order to outrun it. The dog wasn't deterred or out-sped, but rammed Brad and the motorcycle broadside. The result for Brad has been major knee reconstruction surgery and a lingering limp. The Kangal simply ran off.

We saw these extraordinary specimens almost daily, but only had two of what I would consider significant encounters with them. The first was fairly brief and ultimately uneventful, except in our guts at the time and in our memory to this day. Deb and I took the motorcycle for a ride in a smaller *yayla* a slight elevation above that of Brad's encounter. Georgia decided to accompany us on this excursion, which means she ran ahead of us for several miles up rugged, rutted paths. We dismounted our ride to check out a display of odd-to-us vegetation near the edge of the trees. We had been wandering on foot for several minutes, stopping to observe and even take a few photos. I began to walk back toward the bike and Deb was lingering behind a ways when I saw a Kangal advancing toward us at a moderate run across the open meadow. "Deb, move fast to the bike." I was already ahead of her and had to back up in order to join defenses with her. I yelled for her to run faster and her response is comical to us now, but wasn't then. "I *am* running faster!" Before we could reach the bike, our heroine arrived seemingly out of nowhere. Georgia's gorgeous stride put her directly between us and the Kangal. She stood her ground barking and the Kangal halted. He returned her threats with his own deeper bark and made a few short charges forward, but each time she maneuvered between us until we could get on the bike and I could fire it up. Once moving, Georgia continued to stay between us and the Kangal until he finally gave up chase. As always, she stayed within view all the way home.

I'm not ashamed nor proud to admit it, but I ran over a Kangal dog... on purpose...kind of.

I was working in the shop and heard one of our dogs obviously upset about something. I stepped out into the sunshine to see two cows and a young bull heading into the garden. I looked around and didn't see any shepherds in sight, so I assumed these were some wanderers. The shepherds were usually pretty good about keeping their livestock off our property. The ATV was handy so I jumped on it and began to herd them, hoping to steer them back toward the road. Our aging but ever-loyal patriarch, Montana, came to help me. Unfortunately, his presence drew the attention of the shepherd's Kangals. I hadn't been able to see the shepherd down in the valley just below our guesthouses where he was grazing his goats. The two large Kangals roared up the hill and laid into Montana with such ferocity it roused a protective instinct in me reciprocal for all Montana's past service to us. I stood up on the ATV in order to better speed over the rocky terrain. I charged and separated them several times. Then I noticed that one of the guest's eight-year-old boy was down the hillside on foot and way too close for safety, so I turned my attention and the ATV toward him. There was no time to find out if his parents would want him on the ATV or not, consequently I scooped him up and drove him uphill to the dirt road that separated the valley from the picnic area.

In that brief interim, Georgia had joined in and was successfully drawing the Kangals away from Montana, who I could see was already limping and panting heavily. Georgia's swiftness was too much for the Kangals, so they went back after Montana. For all his commitment to the fight, he was getting the worst of it. I couldn't watch him get torn apart. That verbage is *not* an exaggeration for a couple of reasons. Not only do the Kangals have powerful jaws, but they are armed with two-inch metal collars studded with two-inch pointed spikes in order to protect them from other dogs going for their necks when they fight. These collars were the *real* version of the cartoon spiked ones on bully dogs I'd seen as a kid on TV and had assumed were only cartoonists' artistic hyperbole. Not so.

As I reached the four dogs in the midst of tussling and growling, one pairing was faced off momentarily such that I had a sideways vantage. I decided in the instant to give the Kangal a "pop" with the front bumper. I hit him hard enough to knock him off his feet, and he went rolling under one side of the ATV while I bounced over him with both left tires. It did the trick, and he took off like a jumped rabbit. The other Kangal followed him in kind. Poor Montana had a bloody torn ear and cut paw. He literally whimpered as I came to him. He even let me hold and pet him for a few minutes, then limped off. He would, in a few days, recover and return to play the man again when occasions surfaced.

As I came back uphill toward the houses, I realized there was a whole gallery of spectators. A large group of guests had been picnicking on the grass at the crest of the hill and had gathered to watch the Kangal rodeo. I explained the situation and apologized for the scene. One of the men responded for the group, "We're city folks...this was great! Do we owe more for the entertainment?" I assured them it was on the house.

Our pack of three and their respective "doganalities" had grown on Deb and me. We'd come to not only appreciate their general presence, but even to admire their individual qualities. As a bonus, I realized after the spontaneous rodeo that plowing over that Kangal had kind of satisfied in me a reproachful revenge on behalf of Brad for his accident with the Kangal. Put simply, I've developed a new appreciation for the merits of the *canis* genus.

But I still don't want to see a dog licking its...well, you know.

son of the Highlands

Yer bahookie in parsley.
(Scottish expression usually given as a response of disbelief to someone's claim, meaning something akin to "You're all talk" or "You're full of it.")

We're probably all "wannabe" somethings. We each have some mix of realistic goals to pursue or fantasies to play with. But in either case, few of us likely have absolutely nothing we'd change about our lives if we could. Among other things, I'm a wannabe Braveheart. And I'm partway there...at least in my rationalizations. Here's how the watertight analysis flows through my brain:

1) I've always wanted to be more brave (unflappable, calmly confident, poised in my own skin) than I am.

2) My last name being McCracken, I'm of Scottish highlands descent. (I purchased a crest and tartan to prove it...since I won't embrace the possibility of being Irish.)

3) The movie Braveheart not only inspired me like it did millions of other people, I have blood rights to those feelings of inner connectedness.

4) Therefore, I just need to continue stepping out into the scary unknowns of life (Accidental Life) as I have been and...

5) Voila!...I will be increasingly a Braveheart.

As you can clearly see, the stream of logic is irrefutable.

Some people gravitate to the beaches. When plans for vacations or dreams of ideal places pop into mind, visions of white sand, palm trees, crashing waves, and piña coladas hula dance in their heads. (I have to admit I like that scene also, and have had my fantasies of being stranded on a desert island, but it's not my number one "go to.") Others salivate for a trendy studio loft in a bustling downtown niche where art and ethnic eating venues flourish. (Deb and I did love the season we got to experience that very setting in Cincinnati.) Still others fancy themselves on a dude ranch, donning a Stetson and a pair of Luccheses, and riding off into the big red sky. (Now, that *is* an appealing contender sometimes rivaling my epitome.) But...there's nothing that calls to my inner Scot like the mountains. And conveniently, although Deb is not by blood Scottish, she has an organic longing for the craggy peaks and heather-flocked heights, most likely mystically transferred to her in our marriage.

So, finding ourselves perched on *Sakintepe* (Peaceful Peak) in the Bolu Mountain region of Turkey with the charge of ruling over rustic villas... it was a perfect place for living out further Braveheart aspirations.

One of the first projects in which I found myself immersed was the erection of a natural stone barrier for the parking area in front of the owners' house. Seth, his college buddy, and I were into it. The wall was to be an arc cut into the side of a hill that would sit about five feet tall and curve for about seventy feet. That's a lot of tons of rock. Fortunately, all our material was free. The local farmers were thrilled to have us drive the backhoe around the perimeter of their fields and remove the rocks they'd plowed up and tossed aside. Every lift of a massive stone and a toss into the backhoe scoop was that of a highland games competitor, minus the kilt (*that* might have raised some serious concerns in this Mohammedan locale). And it wasn't just this one wall. We made stone paths, stone stairs, stone-lined gardens, stone fireplaces, and a stone pizza oven. There was something very satisfying about stepping back at the end of a back-buster day to see another project of lichen-crusted boulders stacked, fitted, and sometimes mortared together.

F-r-e-e-d-o-m!

Many of the Hollywood images used to portray the hamlets in medieval Scotland could be seen in real life just down the slope from our property. The village was comprised by all of seven houses and, to some degree, one extended family. The signs of a very tight gene pool were evident. The people are agrarian and quite simple. Livestock and human quarters are often separated only by permeated board walls. Everything had the smell of some variety of animal manure. Appropriate words for the design of the community and its architecture might be dilapidated, functional, add-on, patchwork, soiled, poor.

Through much patience and humility, *Sakintepe* owner, Brad, had developed a friendly relationship with this small clan of folks over the previous ten-plus years. As a newcomer, I was gradually building sociable rapport with a few of the men and children. We always waved and greeted as we drove through, it being the normal route to and from the main city at the base of the mountain. Sometimes, I'd stop and visit through the truck window. A few times I gave the men a lift into town. Bit by bit, I was getting used to the guttural, rural dialect. When Brad was asked to bring his backhoe and do some excavation for them, I tagged along.

Since I only had a handful of hours of experience on the machine, Brad decided I should drive it there via the fields, hills, ruts, and trees instead of the road. It was shorter and more of a test for me. *Stoatin! Another opportunity to gain some Celt-like confidence.* After all, big hydraulic equipment is the contemporary equivalent of a yoke of oxen or maybe even a wooden-wheeled catapult, given enough imagination. I did just fine maneuvering my bright yellow beast over the undulating terrain, stopping in the village center to find Brad's friend and get instructions. Brad told me to park it in the middle of the street. I dropped the front scoop to the pavement but failed to give it a little needed extra gas, and the engine died. I was about to start it up again to give the scoop hydraulics one more push down as a brake since we were on a slight downhill grade, but Brad said, "Let your foot off the brake and see...." It stayed put, so we decided "good enough" and we jumped off. A few minutes later, as we were standing in a nearby lane, I heard something scraping and turned around to see (of course) the backhoe rolling in slow motion straight through the middle of the village!

My immediate reaction was to start running. Brad (still healing from the Kangal-related ACL knee surgery) was hobbling and yelling, "Go, Jim, go...Go, Jim, go!" I managed to plow through a very angry village dog that was tied up in my only direct and narrow pathway to the machine. I reached the main street right behind the rolling backhoe. By the time I could catch up alongside it, it was picking up speed. Glancing ahead to its likely route, I could see it was going to miss the Imam's house on the right (*Thank You, Lord!*), but it would probably hit an empty children's swing set, a flatbed trailer or an elderly widow's house. Seeing no people in its path, the decision I made in a couple of seconds of running alongside it – to *not* attempt to jump on, open the door and hit the brakes – was mercifully answered before I gained the necessary courage, or foolishness, to go for it. I watched it miss everything of value, run into an old not-in-use cement watering trough, shove it about five meters, and halt ever-so-gently bumping the flatbed tire...just a smudge mark as the only evidence. The several-ton, two-headed behemoth had rolled seventy-five yards down the main street with no damage done.

As the neighbors gathered around, including the elderly lady whose house just got spared, I was surprised at how Brad spontaneously handled the situation. Grinning excitedly as if something wonderful had just transpired (maybe it *had*), the translation would be something like this: "Aunty, God is big! You must have been praying...God protected you and your house. So many thanks!...it missed everything...no children, nothing...thanks to God!" Everyone just watched as he got in, moved it to the work site, and began the excavation they wanted done (for free of course). My heart incrementally relaxing, I stood around and talked with the men, trying to follow Brad's calm veteran lead. The ladies brought us tea and homemade yogurt drink. The children watched the dozer work the ground. The village dogs stopped barking, laid down, and snoozed. The event passed. I didn't feel like a blue-faced warrior, but more like a red-faced recruit.

When the work was done that afternoon, Brad and I shared a few laughs of relief. And with a slightly raised brow and glance at me in the side of his vision, Brad simply said, "This day *could* have been quite different...." *Cheers, Pal!*

Lost and found. No, not keys or socks or puppies...*me*! I don't know that I'd ever really been lost before, other than a momentary panic in the department store as a kid. It was quite a new experience for me, and not one I care to have again. The meaning of "lost" now carries a heavier connotation as I look back on one of my later adventures in the mountains.

We'd been hosting a team of eleven adults from the States who came as volunteers to stain picnic tables and playground equipment, build horseshoe pits, and add various other amenities to the property. After a long day of work, Brad's wife and co-owner, Ruth, led the team into the woods for an evening hike to watch the sun go down. Deb and Brad stayed at camp to prepare food and mind the place. It had been a busy and physically demanding day, and I felt like I needed to wind down with a little fresh air in my face. I jumped on the dirt bike with the intent of finding the hikers and maybe catch the sunset with them. I didn't know that part of the mountains or woods, but knew the general direction. Fortunately (in grateful retrospect), I told Brad that's where I was headed and I hopped on the bike. I keenly remember that I was a little chilly in just a T-shirt, but decided to not turn around to get a jacket. I'd only be gone maybe twenty or thirty minutes and it was still light out. Right....

After about half an hour of riding up a labyrinth of trails through the thick woods and passing through a couple of small meadows, I still hadn't come across the group or even heard them. It was getting dark, so I headed back toward home. In short order, darkness set in and I realized I was disoriented. I found a small bald I'd been in before, but hadn't been paying attention during the ride to all the turns. It quickly struck me that I was really cold and couldn't tell one mountain ridge from another in the twilight. The first inclination to feel panicky hit me. I shot up a prayer for wisdom and calmness, and tried to determine which of the many mountain ridges was which, but that soon became impossible for me to distinguish. I began to concentrate on the emerging stars and fortunate half moon in order to figure out which way was home.

Two short forays into the brush down trails showed me I couldn't see the sky there and had lost my bearings. I made my way back to the bald area. At that point, I knew it was best to stay put than to wander further from camp and be stuck in the dense, wooded confines. There was nothing productive I could do but wait and call out Brad's name in hopes that my voice would carry enough for him to hear me, realize I'd not come back, and come looking on the ATV. I also thought there was the outer chance that one of the dogs would hear, recognize my voice, and come to the rescue. They would automatically lead the way back home. Then I remembered. *Nuts. It's dinnertime there, so the dogs will never leave.*

Meanwhile back at the camp...the team had taken a *different* shortcut back (thus the reason I never came upon them) and were cleaning up for a late dinner. Deb assumed I was showering, and Brad was busy with chores, totally unaware that I was still gone.

At one point, I heard a distant Muslim call to prayer in what I thought must be the village nearest our place, but immediately the call also went out in the exact opposite direction from another village. I was again uncertain of directions. Plus, I knew the call wouldn't last long enough to help for any distance I might cover and I wouldn't be able to hear it over the motorcycle engine anyway. I needed to stay put. My scouting background and other reading had repeatedly taught me that resisting the urge to wander was often key to being found.

It was in the uncomfortable waiting that another remembrance really set in the trembling. In this very part of Turkey and twenty years prior, an acquaintance and his son were lost in much more serious circumstances. Mike and I had a long conversation at a Christmas party in 1994. Two weeks later, he went snow skiing with his boys at Kartalkaya, which was probably one of the distant ridges I was now squinting to see. He and the ten-year-old son decided to do a little trailblazing, exiting the formal ski area and traversing through the trees. To summarize the horrific next events (which are told in detail in his subsequent book, *Miracle on the Mountain*), the two spent the next nine days without food huddled together in a small nook in the rocks, trapped by a blizzard. Despite literally hundreds of soldiers scouring the mountains on foot and by helicopter, Mike and Matthew were not found. A memorial service for them was held after a week. Mike's training in cold wilderness survival as an Air Force colonel helped him keep them alive throughout the duration. In the end, Mike made the most gut-wrenching decision a father could make – to leave his son to go get help - a decision that ultimately saved their lives. My situation was much less dire, but the remembrance of that time of waiting for news about Mike and my own increasingly chilly air was sending waves of shivers through my body.

About an hour and a half after dark, with a hoarse voice from trying to be heard yelling "Brad" in all four cardinal directions of the compass, I decided I'd likely have to spend the night and find my way back in the daylight. I wasn't worried about dying, but I was *not* looking forward to a very long, miserable night. And my greater concern was that Deb would be scared. I had parked the bike facing what I thought was homeward so I wouldn't lose my bearings as the stars rotated. I began to look for brush I could gather around me as a windbreak.

Later I would learn that the delay in realizing my absence was that Deb concluded I was doing the nightly report or other work. Eventually, Deb, Brad, and Ruth realized no one had seen me. Brad, who isn't one to worry or jump to conclusions but is savvy in that setting, knew I'd either gotten lost or crashed on the mountain. He got the group praying, sent Ruth and a male guest one direction in a pickup, while he and Deb went the other direction he thought I'd probably gone. He told me afterward that he preferred that he, rather than Ruth, find me crumpled in the brush.

Finally, after two hours of trembling, planning for the night, calling out, and wondering if I'd meet any of our local wild boar or bear, I heard a motor in the woods exactly (I might add) from the direction my bike was pointing. I jumped on, revved the motor, flashed the lights, and met Brad and Deb on the other side of the bald. Although I was immensely relieved and still shaking, my first feigned Braveheart comment was, "It's a little chilly up here." For just a flash, Deb wondered if I'd actually just been joy-riding in the dark, but later cried as her truer realization reached the surface. Brad, smiling and telegraphing another of those raised eyebrows, sent me the message that he had been concerned. Then true to the real Braveheart and mountain man that he is, he understatedly quipped, "I'm sure glad to see you on that bike."

evening run to the mountain meadows

In response to that experience, I made a few new rules for myself. Not near dark, make sure somebody knows, and...take a bloody jacket! But what I didn't anticipate was having to wrestle with Deb about applying those rules to *her*. Deb is all about going on an adventure, but she is not one to venture out alone. She claims she gets her courage to do so primarily from me and my penchant to step into the unknown and risky. She's a great follower. The irony of that trust in me sometimes strikes me as quite humorous.

Soon after my "gone missing" escapade, interestingly, Deb began taking walks on her own in the woods...and usually in the late afternoon or early evening. She had things on her mind and, despite my recent illustration to her about how easily one can get disoriented in the wilderness, she wanted the time out there. And it started freaking me out!

I knew she didn't even have the outdoor Boy Scout tracking and trailing training that I had. She's generally more afraid of animals and boogiemen than I am. And for many years, she used to have a particular fear of being lost. But now she was going hiking for an hour or two at times when I wasn't able to do so because of work. I would watch the clock, check the darkening sky, glance toward the trailhead, and generally be nervous until I saw her casually approaching my current worksite. *Why is she doing this?* A few times, I expressed that I was concerned. Deb said she figured if she ever got disoriented, she could just go downhill and eventually get to one of the villages. I knew that was true, but also *not* sufficient in the huge expanses of open mountains around us. Then I started asking if I could tag along. Most of the time she welcomed my company, but I could tell there were times she wanted the solitude and time of reflection. She was stretching *her* independent wings. So, I let her go...and checked the sky, and watched the trailhead...for my budding wannabe Scottish lassie.

As I'm writing this while sitting in a leather recliner with bagpipe music reverberating through my Mac's iTunes, Deb just waved to me as she went out the door for a walk...in our current, tame, residential neighborhood. I'm good with that. Guess I'm still not quite the Braveheart I've aspired to become over the years. Don't get me wrong, though. I still claim the innate, inborn wannabe factor.

"*Yer bahookie in parsley, Jim.*" Maybe so, but I prefer another Scottish expression. "*Failing means ye'r playing.*"

Deb heading for the mountains

exiled on Patmos

"The traveler sees what he sees. The tourist sees what he came to see."
– G. K. Chesterton

I know there's not one right way to travel, but I have to admit that I don't get what I frequently hear to be the way many people travel – whether it's taking vacations, site-seeing, visiting for the holidays, crossing a few states to see grandma or going to a conference – whatever the occasion for being on the road. In short, they *plan* it. Often *all* of it. Reservations for this place, schedule to see that set of "must sees", tickets to watch a well-known presentation...and *that*, sometimes one they've watched on video or even attended before. I know numerous people who have gone to hear Tim Stafford multiple times at Branson, Missouri. My very personal response to that idea of travel? *Shoot me now! Put me out of my misery.*

I confess that there have been times we have done the tourist thing. When we had four days in Athens (Greece, not Ohio), we didn't skip hiking up the Acropolis and traipsing around the Parthenon. I get *that*. And one time I had a six-hour layover in Paris (France, not Texas), a city I'd never seen. I decided to not miss the opportunity, albeit brief in the extreme. Upon de-boarding, I immediately checked my briefcase in the airport's secure stowing area, changed a few bucks into Francs, and threw myself onto the first bus to the Arc de Triomphe. From there, I walked down the Champs Elysees and made sure I scaled the Eifel Tower. Again, I understood how it might seem a bit absurd to be in Paris and not see those touristic standards. But even in my cram-packed, four-hour touring timeframe in The City of Light, to and fro between the Triomphe and the Tower, I also wandered through some backstreet neighborhoods, squeezing myself through the tiny spaces between equally minute parked forms of transportation the French pass off as cars, and tried out the first baguette shop I saw. It would never have crossed my mind to find out which was the "best" pâtisserie according to Frommers, even if I *had* had the time.

Might I miss something that everyone is supposed to see in City X because of not planning out an itinerary? Sure, but most of those things I can get a feel for by reading a gazillion photo-strewn articles online. What I *couldn't* get anywhere else is being invited into a native home for an indigenous meal because I chose to go left where the guidebook clearly says, "go right."

Deb and I made a *gigantic* left turn five years ago by "Breaking Good" - selling our house and striking out on the road. We haven't looked back with regrets nor missed the former, more moored lifestyle. To the contrary, we keep hoisting the anchor and setting ourselves adrift needlessly, just to see where we might float. And, now we find ourselves serendipitously sitting in a place that certainly wasn't programmed into our GPS.

After returning Stateside from our second-round year in Turkey, we were without a plan. *Shocker!* I did have hopes of finding a place I could write my book, but knowing how I'm wired, I'd need someplace really quiet and for an extended period of time. Our current mode of floating didn't lend to such opportunity. One can only cruise from daughter-to-daughter, visiting them and our amazing grandchildren just so long before one runs out of daughters. We needed a place to land for a while. That's when the following email blipped into our "New Mail" folder from an international online resource for which I'd built us a profile:

Hi Jim and Deb!

We are Marco and Diego. We're Italians and we own a small village-resort on the island of Patmos in Greece. We'll be going back to Italy in November and so we're looking for someone who can take care of the property and of our cats, from the beginning of November at least until the end of February or March. Could you be interested? If yes please let us know. Many thanks,

Marco

Gee? Do we want to go stay free of charge for a few months on a Greek isle at an empty beachside resort and simply keep it secure? Hmmm....

Within five days, our respective back-and-forth questions were answered sufficiently, and we had confirmed our intent with an enthusiastic "Yes" response. Five weeks later, cozy in our Delta-Air France seats to Athens, grinning like honeymooners, we clinked wine glasses.

Our arrival on the island of Patmos by eight-hour ferry and at 3:00 a.m. lent a dreamlike impression from the start. The Aegean Sea port's fishy smells. The dark, swirling waters around the still-running ship. The engines rumbling in our ears and under our feet like a minor earthquake. Ropes as thick as my calf slung around dock bollards, creaking from the strain. Sea gulls swooping for anything food-like. Drowsy travelers staggering with luggage down the immense barn-wide gangplank. Our thickly accented Italian hosts hugging us "home."

Our living quarters for the next few months (in which I sit to write) are no less otherworldly. Sitting atop the multi-tiered resort is this 8-by-18-foot cube of Mediterranean white stucco. Inside, rust-colored ceramic floors underlay a desk and minute bathroom. Two steps lead up to a bed and bench loft, shrouded with ethereal, white mosquito net draped artistically around bedposts to the ceiling. One window looks to the inner-island rocky crags. Two other portals are bedside and bed-level, opening to *our* cove. Turquoise bedspreads always coordinate handsomely with the ever-changing blue-greens of the water outside. Only rarely is there not a breeze or gale to carry us sounds and smells reminding us we're not in Ohio anymore. It is magical.

Marco and Diego would only stay two weeks before leaving the place in our care, so they wasted no time familiarizing us with the facility, its workings, and the cats. Yes, the animal-tolerating couple we are, are now the proud superintendents of not one or two, but twelve cats. We only feed three indoors downstairs, and the rest outdoors. Correction – *I* feed and care for the clowder twice a day. Deb's forbearance only goes so far. And I might add, none dare come into our rooftop 144 square-foot paradise. By the end of our tenure here, I hesitatingly own up to the truth that I have actually gotten to know the "catonalities" of our charge...and have even come to - dare I say it - *care* about a few of them. Mike is a blind-in-one-eyed kitten who couldn't be more pathetically adorable, and the one I protect above all others. Second in favor comes Mosè, a tiger-striped shy guy I have to make sure gets his share of victuals. Next in line receiving mercy is Atena, a sleek, sweet-natured beauty who's never given up trying to live with us, always outside our door each morning. Then come the scoundrels. Licorice, obviously pitch black, is creepy, slinking, crouching, and watching my every move. Maria, despite her white coat and biblical namesake, is a haughty hussy, roaming with the boys at night and expecting special treatment. She doesn't earn that favor with me. Finally, a dishonorable mention to Dorian Gray, who in keeping with his ageless celebrity, is a bully who bats around lesser felines to be first to the food. Once, leaping for a scrap of meat in my hand, he ended up hanging by a claw on my left thumb cuticle! Instinctively reverting to my former nature, I sent him sailing across the courtyard with the help of my right foot. And of the other half dozen strays? They don't warrant individual citation. After all, they're just cats.

Back to humans, Marco and Diego would also introduce us to an array of locals who could be resources of help, as well as good company, which some have become. Spiro, the previous owner of the resort, periodically stops by to play the piano he's left in the guys' dining room. His attractively thick, messy ponytail fits his style of play - a mixture of classical training and inner jazz improvisation. We wish he'd come by more often.

Haniel Sofia, a French-Armenian-Egyptian-Greek woman, has become our closest friend and guide. That's what she does for a living, guides tourists to the various places and events on Patmos. During this off-season lull, we aren't her clients, but comrades in various outings. Middle aged, broadly educated, multi-lingual, and energetic, she leads us to restaurants, points out landmarks, gives us impromptu cultural and history lessons, takes us to Christmas and New Year's parties. The latter party took place in a cave house that hosted about twenty folks representing at least seven different nationalities and languages. Another unique excursion was to pick olives, seventeen pounds to be precise, in the orchard of a monastery in order to give to the nuns for pressing.

Sofia also invites us to church and religious events, which has given Deb and me an even deeper glimpse into the Greek Orthodox worship that we had studied and attended on our own several years prior. Regardless of denominations and persuasions, few folks have the privilege to attend a midnight service in the Cave of the Apocalypse, the cave purported as the location of John's writing of the book of Revelation. We were among those who wound six flights of cut-stone steps underground to a candle-lit sanctuary barely taller than my head height. Although accustomed to the icons, beards, incense, gold-leaf, chanting, and even the Greek language, the cumulative of these in the context of such a cryptic, shadowy setting enhanced a sense of awe and wonder. I think that's a big part of the whole idea!

Have you ever arrived someplace to find yourself improperly dressed? Me too. Oddly enough, it had nothing to do with the cultural differences. Sofia invited us to attend a Sunday morning Orthodox service at a small village church. We picked her up, drove up the mountain, parked, and began to walk the road to the church when I looked down and realized I was still wearing my pajama top. I had been waiting till the last minute to change so as not to rumple my intended shirt. It was now too late to turn back, and fortunately my sleepwear was plain enough to pass for a shirt. To make things even more interesting, the priest invited us after the service to join him, his wife, and four of the nuns for breakfast. Father Grigorio and his wife, Presbytera (the generic, ecclesiastical designation of all priests' wives) were warm and engaging. Most entertaining was Deb's seatmate, a 97-year-old nun who spoke no English. Nods, pats, and facial expressions with a little translation was enough...an appropriately scant conversation to complement her long, sparse lifestyle.

Orthodox breakfast, wearing my pajama top

Epiphany has not been a big part of my religious celebration experience. But I'm glad we didn't miss it this year. Joining a sizeable throng of townies down at the port, we gathered around a makeshift stage erected on the edge of the harbor wall. A parade of the island's thirty-some priests in robes and regalia made its way to the platform, where they sang hymns and read Scriptures pertaining to the baptism of Jesus. Then came the more culturally intriguing festivity – a sacred swim meet! The head priest blessed a wooden cross and tossed it into the harbor. Any of the youth who wanted to participate, having positioned themselves strategically around the seawall, hit the water and began splashing toward the cross. It looked like a run of minnows ahead of a hungry bass. The victor (I *knew* he would win, picking him out of the crowd by his ripped physique and game face) kissed the cross and held it high overhead while everyone else on dry land applauded. Returning the cross to what was now the award stand, Mr. Muscles was medallioned with a gold chain and cross, which he kissed...not forgetting to also kiss the hand of the presenting priest. The ceremony ended by the crowd one-by-one filing past the bunched priesthood to be sprinkled with holy water and kiss the wood cross. There's lots of kissing among the Greeks and their Orthodoxy.

Epiphany swim meet, January in the Aegean

Hiking and exploration make up a big focus of our non-study, non-writing time. Deb is pursuing her Master Herbalist training while I write this book. But when we need a break or the surroundings are just too enticing to resist, we throw on whatever layers fit the weather and pick a direction. We were given a map that shows seven formalized hikes scattered over the whole island. Our hope has been to complete them all, and the four we've done already have been fabulous. To describe the terrain and beauty of this compact, rugged dot (only 13 square miles) among the Dodecanese island complex, would be foolhardy. It's not just the colors, shapes and textures, but the connected smells, remoteness, and...mystical nature of the place. To hike it is to tread over history and to traverse through intangible atmosphere formerly, or just possibly *currently,* otherwise occupied.

Hike number one on the map led us to windmills originally built in the 1600s and recently restored, one of them to actual grain-grinding use. From there we approached what looked like Camelot, but we knew to be the monastery of Saint John. Number four followed a rocky coastline to a boatyard and back. Along the route we not only climbed and navigated cliffs steep enough to get our hearts racing, but also stumbled upon an old Greek sun-worshipper who looked like he'd been sunbathing nude for eighty years. His skin was the hue and *apparent* texture of a rhinoceros. We didn't get *that* close and snuck away before he realized he'd been compromised.

Deb scrambling on cliffs

We combined two of the hikes into a longer one since the weather was perfect. Hikes number two & five took us to the highest point on the island and a former hermitage. We ate our packed lunch of black olives, cheese, hard-boiled eggs and fruit, scanning all 360 degrees of the vista. Although no noteworthy accomplishment or significance, it was momentous for me to realize that there was no person higher on the entire island than us at that moment. It felt representative of the privileged existence Deb and I are living out these days. Both ascending and descending on this particular excursion, our olfactory systems were entertained by both lemon and orange orchards.

Patmos' pinnacle, a view to make you ache

Shorter in-town treks also opened up new experiences. One evening after a dinner downtown, walking a new route home put us by the cemetery. Who'd have thought a graveyard at night could be so captivating? The Orthodox think (and I heartily agree) of those who have passed on as alive, not dead. Like many cultures, they visit and decorate the tombs with flowers. However, unlike anything we'd seen before, these Greek above-ground vaults are lit with electric or gas lanterns. But most mesmerizing, they are equipped with mini glass display cases at the head that house a photo and personal effects that represent the life of the deceased. One fisherman's cap and a model boat. An example of a woman's needlework. Racing photos and a model Harley for a motorcycle enthusiast. *I wonder if he crashed.* A microphone of a singer. Deb and I appreciated the personal touch for each loved one. The focus was not on a "dead" person but, more accurately for a faith-based perspective, on one who has transitioned, gone on ahead to more life.

Who gets to travel the world and do these sorts of things? The independently wealthy. But we aren't that by any stretch. The naively irresponsible spendthrift. We've always paid our bills and have no delusions denying that this season logically has an end. The hugely talented travel journalist. Not yet. Which leads me to divulge a fairly private and potentially misunderstood story.

We had been here on Patmos about a month. I walked to the end of our road to a spot that has become my favorite place to watch the waves pound against the rocky shoreline, and to reflect. I was sitting on an eons-pocked, seaside prominence that offers a perfect perch above the surf. I was slipping in and out of simply enjoying the scenery, praying, and thinking about the bigger picture of what Deb and I are doing in this season as Servants at Large. Since I was just sitting, I had picked up several handfuls of small pebbles (most about the size of a kidney bean) and was tossing them at a large boulder about seventy feet below me. As expected, many of these tiny pebbles didn't even make it to the boulder, falling short or being blown sideways by the substantial sea breeze. Those that did make it to the truck-sized boulder *pinged* off it as one would expect rock on rock to do, launching into the surf.

As I specifically evaluated the recent days of writing my book, I wondered if writing could be a viable role for me beyond this book. I have a cursory idea of how difficult it is to write, get published, and to make any kind of living from it. Additionally, I wondered if traveling from place to place could be the backdrop of writing, both providing fresh inspirational material and allowing for quiet contexts for the writing itself.

I kept pondering this possibility and tossing pebbles, each making small splashes, disappearing along the cliff-side or pinging off the boulder. The more I thought about the combination of writing and traveling like our current undertaking, the more it seemed an ideal complement to Deb's and my desires for lifestyle, growth, change, serendipity, solitude – it had it all. I couldn't imagine anything much better. It seemed more of a fit to me than anything I'd considered or attempted before. Then, a mostly rhetorical and ever-so-slightly testing question came to my mind while I threw another pea-sized pebble: *What are the chances of being able to live such a dream? Probably about the same as this pebble landing in that crack on the boulder...*I released the pebble as I inwardly voiced those words. The tiny projectile curved through the wind, landed in the exact foot-long crack I'd targeted, that was so narrow and tight, the pebble barely vibrated... and stayed put!

What are the chances?

Many have expressed in books, poems, and songs a conviction for the metaphor of life as a *journey*. Frost appeals for "The Road Not Taken." Bunyan chronicled the *Pilgrim's Progress*. JT identifies with "Walking Man." Fogelberg sympathizes with challenges "Along the Road" and concludes that the traveler is rewarded when he chooses the more rare "Nexus" and goes the whole distance of life's search. So in keeping with the metaphor...some people end up at crossroads, others try to get a head-start on life, many admire someone really going places, another bemoans trying to get back on track, winners determine to not let someone get in their way, most navigate the twists and turns of life, the over-zealous have to be reminded to stop and smell the roses along the way, while yet others are without direction in life. The verbal pictures are endless. The point is obvious. If life's a journey, then we are travelers.

Most people acknowledge this simile, but to my observation, only few live life as though it's true. To embrace it as an accurate depiction, a person has to accept one of two logical sequiturs. One deduction is that this journey is *all* there is, and therefore one ought to make the most of it, since the journey and destination are one and the same. Strangely, even among people who hold this view, very few seem to walk it out consistently with the axiom. Or the other possible conclusion is that this *isn't* all there is. This life truly is *only* a journey, which begs the question, "Then what is the destination?" As you might guess at this point in my writing, I am of the latter persuasion without hesitation. I don't think I'm necessarily in a minority by embracing such a hopeful view. And still, I *am* somewhat shocked how few in this camp of belief (life after death, in a phrase), like those in the other, don't live as though it's true either.

I empathize with the difficulty. So did Solomon in his grandest of all studies of life and meaning, expounded in the book of Ecclesiastes (my favorite book of Scripture). But even Solomon's dead-end research when looked at "under the sun" (take it literally), thrust him to the conclusion that C. S. Lewis so crisply put in his *Mere Christianity*:

If I find in myself a desire which no experience in this world can satisfy, the most probable explanation is that I was made for another world.

We live here and now, so it's hard to live for anything or anywhere else. But Solomon's conclusion was neither to skip the "now" for a heavenly "then" (a common Puritan overcompensation), nor to deny the "then" for a hedonistic "now" (an Epicurean "Eat, drink and be merry for tomorrow we die" sentiment). Instead, Solomon wisely wrote:

Do not be excessively righteous and do not be overly wise. Why should you ruin yourself? Do not be excessively wicked and do not be a fool. Why should you die before your time? **It is good that you grasp one thing and also not let go of the other***; for the one who fears God comes forth with* **both** *of them.* (Ecclesiastes 7:16-18)

I guess that's at the heart of why I approach life somewhat tongue-in-cheek…accidentally. It's actually very purposeful. It just looks like it isn't. And admittedly, often feels like it isn't. So far, it's working out pretty well to be "purposefully stumbling into meaningful existence." That might be a valid subtitle for not just my book, but Solomon's too.

Just before leaving for Greece, Deb and I made one of our favorite Stateside stops, to visit with my closest former college buddy, Russ, and his wife, Jill. Our few and rare visits over the past four decades always leave me wishing I could live near him. Our talks are deep, and our laughter resurrects past joys. But for me, there has also always been a bit of a sticky discomfort when I see Russ. I hate to say it, but I always feel a bit jealous of him. More specifically, of the course of his career. You see, Russ is one of those guys who always knew what he wanted to do, went for it with gusto, and accomplished it… in spades. His degrees were in law enforcement and criminal justice, because he wanted to be a cop. Right out of college, he was hired as just that. A couple of times in the early years when we dropped in for a visit, I rode his beat with him. To watch him handle a drunk driver, an impudent street punk, an elderly lady, or a store owner... whomever, he was clearly in his element and respected by all. How did it work out? Russ moved up the chain of command to become a detective, and eventually Police Chief. As he neared what could be comfortable retirement, his impeccable reputation in the community earned him the encouragement by many to run for county sheriff. He won unchallenged and now serves in that honorable role. He knew his niche, planned his course, crawled through the trenches, and came out the other end at the pinnacle of possibilities. In short, Russ is what I am not, and has done what I have not done. And it dogged me. Despite all my wonderful experiences and intermittent successes, around Russ I always felt like the wandering soul who could never quite find his "fit."

I had never shared this very personal feeling, stashed away in our otherwise aboveboard friendship. Until this past visit, that is, when I finally came clean to the Sheriff. At first, the grin on his face made me wonder if he was actually being smug enough to enjoy it! Then he got up and walked away, saying, "I gotta show you something." He logged into his computer and pulled up a YouTube video. "This is what *I* picture when I compare you and me." It was the intro to a 1969 TV show I'd totally forgotten – *Then Came Bronson*.

Roll the tape...

Bronson, in his black stocking cap and leather jacket, pulls up to the stop light on his motorcycle, loaded with a duffle and sleeping bag. Beside him is a guy with a nondescript fedora in a cream-colored station wagon. Looking bored and wiping the weariness from his face, he glances sideways at Bronson.

Guy: *Taking a trip?*
Bronson (not fully hearing): *What's that?*
Guy: *Taking a trip?*
Bronson smiling: *Yeah.*

Guy: *Where to?*
Bronson: *I don't know. Wherever I end up, I guess.*
Guy (shaking his head): *Man, I wish I was you.*
Bronson: *Really?*
Guy: *Yeah.*
Bronson: *Well, hang in there.*

The light changes to green, both smile at each other and nod understandingly, and Bronson takes off down the highway, then through the salt spray on a beach, then over a mountain pass bridge...and into the mist.

Russ looked at me and leveled, "Mac, in my mind, I'm the guy in the station wagon, and *you're* Bronson!" We laughed and shook our heads, mutually amazed by the other's revelation. As the Turkish version of this "greener grass"

with Sheriff Russ, a mutual admiration and love

syndrome goes, "Your neighbor's duck looks like a goose, and his wife like a teen-ager." Perspective is a wonderful thing. I hope Russ is as encouraged by my confession as I am by his.

Accidental Life? I'm more than okay with it. And my sidekick, Deb, is okay with it, too. Where from here? We haven't the foggiest. What about the risk of the unknown? In our conjoined mind, there's something that would be worse...by far. To play it safe, *not* risk it, and always wonder in the years to come...*What might have happened if we had...?*

Jim McCracken

poetry in motion

[Daughter Kate's gift of poetry to us when we were "Breaking Good"as Servants at Large...who, being the "Chipette off the old Blocks" that she is, wrote off-the-cuff and without edit]:

My Ode to the Gypsies
Kate McCracken Bertrand

There once was a couple
Who had little trouble
With things such as boxes and lines
Some lines they would bend
Some boxes they'd mend
But for other things they would just pine

See, they wanted a path
Of a similar math
To the arithmetic in their heads
But such a road was not found
Though they looked round and round
And this troubled them oft' in their beds

"Simplicity!" they'd cry
As life hustled by
With complexities galore to be had
Looking for matter
Amidst all the clatter
Would sometimes make both oh so sad

Accidental Life

But then one would grin
The other's confidence win
For they both loved the other one so
He'd say "I've a plan!"
She'd say, "You're my man!"
And on another adventure they'd go

So together they walked
And, as always, they talked
Searching no more for some hidden trail
For now they were making
The path they were taking
And with HIM in their hearts, who could fail?

So perhaps one fine day
If you're lucky they say
You may see this odd couple go by
They may stop for a while
Helping hands and a smile
Till on to their journey they fly

The Gypsies, a Turkish cafe and beyond...

www.ingramcontent.com/pod-product-compliance
Lightning Source LLC
Chambersburg PA
CBHW020357080526
44584CB00014B/1055